THE
AMBIVALENT
MIND

THE AMBIVALENT MIND

The Neuropsychology
of Left and Right

Michael C. Corballis
and Ivan L. Beale

Nelson-Hall nh Chicago

LIBRARY OF CONGRESS CATALOGING IN PUBLICATION DATA

Corballis, Michael C.
  The ambivalent mind.

  Bibliography: p.
  Includes index.
  1. Left and right (Psychology) I. Beale, Ivan L.
II. Title.
BF311.C674 1983   152.3'35   83-4026
ISBN 0-88229-475-X

Manufactured in the United States of America

10 9 8 7 6 5 4 3 2 1

The paper in this book is pH neutral (acid-free).

"Perils of Modern Living" by Harold P. Furth reprinted by permission; © 1956 The New Yorker Magazine, Inc.

Contents

Preface

Left and right have always exerted a certain fascination. For one thing, there seems no *essential* difference between them, in the sense that there is a difference between up and down or front and back. A perplexed child, unable to decide which is the left or right side of his or her body, might therefore be said to be ambivalent as to which is which.

There is another sense in which a person's mind might be said to be ambivalent. According to current folklore the two sides of the human brain represent different mental styles: the left cerebral hemisphere is said to be rational, analytic, rigid and predominantly Western in its mode of thought, while the right hemisphere is intuitive, holistic, creative, and predominantly Eastern. We are ourselves ambivalent as to the legitimacy of its distinction, however, and we believe it to be largely a modern manifestation of an age-old urge to associate opposite poles of various dichotomies, such as male and female, light and dark, odd and even, with right and left. This labelling was hitherto associated with the right and left hands, but with the discoveries over the last century of asymmetries between the two sides of the brain the dichotomizing has gone to our heads.

Fourteen years ago we began a series of laboratory studies of the transfer of left-right information between the two sides of the brains of pigeons. At that time we had no idea that those experiments would lead to a simple concept of brain function that would provide a framework for exploration of a wide variety of apparently unrelated psychological puzzles, all having some relevance to the concepts of left and right.

Much has already been written on many of these individual puzzles, both in scientific journals and in the popular press. In this book, though, we draw these puzzles together in a common framework, not only to show their interrelationships, but also to throw light on their explanation. This framework permits a re-evaluation of some old ideas on the role of cerebral dominance in dyslexia and stuttering and lends perspective to theories of the origins and inheritance of handedness.

In recent years there has been a burgeoning of interest in many of the phenomena discussed in this book, particularly specialization of function of the two cerebral hemispheres in humans. Popularizations of this area of research have often been extravagant in their interpretations, and we hope that this book will present a more realistic picture of cerebral specialization by placing it in its proper context of overall functional symmetry.

The book is divided into four parts. In the first, we examine the nature of left and right and what it means to tell them apart. We trace the origins of bilateral symmetry in animals and humans and explore its significance for behavior. Questions addressed include the following: How can symmetrical animals learn to tell left from right? Why do we tend to treat left and right as equivalent? What does the salience of bilateral symmetry in our visual world suggest about the organization of the brain?

The second part emphasizes asymmetries of function, especially in humans. Topics considered include the origins, variations and inheritance of handedness, the nature of specialization of function of the two cerebral hemispheres and the development in children of a left-right sense.

In the third part we discuss two pathological conditions, specific reading disability and stuttering, that are sometimes said to be associated with incomplete or poorly established lateralization of the brain. Hence the disabled reader might be regarded as ambivalent as to whether a certain symbol is a ''bee'' or a ''dee'' and the stutterer might suffer from ambivalence as to which side of the brain controls speech. The so-called "dominance theory" of these disorders was prominent in the 1920s and 1930s, but fell from favor after World War II. It is suggested that the time may be ripe for a revival of this theory in at least some cases of reading disability and stuttering.

In the fourth part we entertain the possibility that there might be some link between the asymmetries to be observed at the levels of neuropsychology, human physiology, biochemistry and particle physics. That is, is there a common thread that unites human handedness and cerebral lateralization, the asymmetries of the heart and other internal organs, the asymmetry of living molecules and the asymmetry of the weak subatomic forces that defy the Law of Conservation of Parity? We tentatively suggest that there is, but confess to some ambivalence about it.

The book is intended as a summary and synthesis of the current state of knowledge of psychological aspects of functional symmetry and asymmetry in man and animals. We have tried to write in a style comprehensible to the interested nonspecialist, but we are aware that the result is uneven. Our topic covers a wide range of disciplines, from psychology to embryology, philosophy to genetics, archeology to particle physics, religion to biochemistry. Moreover, there has been an explosion of published information in neuropsychology, which is at the core of our subject, and we have felt obliged to give as fair and complete a picture as possible. A good deal of the popular literature on the topic, especially that dealing with handedness and the two sides of the brain, has been ill-formed, oversimplified and sensationalist, and part of our aim in writing this book was to restore a balanced perspective. Even so, some of our own biases will be apparent; given the rapidly changing state of the field, it is neither possible, nor, we think, desirable, to maintain a completely neutral stance.

Aside from its theoretical interest, the book contains practical information for those concerned with remedial reading instruction on the role of handedness and cerebral dominance in the development of reading and other academic skills. There are useful messages for educators generally and especially for teachers of reading and speech therapists.

We hope that the book will be of value to specialists as well as to nonspecialists, if only because of the large number of references we have cited and listed. Some readers will no doubt treat the book as a bibliography, and perhaps ignore our attempts to make sense of the material. Our earlier book, *The Psychology of Left and Right,* was published in 1976 by Lawrence Erlbaum Associates. That book was intended primarily for psychologists and those in related disciplines. In writing the present book our initial aim was to cover essentially the same material for the less specialized reader. We soon discovered, however, that there was a good deal of new material that had appeared in the meantime, that there were several important errors and omissions in the earlier book, and that our own ideas had changed somewhat. The present book is therefore a complete revision and extension of the earlier one, and our attempts to achieve a more popular style were to some extent defeated by the wealth of new material to be covered.

Acknowledgments

A great many people have contributed to our thinking on left and right over the years, and we cannot possibly list them all. Some, however, must be singled out for special thanks. Michael J. Morgan of the University of London was responsible for giving us a biological perspective and introducing us to the important genetic and embryological questions about lateralization of function; he is not responsible, however, for our errors and misconceptions. Lauren J. Harris of Michigan State University provided us with valuable historical information, both in his writing and in informal discussion.

We thank all those who helped with the preparation of the manuscript; Alison, Dorothy, and Robert for typing and Heather and Sara for illustrations.

Last, but certainly not least, we thank our children Paul, Timothy, Anya, Sara, and Lisa, and especially thank our wives Barbara and Isobel, for their indulgence of our obsession with left and right during the years we have been thinking about this book. We are grateful for their unfailing encouragement at times when, we now realize, they would have been right had they left!

PART ONE

Left, Right, and Bilateral Symmetry

Tyger! Tyger! burning bright,
In the forests of the night,
What immortal hand or eye
Could frame thy fearful symmetry?
                    [William Blake, ''The Tyger'']

Chapter 1

Defining Left and Right

I do not like these "left" and "right" classifications; they are conditional concepts, they are loosely bandied about, and they do not convey the essence. [Alexander Solzhenitsyn, *The Gulag Archipelago*]

Among the dimensions that are used to locate things in space, or to describe their shapes, the left-right dimension is rather special. For one thing, people are often confused about which is left and which is right, but they are seldom confused about up and down and back and front. Also, left–right symmetry, or symmetry about a vertical axis, is much more noticeable than up–down symmetry, or symmetry about the horizontal. As we shall see, this is related to the fact that the human body, like the bodies of other animals, is itself to a large extent symmetrical with respect to left and right. But this overall symmetry itself adds an element of mystery to two strikingly asymmetrical phenomena; the first of these is handedness, and the second is the functional asymmetry of the human brain.

Our two hands, like the two sides of our brain, look to be almost perfect left–right mirror images of one another. Yet there is a striking asymmetry of function between the hands, as any right hander can tell by trying to write with the left hand. Over the past hundred years it has become increasingly apparent that there are equally remarkable asymmetries of function between the two hemispheres of the human brain, asymmetries that seem to belie the brain's basic anatomical symmetry. Thus, the close anatomical resemblances between the two hands and between the two sides of the brain are seemingly contradicted by important differences in function.

Our concern in this book is with the primarily psychological questions about left and right that arise from the symmetry and emerging asymmetries of the body and brain. Before we can expound on these themes, we must first clarify the geometry of the left–right dimensions in relation to the other axes of three-dimensional space. We shall see that even from a geometric point of view the distinction between left and right is rather special. It almost inevitably involves a psychological component because it requires reference to the sides of one's own body, whereas the top, bottom, back or front of an object can usually be identified in terms of properties intrinsic to the object itself. We shall also need to clarify the nature of mirror images, because an important test of the ability to tell left from right involves the discrimination of patterns or objects that are mirror images of one another.

THE AXES OF SPACE

When we describe the spatial characteristics of solid objects we usually do so with reference to three axes: the up–down axis, the front–back axis, and the left–right axis. The left–right axis is in a sense the most uncertain, because it cannot be specified until the other two have been established. One cannot speak of the left or right sides of a sphere, such as a tennis ball, because there is no true top and bottom and no true back or front. Similarly, an upright cylinder, such as a bottle, has a top and bottom but no back or front (unless it has a label, perhaps), and so again we cannot specify a left–right axis. Sometimes we may make exceptions to these rules by superimposing our own body axis onto the object in question; for instance, it may be legitimate to speak of the left and right of a tennis ball one is holding, with the implicit understanding that the right side is the side that is toward one's *own* right.

The up–down and front–back axes can generally be specified in terms of reasonably constant physical characteristics. For instance, the up–down axis is the axis that is perpendicular to the surface of the earth (or, as space travellers might insist, of whatever celestial body one inhabits). The top of an object is that part which is normally farthest from the earth's surface while the bottom is closest to it and is usually in contact with it. Of course an object may be upside down, but this is meaningful only if there is some normal or proper orientation of the object relative to the earth's surface; a tennis ball cannot be upside down. The persistent pull of gravity, which keeps most objects in contact with the earth, also means that most objects with a well defined up–down axis are asymmetrical with respect to up and down. Their tops are not like their bottoms. This means that top and bottom can generally be identified in terms of relations internal to the object itself. For instance, bottles are generally wide at the bottom and narrow at the top, and they are closed at the bottom and open at the top. Animals have legs on their undersides and their heads are usually at the top of their bodies. There are therefore fairly general rules that enable us to quickly determine which is the top or bottom of familiar objects or categories of objects. Even in the case of drawings that do not represent real objects, people seem to agree fairly well as to which is the top and which is the bottom; if asked to rotate a picture so that it is upright, people generally orient it so that the widest part is at the bottom and it tapers upwards, although other considerations also come into it.[1]

The back–front axis also can be characterized in terms of the structure of the object in question, although this may be a little more tricky than is the case with up and down. Indeed, it may require a more subtle sense of metaphor. In the most primitive sense perhaps, back and front are defined in relation to linear motion; the front of an object is the leading surface with respect to the object's preferred or habitual direction of motion. But houses also have fronts and backs even though most of them do not move (to confuse the issue, mobile homes typically move sideways!). The front may therefore be identified in terms of some salient feature, such as the main entrance to a house, the label of a bottle, or the face of a clock. The essential metaphor here may be that of the human face, which is typically more interesting, expressive, and functional than is the back of the head (we know of rare exceptions). Even the distinction between the front and back of the head may be derived ultimately from motion; the eyes, nose, and mouth are located on the leading surface precisely in order to facilitate such activities as navigation, exploration, food-seeking, and attack. Whatever the rules underlying the identification of front and back, there is seldom any doubt as to which is which; the very terms "front" and "back" imply an asymmetry, so that the distinction can be made in terms of the object itself.

The left–right axis is last in the hierarchy of spatial dimensions because it cannot be identified until the up–down and back–front axes have been established. Moreover, it is difficult to define which is left and which is right in physical terms, because the everyday physical world exhibits no consistent left–right biases. If one imagines any physical object that is free to move around on the surface of the earth one can easily identify asymmetrical influences with respect to top and bottom, and back and front; gravity creates the up–down asymmetry, and the demands and consequences of movement bring about the asymmetry between front and back. But the absence of any consistent left–right bias means that there is no consistent left–right asymmetry to provide us with a clear *definition* of which is left and which is right. As a rule, we can find no general properties of objects to enable us to distinguish their left sides from their rights sides except in the case of some objects made by humans. The only consistent asymmetry is that of our own bodies, and consequently we must judge the left and right sides of other objects in relation to the left and right sides of ourselves. This is why the left–right dimension has a uniquely psychological character.

Actually, it is not quite true to say that the physical world offers no consistent basis for defining left and right. The molecules of living tissue exhibit consistent asymmetries; for instance the DNA molecule is a double clockwise helix. Even the basic laws of physics exhibit a consistent asymmetry at the level of so-called ''weak'' nuclear interactions, and this asymmetry might serve as the basis for a universal definition of the difference between left and right. We shall have more to say on these fundamental asymmetries in the final chapter of this book when we attempt a more global synthesis of the problems posed by the left–right distinction. In the meantime, we may simply note that the asymmetries of living molecules or of nuclear interactions are quite useless as *practical* bases for defining left and right, since the average person has no access to the information they provide.

THE PSYCHOLOGICAL COMPONENT

The psychological component underlying the left–right distinction is evident in the way dictionaries define the terms ''left'' and ''right.'' Here are the versions given by the Oxford English Dictionary (1933 edition):

Left.   The distinctive epithet of the hand that is normally the weaker of the two, and of the other parts of the same side of the human body (occasionally of their clothing, as in *left boot, glove, sleeve*); hence also of what pertains to the corresponding side of any other body or object. Opposed to *right*.

Right. The distinctive epithet of the hand that is normally the stronger; by extension also of that side of the body, its limbs, their clothing, etc.; hence in a transferred sense of corresponding parts of other objects. *Right bank* (of a river), that on the right of a person facing down the stream.

One might quibble with the choice of physical strength as the defining criterion to distinguish the left from the right hand, since the hands also differ with respect to other, perhaps more obvious attributes such as preference and skill (hence the term "dexterity"), although it is true that in most right-handed people the right hand is capable of the stronger grip. The point is that handedness is the most salient characteristic upon which to base the definition of left and right, and this inevitably throws us back on an appreciation of which is our *own* left and right in judging the left and right sides of other objects.

Of course handedness is not the only possible basis for the definition of left and right and is indeed in some respects unsatisfactory. Some people are left handed and must essentially reverse the definition; worse still, some people are ambidextrous. Children under the age of about six years are often confused as to which is their left or right hand, and some people remain confused even in adulthood. A more universal definition might refer to the leftward displacement and asymmetry of the heart, which holds for all but the merest fraction of the human population, and indeed for vertebrates generally. However, people are not really aware of this asymmetry, and it therefore does not serve as a useful practical basis for distinguishing left from right. Cerebral asymmetry is also more universal than handedness in that some 95 percent of the human population have speech represented primarily in the left cerebral hemisphere of the brain, whereas only about 90 percent are right handed. But again we are not normally aware of cerebral asymmetry per se, although cerebral asymmetry may well contribute to our internal sense of which is left and which is right.

The special character of the left–right distinction can be demonstrated with reference to Figure 1.1. It will be quickly apparent to most readers that this looks like a letter *R* that is more or less upside down. The up–down axis can be readily discerned from the internal structure of the figure itself and from one's knowledge of what an *R* is like. But what is

FIGURE 1.1.
Is this letter normal or backward?

not so immediately obvious is that this is a *backward R*. Most people determine that this is so by turning the *R* around so that it is upright, and then they can judge that it is left–right reversed. It is possible to accomplish this "turning around" by a mental rotation; that is, by *imagining* what the figure would look like if rotated back to the upright. This mental rotation takes about one third to one half of a second—about the same time it might take to rotate the book to make the *R* upright—and the act of imagining what this figure would look like up the other way can be considered comparable to the act of actually seeing it up the other way.[2] What this illustrates is that we cannot normally assess the left–right orientation of a figure unless we somehow, physically or mentally, align it with our own body axes, whereas up–down orientation can be determined quickly from the characteristics of the pattern itself.

    The same is true of three-dimensional objects. We can quickly recognize a shoe as a shoe, or a glove as a glove, but it takes a deliberate act of mapping the object in question onto one's own body coordinates (or vice versa) if we are to determine whether it is a left or right shoe, or a left or right glove. A capsized automobile is fairly easily identified and seen to be upside down, but again we must relate it explicitly to our own body axes if we are to establish whether it is a left-hand drive or a right-hand drive vehicle. If you need convincing, try the puzzle illustrated in Figure 1.2. Fortunately, people are generally fairly skilled at carrying out these mapping operations mentally and, for example, can therefore tell whether a shoe is a left or a right shoe without actually having to try it on.

FIGURE 1.2.

Which of these vehicles has the left-hand drive?

WHY DO MIRRORS REVERSE LEFT AND RIGHT?

The unique and confusing status of the left–right dimension is further illustrated by the puzzling observation that mirrors seem to reverse left and right but not up and down or back and front. The person who stares back at you from the looking glass may seem very like yourself, except that his or her watch is on the other wrist, or the hair parting on the other side. Why is one's "mirror twin" of opposite handedness? Why should the left–right dimension be singled out for special treatment?

This question has occupied philosophers for over 2,000 years. In his monumental philosophical poem, *De Rerum Natura,* Titus Lucretius Carus, known as Lucretius (*c.* 99–55 B.C.), discussed the matter as follows:

. . . in mirrors the right hand side of our body
Always appears on the left, because when the
                        on-coming image
Strikes the plane of the mirror, it is not turned
                        backwards unaltered,
But, beaten flat, it rebounds direct, undergoing
                        inversion;
Just as if you should take an undried mask made of
                        plaster,
Dash it 'gainst pillar or beam without distorting
                        the features
So that the daub throws backwards the facial contours
                        inverted.
Now will the right eye become the left and the left
                        eye conversely
Come to the right.[3]

Lucretius' graphic account perhaps does not really explain why the left–right dimension should be singled out for special treatment. Moreover, he was somewhat perplexed by the fact that a curved mirror, as in Figure 1.3, does not reverse left and right at all, but presents a reflection whose left–right orientation is normal:

Further, cylindrical mirrors whose concave sides are
towards us
Send us back idols which have their right on the
same side as ours;
Either because as they pass between the mirror's
two edges
They, on returning to us, undergo a twofold
reflection;
Or it may be that our image, as soon as it reaches
the mirror,
Urged by the curve to wheel about, turns round and
confronts us.[4]

To add to the confusion, we may note that if we turn a curved mirror sideways, as in Figure 1.4, it turns the reflection upside down!

A lucid account of why mirrors do what they do is provided by Martin Gardner in his excellent book, *The Ambidextrous Universe*.[5] In truth, as Gardner points out, a mirror has no preference for left and right, but

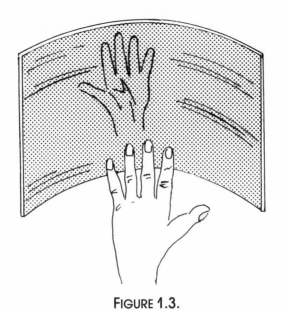

FIGURE 1.3.

A curved mirror presents a reflection that is not a reversed image.

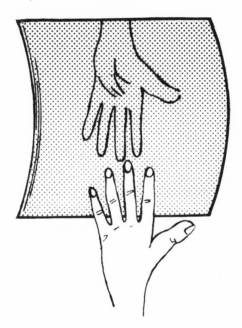

FIGURE 1.4.

A curved mirror can also turn things upside down.

11

simply reverses about its own plane. When you stand in front of a plane mirror what you see is actually a back–front reversal of yourself. A left–right reversal is obtained by standing alongside a mirror, an up–down reversal by standing on top of one. But all three mirror images are really the same, in the sense that if your mirror image could materialize into a real person it would be the same person in each case. We tend to describe that person as the *left–right* reversal of you, but that is simply a matter of convenient description; it is not the fault of the mirror.

But why, then, should the most convenient description refer to left–right reversal? Gardner points out that this has to do with the bilateral symmetry of our bodies. It is perceptually and anatomically simpler to think of a switch between the two sides of the body than to think of one's front changing with one's back, or one's head with one's feet. There is relatively little violence done to the description of the human body if one simply maps the left onto the right, and vice versa; mapping the front of the body, with all its interesting organs, onto the relatively featureless back, and vice versa, is almost unthinkable—it would require an inordinate amount of surgery. But in the case of two mirror-imaged objects that have no plane of symmetry, such as the weathervane-like figures shown in Figure 1.5, there is really no preference for one interpretation

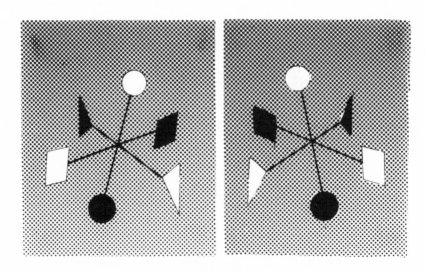

FIGURE 1.5.

No matter how you rotate these two objects, one cannot be superimposed on the other. They are **enantiomorphs**.

over another. One could go from one object to another by reversing about any of the three planes formed by the intersecting lines, or indeed by reflecting about any plane at all.

But if the observation that mirrors seem to reverse left and right and not up and down or back and front is just a matter of interpretation, related to the fact that the human body is to a high degree bilaterally symmetrical, then how might we explain the following? A person may put a glove on her left hand, and the reflected person in the mirror is seen to be wearing a glove on her *right* hand. Why is it not the case that a person who wears a hat on his head is seen in reflection to wear a hat on his feet?[6] (Not, we hope, another pernicious sex difference.) Surely left and right *have* been singled out for special treatment? Again, even this observation is related to the bilateral symmetry of the body, for suppose the gloved person were unfortunate enough to have lost her right hand in an accident, and to have had it replaced with a hook; the reflected person would still have the glove on her hand, not on her hook, just as our other reflected friend continues to wear his hat on his head and not on his feet.

As for curved mirrors, Lucretius' first explanation was essentially correct; they actually create a double reversal, which restores the parity of the original. Moreover, these two reversals are about different planes. If you stand in front of a vertically oriented curved mirror, as in Figure 1.3, the mirror reverses back and front (just as a plane mirror does) but it also reverses left and right. These two reversals are geometrically equivalent to a rotation of 180° about the vertical, so that you essentially see yourself as others really see you. Lucretius' second explanation was therefore also correct, and equivalent to the first. If the mirror is oriented horizontally, as in Figure 1.4, it reverses back and front as well as up and down, which is equivalent to a rotation of 180° about the horizontal.

Geometric Relations between Mirror Images

Objects that are mirror images of one another, such as a left and a right shoe or the two objects shown in Figure 1.5, are known as *enantiomorphs*. Any object that is symmetrical about one or more planes is identical to its own enantiomorph. You are nearly the same as your own enantiomorph, to the point that you might wear the same clothes, but you are not quite so. The two of you are of opposite handedness and have hearts and internal organs that are displayed to opposite sides, and so on. In general, enantiomorphs are not the same in the sense that one could not make a mold from one and fit the other into it; yet in another sense they *are* the same. One can characterize a shape in terms of the distances between all pairs of points on its surface. Such a characterization uniquely specifies a shape *except* that it fails to distinguish between enantiomorphs. For every distance that can be measured between two points on the surface of a left shoe, there is a corresponding distance on a right shoe.

This paradox was of particular interest to the German philosopher Immanuel Kant (1724–1804). In his *Prolegomena to Any Future Metaphysics,* he wrote: "What can more resemble my hand or my ear, and be in all points more alike, than its image in the looking-glass? And yet I cannot put such a hand as I see in the glass in the place of its original . . . ."[7] Kant inferred from this that space itself must be structured in such a way as to establish the "handedness" of a given shape. There is no intrinsic measurable property of a left shoe that establishes it as distinct from a right shoe; and yet it *is* a left shoe, in the sense that it fits a left foot and not a right foot. According to Kant, then, it must gain its quality of "leftness" by its relation to some immutable property of space. Kant also thought of space as *a priori* rather than based on experience and as subjective rather than objective.

Kant has been much criticized for his conclusions, especially by philosophers of a more empiricist bent such as Bertrand Russell who objected to his metaphysical and indeed somewhat mystical conception of space.[8] And yet we can salvage at least something from Kant's analysis. The fact is that the "handedness" of each of a pair of enantiomorphs can really be established only in relation to some standard. Our usual reference is to our own handedness, or more generally our own internal sense of which is left and which is right. As we have already explained, we can know whether a shoe is a left or a right shoe only by referring it to our own internal coordinates. If we ourselves were perfectly symmetrical we could not label a shoe as "left" or "right"—a point we shall make more explicit in the following chapter. Kant was therefore correct in identifying a subjective element in the knowledge of which is left and which is right, and thus to the distinction between enantiomorphs. We also hinted earlier that it *is* possible to establish a purely physical basis for the distinction between left and right in the asymmetry in the laws of physics at the level of weak nuclear interactions. We may find here, perhaps, a basis for Kant's notion of an *a priori* structure underlying physical space. Kant may well have erred in constructing a conception of space that was too transcendental, too far beyond observable reality, but in some respects he was 200 years ahead of this time.

With Kant's help, we have perhaps clarified the bases upon which enantiomorphs may be distinguished, but we have not really resolved the paradox that they are identical with respect to internal structure. There is probably no real mystery in this. The distance between any two points is unaltered by mirror-reflection, and so the tabulation of all possible distances between pairs of points on the surface of an object also remains unaltered when the object is reflected about a plane. Some descriptions survive mirror-reflection, others do not; for instance the location of an object is altered by mirror-reflection, depending where the plane of reflection is located. Indeed, we may tend to prefer certain descriptions precisely because they *are* invariant with respect to mirror-reflection.

That the intrinsic "shape" of an object is unaltered by a reflection about a plane can also be understood in terms of a basic geometric property: mirror-reflection of a three-dimensional object is equivalent to rotation through a fourth dimension! One can turn a left shoe into a right shoe by the simple expedient of flipping it over in four-dimensional space. To gain some grasp of why this is so, imagine two plane figures that are mirror images in *two*-dimensional space, such as a *b* and a *d*. One can convert one to the other by simply turning it over through the third dimension, provided of course that we can prize it out of the plane of the paper. Similarly, if we could escape the three-dimensional constraints of our physical universe, and discover—if only momentarily—a fourth dimension, we could very simply convert Mr. Jack Nicklaus into the greatest left-handed golfer of all time. (This is not intended as a left-handed compliment.)

SUMMARY

Although this chapter has been concerned primarily with questions about physical space, and in particular with the status of the left–right dimension in the description of physical objects, we have seen that for all practical purposes the difference between left and right requires reference to one's own bodily coordinates. The left–right axis is therefore unique in that it is psychological rather than physical—although one *can* discover a physical basis in the relatively inaccessible phenomena of weak nuclear interactions. The constraints imposed by gravity and by motion serve to identify and polarize the up–down and back–front axes, respectively. The left–right axis is then established by elimination, but there is no consistent force or bias to polarize it, at least in the everyday laws of nature.

It is for essentially the same reason that we choose to describe mirror images, or enantiomorphs, as *left–right* reflections of one another. The top and bottom, and the back and front, of your reflection in a mirror are clearly identifiable from the intrinsic properties of the dashing figure before you, but the very symmetry of your body leaves the left–right axis only weakly specified. The simplest interpretation, the one that maximizes the likeness between you and your reflection, is that it is a left–right reflection of yourself. This interpretation, although perceptually and psychologically the most compelling, fails to describe what the mirror is actually doing, which is to reflect about its *own* plane.

In the next chapter, we shall expand upon the psychological character of left and right by carefully defining what it means to be able to *tell* left from right. It will then be easy to show that this ability requires some asymmetry within the person or organism that does the telling. In other words, a symmetrical organism cannot tell left from right.

Chapter 2

Telling Left from Right

We saw in the previous chapter that left and right are defined in terms of the human body. To be able to *tell* left from right, then, is to be able to label each side of the body distinctly and consistently. The labels could be the words "left" and "right" themselves, although we shall have to consider labels that are not words at all but are actions. The main reason for this is that we shall want to test whether animals can tell left from right; although some animals might be taught to use words (parrots, for example), most would have difficulty, and simpler methods for testing their ability are therefore necessary.

One way to find out whether a person can tell the left from the right side of his body is to ask questions like "Show me your left hand," or "Touch your right ear," and observe whether the person responds with the hand or ear on the correct side. This is essentially a test of the person's ability to *decode* the labels "left" and "right" into appropriate spatial responses. We refer to tests like this as tests of *left–right response differentiation.*[1] The labels need not be the words "left" and "right," and indeed need not be words at all. For instance, we might try to teach a dog to lift its left paw whenever a buzzer sounds and its right paw whenever a bell rings. If the dog can do this, we can then say that it can tell left from right; the labels are the buzzer and the bell, respectively. There is nothing in these labels that points to the left or right side,

17

so the dog must refer to its own knowledge of which is which in order to respond correctly.

The other principal way to find out whether a person can tell left from right is to indicate one or other side of his body and ask him to identify whether it is the "left" or the "right" side. In this case the task essentially requires the person to *encode* the sides of the body into the labels "left" and "right." The task itself involves stimulus events, such as touching or pointing to one or other side, that are mirror images with respect to the person being tested. We therefore refer to this test as one of *mirror-image stimulus discrimination,* or simply *mirror-image discrimination.*[2] Unless we specify otherwise, we shall take it that the term "mirror-image" refers to *left–right* mirror images with respect to the person or animal being tested. Once again, the labels need not be the terms "left" and "right" and need not be verbal. For example, we might try to condition a dog to salivate when it is touched on the left side of the body but not to salivate when it is touched on the right side. In this case the dog is supposed to signal its knowledge of which is left and which is right by salivating or not, as the case may be—provided of course that it can *tell* left from right. In fact, as we shall see in the next chapter, it appears to be virtually impossible to condition dogs to accomplish this discrimination.

We can extend the test of mirror-image discrimination to include discrimination of any pairs of events, or stimuli, that are left–right mirror images of one another. For instance, discrimination of the lowercase letters *b* and *d* requires the ability to tell left from right. Discrimination of *b* from *p* does not require the ability to tell left from right, however, because these letters are up–down mirror images of one another, not left–right mirror images. On the other hand, we can say that it does require the ability to tell left from right in order to distinguish objects or patterns that are mirror images if these objects or patterns can appear in *any* arbitrary orientation. We could not discriminate a left shoe from a right shoe unless we could tell left from right, assuming there is nothing systematic in the way the shoe is presented. We might discover that a particular shoe fits a certain foot, but that is no help because we still would not know whether the foot is a left or a right foot. But if the shoe is always presented to us with the open side toward us and the toe pointing to our right, then we could label a left shoe as distinct from a right shoe by virtue of the fact that the rounded side would be uppermost for a left shoe, but on the lower side for a right shoe. These different possibilities are illustrated in Figure 2.1.

In the case of mirror-image patterns or objects that can appear in *any* orientation, the task of discriminating among them may involve more than just the ability to tell left from right. It may also require an act of mental rotation in order to refer the pattern or object in question to one's own body coordinates. For instance, a child may correctly identify her own left and right sides, but fail to label the left and right sides of a person facing her because she cannot mentally accomplish the 180° rotation necessary to align that person with her own body coordinates. In fact, children sometimes systematically reverse the labels "left" and "right" when identifying the sides of other people.[3] This shows, incidentally, that they *can* tell left from right, but that they cannot perform the mental mapping operations required to successfully apply the verbal labels "left" and "right"! Again, a person might know which is his own left or right foot, but have difficulty in identifying a shoe as "left" or "right" because he lacks the spatial imagination to mentally try the shoe on.

It is extremely important to note that in tests of telling left from right,

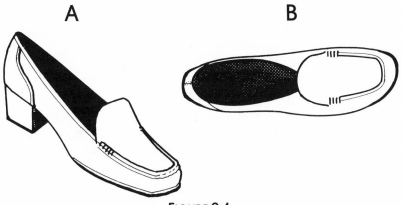

A   **B**

FIGURE 2.1.

If a shoe is presented in **any** orientation, as in (A), you would need to be able to tell left from right in order to decide whether it is a left or a right shoe. But if it is always presented with, say, the open side toward us and the toe pointing to the right, as in (B), then you could decide whether it is a left or right shoe without being able to tell left from right. It is a left shoe if the rounded side is uppermost, a right shoe if the rounded side is on the lower side.

the labels that are attached to the two sides must not themselves be left–right mirror images. Just as the ability to copy script does not prove that one can read, so the ability to attach mirror-image labels to mirror-image events or stimuli does not prove that one can tell left from right. In the natural world, most asymmetrical behavior is of this type and reveals nothing of the ability to tell left from right: a cow might swish its tail to one or other side to brush off a fly, a sheep might turn left or right to follow a winding track, a falcon might swoop left or right to seize a prey. Tests of the ability to tell left from right must be carefully contrived so that left and right are mapped onto labels that are not themselves left–right mirror images. One is hard pressed to find examples of such tests in the natural world; that is, animals are hardly ever called upon to tell left from right. Humans are sometimes required to be able to tell left from right, as in shaking hands (i.e. knowing which hand to hold out) or in giving and receiving directional instructions (e.g. "Take the second turn on your left"). In the case of scripts that are written in a consistent left–right direction, both reading and writing also require the ability to tell left from right. Discrimination of *b* from *d* and *p* from *q* are both mirror-image discriminations, and the ability to write a word or a sentence forward rather than backward requires left–right response differentiation. Most parents and teachers will note that these are precisely the kinds of tasks that young children find difficult when they are learning to read and write.

It is also important to understand that mirror-image discrimination has to do with the way one interprets the world rather than with the way one actually sees it, although the distinction may sometimes be a fine one. For instance, a child may have not the slightest difficulty in seeing which way round a *b* is, but yet have extreme difficulty in labeling it as a "bee" rather than a "dee." A child who is unable to tell left from right might easily be able to tell that the letters *b* and *d* are different, but yet be unable to label them appropriately. A child may be able to point in the direction that an arrow is pointing without knowing whether he or she is pointing left or right. Limits on the ability to tell left from right are not really limits on perception, they are limits on one's ability to apply labels.

Most tests of the ability to tell left from right are actually tests of *memory*. The simple reason for this is that when labels must be attached to the sides of the body, or to patterns or objects that are left–right mirror images, these labels have to be taught. The child must learn the correct labels for *b* and *d*, and the difficulty he or she may have resides not in his or her perception of which way round they are, but in his or her memory for which label goes with which letter. The simple acts of recognizing or recalling the left–right orientations of events or scenes are themselves tests of the ability to tell left from right. If you recognize a photograph or a slide of a scene as being in the same orientation as the original scene (or if you recognize it as in the opposite orientation, for that matter), you are demonstrating mirror-image discrimination. Here the labels are "same" and "different" (or "opposite"), and the potential stimuli are the photograph of the original and its mirror image. Similarly, if someone asks you which way round something was—such as whether you were sitting on the left or right of someone at the dinner table—and you indicate the answer, you are effectively demonstrating left–right response differentiation. You may give the answer verbally, but this generally implies and indeed stands for an explicit indication by means of some action, such as drawing a plan of the seating arrangements.

Some years ago one of us, who shall be nameless, was discussing these matters with a well known psychologist, who shall also be nameless. The psychologist claimed to have no difficulty remembering which way round things were. He also claimed to be familiar with Whistler's famous painting of his mother, known formally as *Arrangement in Black and Gray: The Artist's Mother,* but when asked whether the portrait was in left or right profile he made the wrong choice. These are moments to cherish. We invite the reader to consult his or her own recollection of this painting and state which profile is depicted. Naturally, we cannot ourselves recall the proper orientation.

Psychologists quite often set up tests in which a person or an animal must choose which of two simultaneously displayed mirror-image patterns is "correct." For instance a child might be shown a *b* and a *d* and asked to point to the "dee." Or a hungry cat might be confronted with two doors, one with a 45° (/) diagonal line across it and one with a 135° (\) diagonal line across it, and must learn to choose the one with the 135° line in order to gain access to food. Such tests are often described as tests of mirror-image discrimination because the subject must know which of two mirror-image patterns is the appropriate one to choose. But there is often an ambiguity here. If the patterns are displayed side by side, they form a bilaterally symmetrical pair, and the subject essentially has to make a left or right response. Usually the two patterns are interchanged from time to time on a random basis, so that the subject must make a left response to one symmetrical combination and a right response to the other. This is illustrated in Figure 2.2. Strictly, then, this is a test of left–right response differentiation rather than one of mirror-image discrimination. In practice, however, it may depend on the subject's strategy. If he tends to focus on the patterns one at a time, the task may be one of mirror-image discrimination, but if he treats the stimulus pair as a single configuration the task is one of left-right response differentiation. Either way, the task does call for the ability to tell left from right, so the point may seem academic. We suspect, however, that the two kinds of tests may make somewhat different demands and the ambiguity of this so called "simultaneous mirror-image discrimination" is perhaps best avoided.

Readers who are anxious to rush off and test their children, cats, or guinea pigs for the ability to tell left from right should note one final

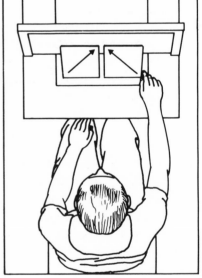

FIGURE 2.2.

This situation illustrates the ambiguity of simultaneous mirror-image discrimination. The subject might be making a left response to one symmetrical display and a right response to the other; alternatively, he might simply choose the arrow that points to the left in each situation.

point. In tests of either mirror-image discrimination or left–right response differentiation, the tester should be careful to avoid constant left–right asymmetries in the environment which might serve as cues as to which is left and which is right. For instance, if the tester always stands on the right hand side of a child, the child might simply note that a *b* has the rounded edge facing toward the tester while a *d* has the rounded edge away from the tester, and so discriminate them without having to refer to his own knowledge of which is left and which is right. Or if a cat must discriminate between two doors displaying mirror-image patterns, and both doors are hinged on the left, this simple asymmetry could provide the relevant left–right information. In practice, it may be virtually impossible to eliminate all left–right cues in the environment, since the environment is seldom perfectly symmetrical. One way to achieve close to optimal conditions in mirror-image discrimination is to test the animal in darkness, save for the patterns to be discriminated.

In summary, the task of deciding whether a person or an animal can tell left from right is deceptively subtle. The important question is whether the subject can associate different non-mirror-image labels consistently with opposite sides of the body under conditions in which there are no consistent left–right cues in the environment. No test can be considered final. A subject may fail to accomplish a mirror-image discrimination because of a failure in spatial mapping, or for any number of other reasons such as lack of interest or motivation, poor vision, or a desire to cheat, and not because of inability to tell left from right. Again, a subject may be unable to tell left from right, but may successfully learn a mirror-image discrimination or a left–right response differentiation because of the presence of some environmental asymmetry unnoticed by the tester. In the next chapter we shall review some actual experiments on the ability of animals to tell left from right and we shall touch on some of these methodological issues again. Before we do this, however, we must establish the very important point that a symmetrical organism cannot tell left from right.

RESTRICTIONS IMPOSED BY BILATERAL SYMMETRY

It will perhaps be clear already that the ability to tell left from right requires some structural, bodily asymmetry. We saw in Chapter 1 that left and right are effectively *defined* in terms of the sides of the body, and if there is no way to distinguish the sides of the body with non-mirror-image labels, then there is no way to tell left from right. A perfectly symmetrical person could never tell which is his left or right hand, could never discriminate a b from a d, could never learn to write in a consistent direction.

The first person to appreciate this point was the versatile nineteenth-century Austrian scientist, Ernst Mach. Specifically, he thought that confusion of left–right mirror images was due to the symmetry of the visual system.

> It is extremely probable that sensations of space are produced by the motor apparatus of the eye. Without entering into particulars, we may observe, first, that the whole apparatus of the eye, and especially the motor apparatus, is symmetrical with respect to the median plane of the head. Hence symmetrical movements of looking will determine like or approximately like space-sensations. Children constantly confound the letters b and d, and also p and q. Adults, too, do not readily notice a change from left to right unless some special points of apprehension or intellect render it perceptible. The symmetry of the motor apparatus of the eye is very perfect.[4]

This account is perhaps not totally explicit and seems to suggest, erroneously, that a symmetrical visual system would create a *perceptual* confusion between mirror images, whereas we have already pointed out that the restriction imposed by symmetry is on labeling rather than on perception per se. Moreover, the restriction imposed by bilateral symmetry is not limited to the visual system or to the discrimination of mirror images—it applies to *any* test of the ability to tell left from right.[5]

We can demonstrate that this is so with reference to a mirror. Any mechanism that is perfectly bilaterally symmetrical would be unaltered by mirror reflection; the looking glass version would be identical to the original. Imagine such a mechanism responding to some stimulus. Mirror reflection would reveal the *same* mechanism giving the mirror-image response to the mirror-image stimulus. That is, a bilaterally symmetrical mechanism *must* give mirror-image responses to mirror-image stimuli, and this is sufficient to guarantee that it could not accomplish either left–right response differentiation or mirror-image stimulus discrimination as defined earlier in this chapter. For instance, imagine a symmetrical child calling a b a "bee" and a d a "dee"; mirror reflection would reveal the *same* child calling a d a "bee" and a b a "dee"— an impossible state of affairs. Again, imagine a symmetrical dog lifting its left paw to a buzzer and its right paw to a bell; mirror reflection would show the *same* dog lifting its right paw to a buzzer and its left paw to a bell—another contradiction. It follows that these behaviors cannot occur.

Imagine Alice through the looking glass, in a world where everything except Alice herself is mirror reversed. We must also imagine that she has some way of averting the annihilation that would result from the contact of matter with antimatter—a point overlooked by Lewis Carroll. Let us further suppose that Alice is perfectly bilaterally symmetrical. There is then no way in which she could detect that the world she is in is not the real one. If it were the world that remained the same while Alice were reflected, nothing would be different because Alice, being symmetrical, would be quite unaltered by reflection. In terms of her relation to the world, and therefore of her ability to recognize and respond to it, the situation is exactly as it would be if the world were reflected and Alice were not. In either case, then, the world would appear to Alice to be quite unaltered.

The fact that Alice *did* notice some odd things about the looking glass world can therefore be said to prove that Alice must have been asymmetrical, or rather that her creator was. Martin Gardner confirms this for us in his introduction to *The Annotated Alice*.

> In appearance Carroll was handsome and asymmetric—two facts that may have contributed to his interest in mirror reflections. One shoulder was slightly higher than the other, his smile was slightly askew, and the level of his blue eyes was not quite the same.[6]

It was also known that, politically, he leaned to the right.

Some intelligent readers have proven resistant to our reasoning,[7] so we therefore issue a challenge. We invite anyone to construct a symmetrical device that can tell left from right by either of our test criteria. If anyone can do so we shall eat our words—indeed, we shall eat this very book, covers and all. However, there is one option we shall disallow, that of using those weak subatomic forces thought to disobey the law of conservation of parity. Nonconservation of parity implies that certain dynamic laws do not survive mirror reflection, so that in principle it might be possible to construct a symmetrical device whose behavior *would* meet our criteria, although there is some question as to whether such a device could be strictly symmetrical. But we doubt in any case that this possible exception has any relevance to the practical issue of telling left from right, since the domain in which nonconservation of parity applies is far removed from that of the neural and behavioral events involved in discrimination and choice.

The restriction imposed by bilateral symmetry is of some practical importance because although no animal or organism is *perfectly* bilaterally symmetrical, most are approximately so. We shall see in the next chapter, moreover, that most animals have difficulty telling left from right, although few animals may be completely unable to do so. It seems entirely reasonable to conclude that the difficulty of telling left from right is related in some way to the bilateral symmetry of the body and of the central nervous system. We shall speculate in more detail on this relation in Chapter 4, after we have examined the evidence on left–right confusion.

Chapter 3

Can Animals Tell
Left from Right?

Pooh looked at his two paws. He knew that one of them was the right,
and he knew that when you had decided which of them was the right,
then the other was the left, but he could never remember how to begin.
"Well," he said slowly. . . [A.A. Milne, *House at Pooh Corner*]

Here we find Pooh faced with the task of attaching the verbal labels
"left" and "right" to each of his paws. His two paws are approximate
mirror images but the labels "left" and "right" are not. The task is
therefore a genuine test of Pooh's ability to tell left from right; it is an
example of mirror-image discrimination. Pooh seems to be failing the
test. We can see from his thoughts that he is confused and it seems fair to
conclude that he cannot tell left from right. It is easy to know about
Pooh, since we are privy to his thought, but how do we find out about
real animals?

As we explained in Chapter 2, the relevant procedures are those
which test *mirror-image stimulus discrimination* or *left–right response
differentiation*. We remind the reader of our definitions and discussions
of these tests, for there are many procedures which might seem to test
mirror-image discrimination but which fail to meet our criteria. We also
noted that experiments are easily contaminated by extraneous cues
which might enable the animal to solve the problem without reference to
left and right at all. Consider, for example, how Pooh would be assisted

by the presence of a mole or a scar on his right paw. Some of the experiments we shall mention were not explicitly concerned with the left–right problem at all, and the experimenters were not concerned with eliminating extraneous left–right cues. It is likely that there were obvious extraneous cues in at least some of the experiments we shall describe, and in this respect we can expect the evidence to *overestimate* the ability of the animals tested to tell left from right. If Pooh knew his right paw simply because of the mole he need not know left from right to be able to raise his right (or left) paw on command.

On the other hand there are also ways in which the evidence from experiments might *underestimate* the ability of an animal to tell left from right. A particular test of mirror-image discrimination of left–right differentiation might prove difficult for some reason unrelated to left and right; the patterns might be too complex to be discriminable, the subject might be bored or uncooperative, or the training procedure might be ineffective. Suppose, for example, that we attempt to train a rat to choose one of two mirror-image stimuli, but because of its short-sightedness it is unable to see the stimuli from the point where it must make its choice. Its choice will never be influenced by stimuli it cannot see, and no amount of training will change that.

It is practically impossible to *prove* that an animal cannot tell left from right. Attempting to decide this question puts us in the position of an angler who fishes all day in a certain pond and catches nothing. He is reluctant to conclude that there are no fish in the pond; another angler, using different bait or tackle, might easily prove him wrong. Suppose the angler fishes three ponds, using the same bait and tackle, and catches fish in all but one. At least now he can make a useful comment on the *relative* chances of success in each pond using a particular tackle. Like the angler, we shall do better to consider the relative difficulty of left–right tasks compared to other sorts of tasks. As we shall see, most animals do seem to be able to solve at least some left–right tasks, albeit with difficulty, given sufficient training.

MIRROR-IMAGE DISCRIMINATION

Mirror-image stimulus discrimination requires an animal to make different, non-mirror-image responses to stimuli that are left–right mirror images. We made the point in Chapter 2 that this test strictly requires that the stimuli be presented one at a time. If the stimuli are presented simultaneously, side by side, and are interchanged randomly, the test is then really one of left–right differentiation, although the animal may effectively treat it as one of mirror-image discrimination by attending to the stimuli one at a time. However, it is convenient to include experiments on simultaneous discrimination in this section rather than under the heading of left–right differentiation.

In order to establish that animals find it difficult to discriminate left–right mirror images because of a difficulty telling left from right, we need to be able to make a comparison with other stimuli that do not involve a left–right difference. To return to our fishing analogy, we need to compare the effectiveness of the same tackle used in different ponds. This comparison is usually referred to as experimental control; it is a device for eliminating some of the alternative explanations for a particular experimental result. The fact that fish are caught in ponds 1 and 2 means that failure to catch fish in pond 3 is not a result of inappropriate tackle, bait, or technique. If we are testing an animal's ability to discriminate left–right mirror images, we might usefully include control stimuli such as up–down mirror images for purposes of comparison. For instance, we might compare discrimination of the left–right pair ⊂ and ⊃ with discrimination of the up–down pair ∪ and ∩. If our subject can learn to discriminate up–down but not left–right mirror images of the same shape, we can conclude that it is the left–right difference that poses the difficulty, and not some other aspect of the stimuli or training procedure.

However, there is one special but frequently encountered case in which there is no such control. This is the case of mirror-image obliques—lines, rectangles, or grids oriented at, say, 45° versus 135° or 60° versus 120°. Any such pair of mirror-image obliques can be considered to be either left–right or up–down mirror images, since reflection of an oblique about the vertical or horizontal axis achieves the same result. Experimenters have usually compared the discrimination of mirror-image obliques with that of horizontal versus vertical. As we shall see, this does not always provide an altogether appropriate control.

In the previous chapter we noted that the inability to tell left from right need not imply any perceptual deficit. An animal may be able to *perceive* correctly the left–right orientation of each of two mirror-image stimuli yet be unable to tell which is which in discrimination training. Ideally, then, experiments should also be designed to distinguish perceptual factors from those which have to do with telling left from right. In fact, this ideal is seldom achieved. This issue has special relevance to the discrimination of mirror-image obliques, since it is known that perception of lines or bars is worse if they are sloping obliquely than if they are horizontal or vertical.[1] This factor obviously complicates the interpretation of experiments using mirror-image oblique lines, since it is difficult to separate poor perception from difficulties in labeling. That is, mirror-image obliques may be difficult to discriminate either because they are mirror images or because they are obliques, and in some experiments it is impossible to tell which explanation is correct.

Bearing in mind these general considerations of experimental control, we may now take a look at some experiments that bear on the question of whether animals can solve mirror-image discriminations. As might be expected, not many species have been studied. Those that have were chosen usually on account of their availability in research laboratories where colonies were maintained for purposes quite unrelated to questions about left and right. Nevertheless, a reasonable range of vertebrate families is represented.

Rats

From the earliest days of experimental psychology extensive use has been made of the laboratory rat as a convenient subject on which to work out the laws governing behavior. The neuropsychologist Karl Lashley, working at Harvard University in the 1930s, carried out many studies of visual discrimination in the rat.[2] These experiments stemmed largely from Lashley's desire to understand the functional organization of the rat brain, but the fortunate inclusion of mirror-image stimuli in his experiments provided results that bear on our interests also.

In order to discover whether his rats could discriminate between a particular pair of visual stimuli, Lashley mounted the stimuli on cards. The cards were used in a training apparatus where they blocked two openings leading to a food tray. Lashley trained the rats to knock down an unsecured card to gain access to the food. If the unsecured card always displayed one particular stimulus the rat might be expected to learn to recognize the unsecured card from the stimulus displayed on it. If the rat learned always to approach the unsecured card rather than the secured card, it could reasonably be concluded that the rat could discriminate between the stimuli displayed on the cards.

The training apparatus, generally referred to as the Lashley Jumping Stand, is shown in Figure 3.1. The rat jumps 20 centimeters from a small platform to the stimulus cards. A jump to the correct card knocks down the card and gives access to the food tray on the platform behind. A jump to the incorrect card results in the rat falling into the net below.

In the illustration the stimuli are a black square and a black triangle. Lashley's experiments involved first familiarizing the rat with the jumping stand by allowing it to explore the stand with the stimulus cards not fully blocking the holes and with the jumping platform pushed up to the cards. The rat learned to find food in the tray, and later, to jump against the cards to get to the food.

The jumping distance was gradually increased to 20 centimeters. The rat was deprived of food for a day to provide an incentive to jump. Formal training with the mirror-image stimuli was carried out in daily training sessions of ten trials per day. Each trial involved setting up the stimulus cards, positioning the food tray and placing the rat on the stand, and

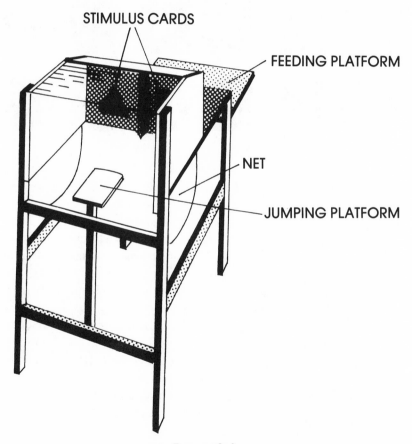

STIMULUS CARDS

FEEDING PLATFORM

NET

JUMPING PLATFORM

FIGURE 3.1.

Lashley used a jumping stand like this one for testing discrimination in rats.

ended with either a correct jump followed by eating, or an incorrect jump followed by recovery from the net. The two stimulus cards were assigned to left or right positions according to an irregular order, so that if the rat ignored the stimuli and always jumped to the left card, say, it would be correct on only half of the trials.

Using this simultaneous discrimination-training procedure, Lashley trained fifteen rats on both left–right and up–down mirror-image pairs of stimuli consisting of triangles and U-shapes (see Figure 3.2). Training was continued until each rat made twenty consecutive correct

FIGURE 3.2.

Lashley tried to teach rats to discriminate between the figures in each pair.

jumps. As it turned out, the left–right mirror-image triangles presented no more difficulty than the up–down mirror-image triangles, but the left–right U shapes proved much harder than the up–down ones. With the left–right U shapes, 5 rats failed to master the problem in 150 trials, and the remaining ten averaged 120 trials to mastery. On the up–down U shapes, all but two rats mastered the problem in an average of 70 trials. In another experiment, Lashley trained twenty rats on the mirror-image pairs of N and S shapes shown in Figure 3.2. Here *all* failed to learn in 150 trials. Note, however, that each pair represents up–down as well as left–right mirror images. Another two rats were trained on a clockwise versus an anticlockwise spiral. Neither progressed beyond chance performance in 300 trials.

Of Lashley's three experiments, only that with the U-shapes and triangles has a clear meaning because only in that case were appropriate control stimuli used. As we have seen, there are really no suitable control stimuli for oblique-type stimuli such as N, S, or spirals. Mirror-image stimuli of this type may have been difficult because they involve left–right discrimination, or for some unrelated reason such as their complexity. Even so, these results are at least consistent with the idea that left–right discriminations are very difficult.

Following Lashley's work, over three decades passed before rats were again put to the test on mirror-image problems, this time by Marcel Kinsbourne who was then at the Institute of Experimental Psychology at Oxford University.[3] Kinsbourne gave twenty-eight rats simultaneous-discrimination training on various pairs of P-shaped stimuli. Non-mirror-image pairs were the easiest to discriminate. Only one out of six rats mastered the up–down mirror-image problem in 200 trials, but *none* of the seven rats trained on left–right mirror images were able to solve the problem, even to the weak criterion of 9 out of 10 correct.

An interesting experiment by Karen Tee and Austin H. Riesen shows that rats have difficulty discriminating mirror-image oblique lines, and that this difficulty is not perceptual.[4] The rats were trained on two different kinds of task. They were confronted with two doors and had to push open the correct one in order to avoid receiving a mild electric shock. One task was a simultaneous-discrimination task in which different patterns were displayed on the doors, and the rats had to learn which pattern was correct. The other task was a matching task in which a third pattern was placed between the doors, and the rats had to choose the door displaying the pattern that matched this middle one. For both tasks, the patterns were either mirror-image oblique parallel lines, or horizontal versus vertical parallel lines (see Figure 3.3).

The matching task proved of equal difficulty regardless of whether the patterns were oblique lines or horizontal versus vertical lines, and of difficulty equal to that of the discrimination task when the patterns were horizontal and vertical lines. But the discrimination task with oblique lines was considerably more difficult, and six of the twelve rats failed to master it at all. This was the only case in which the animals were required to tell left from right. Moreover, the fact that the rats could accomplish the matching task with oblique lines demonstrates that they had no difficulty in correctly *perceiving* the orientations of the lines. The problem in the discrimination task was therefore one of *labeling* which was which.

Cats and Dogs

Having now dealt with rats, it is natural to follow them up with cats. The evidence is rather confusing, but it is worth our consideration here because it demonstrates the importance of using a variety of training procedures. Stuart Sutherland, then of Oxford University, trained four cats to discriminate mirror-image oblique rectangles and four others to discriminate horizontal from vertical rectangles using a simultaneous-discrimination procedure.[5] During training, a cat would be released into a small enclosure containing two escape doors separated by a partition. The doors displayed patterns, one of which could be displaced to give access to food. Using this procedure, the two sets of stimuli proved equally difficult.

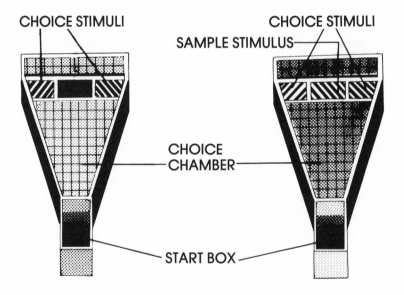

FIGURE 3.3.

Tee and Riesen used these two chambers to test the ability of rats to discriminate between mirror-image oblique lines. For the task depicted on the **left**, the rat had to remember which stimulus was the correct one. For the task depicted on the **right**, the rat had to decide which of the choice stimuli matched the sample stimulus. With mirror-image stimuli like those depicted, the task involving memory (left) proved more difficult than the one involving matching (right), but the tasks were of equal difficulty when the stimuli were not mirror images.

Sutherland sought to control for the possibility that the cats were responding to the configurations made by the two patterns together, rather than to the individual patterns—an issue we raised in Chapter 2. He therefore retrained the cats using a different procedure, called successive discrimination, where only one stimulus was presented on each trial. On half the trials the correct shape only was presented with a blank door on the other side; on the other half the incorrect shape only was presented. When the incorrect shape was displayed the blank door gave access to food. All the cats were still able to respond correctly on this new task. They made a few more mistakes than before, but with both sets of stimuli fared equally well. With continued training, the cats improved slightly in the horizontal–vertical task, but not on the oblique task. In short, the cats seemed to have no special difficulty with mirror-image obliques. Sutherland himself seemed surprised at their prowess, commenting thus:

> The fact that, when only one stimulus was presented at a time, the animals still discriminated as accurately between the oblique rectangles as between the horizontal and vertical rectangles was in marked contrast to my own powers of discrimination in relation to these shapes. In setting up the oblique rectangles in the correct sequence, I had to proceed slowly and to double check every setting for fear of making an error. No such difficulty was experienced with the horizontal and vertical rectangles.[6]

Despite Sutherland's findings, two more recent studies seem to suggest that cats do have some difficulty with mirror-image discriminations. Jill Parriss taught four cats to discriminate mirror-image obliques, and also to discriminate horizontal from vertical lines.[7] She presented the stimuli one at a time, so that the task involving oblique lines was a genuine test of mirror-image discrimination. This task proved more difficult than the discrimination of horizontal and vertical, regardless of which task was learned first. J. M. Warren confirmed Sutherland's finding that mirror-image obliques were no more difficult than horizontal versus vertical when the simultaneous-discrimination procedure was used. However his cats did find it more difficult to discriminate U-shapes if they were left–right mirror images than if they were up-down mirror images.[8]

We know of only one relevant experiment on dogs, or rather, on *one* dog. This was reported, not surprisingly, by the great Russian physiologist and psychologist Ivan P. Pavlov, who mentioned that two colleagues of his had been unable to teach a dog to salivate in response to a touch on one side of the body, and not to a touch on the symmetrically opposite place on the other side.[9] Pavlov did not mention any control tasks involving touches that were not mirror images, but he did state that the difficulty of discriminating the mirror-image touches disappeared when the principal nerve fibers linking the two hemispheres of the brain were severed. We shall have more to say on the significance of this finding in Chapter 4.

Monkeys and Chimpanzees

In experiments on primates, including monkeys, chimpanzees, and even human children, it has been common practice to use an apparatus known as the Wisconsin General Test Apparatus, or WGTA for short

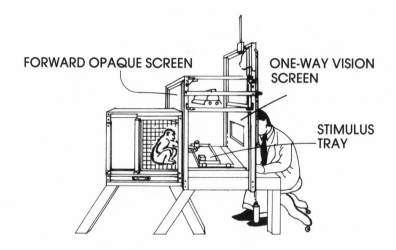

FORWARD OPAQUE SCREEN

ONE-WAY VISION SCREEN

STIMULUS TRAY

FIGURE 3.4.

Psychologist Harry F. Harlow developed the Wisconsin General Test Apparatus (WGTA) for testing discrimination in primates.

(see Figure 3.4). It was developed at the Wisconsin Primate Laboratories by Harry F. Harlow, a psychologist known for his work on the effects of rearing practices on the emotional behaviour of monkeys. Unlike the training apparatuses already described, the WGTA does not require the animal to move anything except its arms, and training can be carried out without the animal leaving its home cage. The WGTA is simply pushed up to the cage and the animal can reach through the bars of its cage to open either of two doors on which stimulus patterns are displayed. Both doors cover foodwells, only one of which is baited. Between trials an opaque screen can be lowered to shut off the animal's view while the stimuli are repositioned and a foodwell baited.

In one experiment, 12 rhesus monkeys were taught in the WGTA to discriminate 48 different pairs of stimulus patterns, ranging in complexity from V-shapes to E- and K-like shapes (see Figure 3.5).[10] The discriminations were divided equally into those between up–down mirror

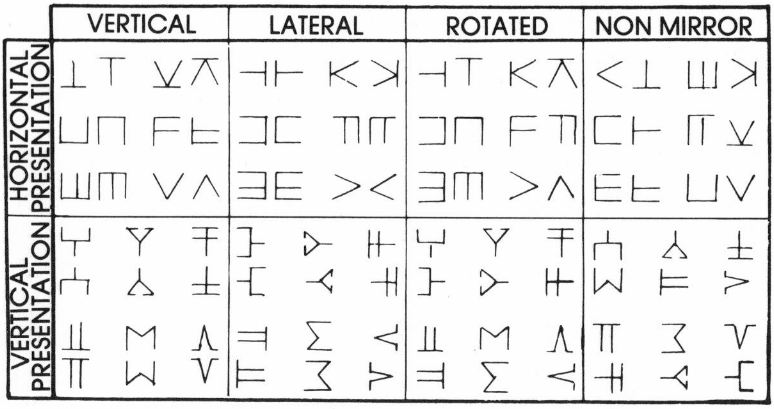

	VERTICAL	LATERAL	ROTATED	NON MIRROR
HORIZONTAL PRESENTATION	⊥ T ⅄⅄	⊣⊢ K ⋊	⊣T K⅄	< ⊥ Ш⋊
	Ⴑ⊓ Ⲫ⊢	⊐⊏ ⫪⫪	⊐⊓ Ⲫ⫪	C⊢ ⫪⋎
	Ш⊓ V∧	⊒E ><	⊒⊓ >∧	E⊢ ⊔V
VERTICAL PRESENTATION	4 Y Ŧ	⊣ ⋗ ⊩	Ч Y Ŧ	⊓ ⋏ ⊥
	⊓ ⋏ ⊥	⊏ ⋖ ⊩	⊢ ⋗ ⊩	W ⊨ ⋗
	⊥ M ⋏	⊐ Σ ⋗	⊥ M ⋏	⫪ ⊒ V
	⫪ W V	⊨ ⋜ ⋗	⊒ Σ ⋖	⊩ ⋖ ⊏

FIGURE 3.5.

Riopelle and his colleagues taught these discriminations to rhesus monkeys.

images, left–right mirror images, rotations (in which each stimulus was compared with the same stimulus rotated 90°), and various non-mirror-image pairs. The stimuli were displayed on doors that were either side by side or one above the other, the latter arrangement resulting in generally slower learning. Regardless of the arrangement of the doors, however, the up–down mirror images proved the easiest to discriminate, and the left–right mirror images the most difficult.

In another experiment four chimpanzees were taught to discriminate a variety of pairs of stimuli, including simultaneously presented mirror-image oblique lines and horizontal versus vertical lines.[11] Because of procedural variations, it is difficult to compare performance on the two tasks accurately. Nevertheless, twice as many trials on the average were required to learn the mirror-image problem as to learn the horizontal–vertical problem.

Octopuses

Stuart Sutherland, whose work with cats has already been described, tried to teach octopuses to discriminate various stimulus pairs, including mirror-image oblique rectangles, horizontal versus vertical rectangles and T-shapes presented either as left–right or up–down mirror images.[12] Training was carried out at the Stazione Zoologica in Naples, where octopuses were kept in individual tanks and shapes were presented one at a time at the end of the tank away from the octopus's home. Animals were trained to attack one shape and not the other by rewarding attack on one shape with a piece of sardine and punishing attack on the other shape with a 10-volt electric shock. Shapes were presented on the end of a transparent Perspex rod, and were moved up and down in the water by hand through a distance of about three centimeters three times a second. The shapes remained in the water for a maximum of 30 seconds unless attacked earlier. The octopuses failed to learn to discriminate the oblique rectangles, but had little difficulty with the horizontal and vertical ones. The T-shapes proved very difficult, especially the left–right mirror images. In a later experiment Sutherland trained the discrimination of U-shapes presented as left–right or up–down mirror images.[13] The octopuses were able to learn the up–down problem, but were still not discriminating between the left–right stimuli after 400 trials. In the octopus, then, it appears that the problem of telling left from right is particularly severe.

Goldfish

In collaboration with Sutherland, Janet Mackintosh trained goldfish to discriminate between simultaneously presented pairs of rectangles at one end of a fish tank.[14] The rectangles were presented either as mirror-image obliques or as horizontal versus vertical. One stimulus of each pair was baited with a pellet of food not apparent until the stimulus was closely approached. The obliques were much more difficult to discriminate than were the horizontal and vertical rectangles. Half of the fish failed to learn the mirror-image discrimination, whereas all but one of the 16 fish mastered the horizontal–vertical problem.

Pigeons

The homing pigeon was first introduced to psychology laboratories as an experimental subject during the 1940s when B. F. Skinner of Harvard University explored the feasibility of using trained pigeons to guide missiles used in warfare. This project was abandoned in favor of radar control, but the pigeon had by then proved its value in psychological research and now vies with the rat in popularity.

Discrimination training with pigeons is usually carried out in a small ventilated box, sometimes known as a Skinner box. On one internal wall of the box there are up to three circular disks, or keys, of about one inch in diameter. Stimulus patterns can be projected onto these keys from behind. If the pigeon pecks the correct key, grain is occasionally presented in a lighted hopper below the keys, as illustrated in Figure 3.6.

Robert J. Williams, a master's student at the University of Auckland, compared discrimination of left–right mirror-image pairs with discrimination of up–down mirror-image pairs.[15] The patterns to be discriminated were presented successively on the center key, and consisted of bisected circles that were half red and half green. Left–right and up–down pairs proved equally difficult when the birds viewed the patterns with both eyes open, and when they had to peck the center key in order to procure grain. The left–right pairs proved the more difficult to discriminate, however, when the birds had to peck one of the keys to the left or right of the center key, depending upon which was lighted up, in order to obtain access to the grain, although the stimuli themselves were still projected on the center key. The left–right problem was also more difficult than the up-down one when the birds had one eye covered up. This is rather surprising, since the very fact of having an eye covered would have created a consistent left–right asymmetry that could have served as an external cue.

Williams' experiment showed that pigeons find left–right mirror images only slightly more difficult to discriminate than up–down mirror images; indeed, the added difficulty is only apparent when the task is made more complicated in ways irrelevant to the discrimination itself. Some years earlier, moreover, it had been shown that pigeons could discriminate mirror-image obliques about as well as they could discriminate horizontal from vertical.[16] Nevertheless, other evidence reveals that pigeons also display a natural tendency to treat left–right mirror images as equivalent. For instance, if a pigeon is taught to peck a key displaying an oblique line and is then tested with the line in various different orientations, it pecks almost as much to the mirror-image of the original line as to the original itself, and somewhat less to other orientations. This was first demonstrated in 1966[17] and was repeated in our own laboratory in 1972.[18] Our own experiment also showed that pigeons in which the major neural commissures joining the two sides of the brain had been disconnected did not show strong generalization to the mirror image of the training stimulus. This result, illustrated in Figure 3.7, will be discussed again in Chapter 4.

It is perhaps surprising that pigeons should generalize readily from a particular stimulus to its own mirror-image, yet have no great difficulty learning a mirror-image discrimination. However, there is some evidence that they may learn mirror-image discriminations by developing consistent response or postural asymmetries. For example, we have ob-

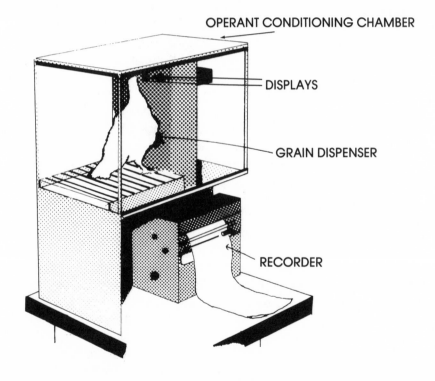

FIGURE 3.6.

The Skinner box has been used in teaching discriminations to pigeons.

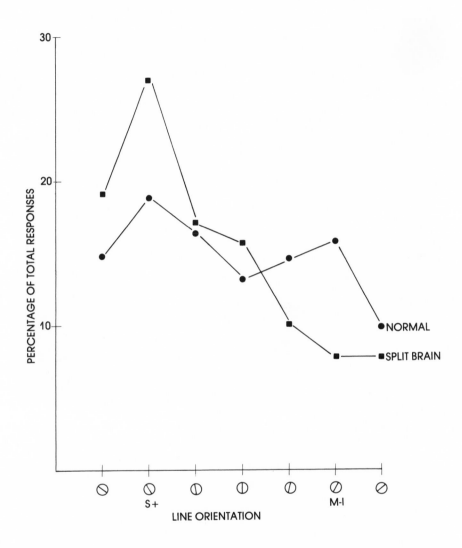

FIGURE 3.7.

Our graph shows the percentage of pecks that pigeons made to lines of varying orientation after they had been trained to peck to a line of 135° (S). Notice that normal pigeons pecked almost as often to the mirror-image (M–I) line of 45°, while the split-brained pigeons did not.

41

served that pigeons learning to discriminate mirror-image obliques apparently solved the problem by cocking the head to one side so that the 45° and 135° lines then became vertical and horizontal with respect to the axes of the tilted head. This asymmetrical strategy is illustrated in Figure 3.8. Pigeons may also adopt other kinds of asymmetrical response strategies. Together with J. Christopher Clarke, one of us

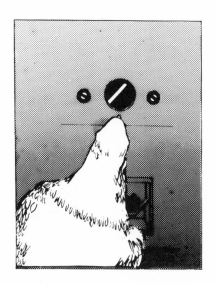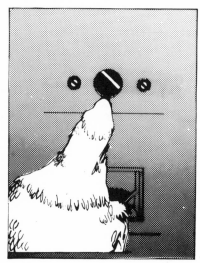

FIGURE 3.8.

Illustration, redrawn from a photograph, shows how a pigeon cocks its head to one side in learning to discriminate mirror-image oblique lines. Notice that the lines are no longer mirror images with respect to the bird's head.

(I.L.B.) taught 2 pigeons to discriminate a circular disk that was red on the left and blue on the right from one that was blue on the left and red on the right. It was observed that the birds solved the discrimination by standing to one side of the key that displayed the stimuli and apparently attending only to that side.[19] Subsequent tests revealed that the birds had effectively learned a simple color discrimination. When a series of simple colors was displayed on the key the pigeons pecked mainly that color that had been displayed on that side of the correct stimulus to which they had attended during training.

Of course, the ability of birds to maintain a postural or response asymmetry can be taken as evidence in its own right that they can tell left from right; in effect, the birds solved a mirror-image discrimination by making a left–right response differentiation. We shall suggest, however, that simple response asymmetries are fairly easily acquired by most species. Bear in mind, though, that if the pigeon's training box is at all asymmetrical, the pigeon need only copy that asymmetry to make a consistently asymmetrical response; it need not tell left from right to do this. Notice for example that in the training box pictured in Figure 3.8, the slots in the screws on either side of the key both slope up to the left. Perhaps the pigeon used these to remind itself which way to cock its head when observing the stimuli on the key.

Humans

Most normal human adults appear to be able to tell left from right without undue difficulty. Some individuals appear to have special trouble, however, and in 1924 the German psychologist Kurt Elze coined the term "right–left blindness" to refer to such cases.[20] Elze wrote of army recruits in Czarist Russia who were so bad at telling left from right that they were drilled on parade with a bundle of straw tied to the right leg and a bundle of hay to the left. Folklore has it that children raised in the Roman Catholic faith often quickly make the sign of the cross in order to tell which is their right hand. This may be interpreted either as an appeal to a higher authority, or as an illustration of a principle we have already enunciated—namely, that asymmetries emerge more readily in motor systems than in perceptual ones.

Children nearly always have difficulty telling left from right, especially when trying to learn which side of the body is which, and when learning to read and write. We shall discuss this in more detail in Chapter 10, where we consider the development of the left–right sense. Sometimes left–right confusions persist and may be a component in specific reading disability or dyslexia. This is a topic we shall also reserve for special discussion in Chapter 11. There is also evidence that women report a greater tendency to left–right confusion than do men.[21] This is somewhat paradoxical since reading disability is much more common among boys than among girls. Perhaps women are simply more likely to admit to being confused, but are in reality no more confused than men are.

Our main concern in this chapter is not with pathological cases, nor with the development of the left–right sense, but rather with the ability of normal adult humans to tell left from right. The human equivalent of the laboratory rat or pigeon is the long-suffering undergraduate. Clearly it would be a waste of time and public funds to compare the number of trials it takes undergraduates to learn left-right mirror-image discriminations with the number it takes them to learn up–down discriminations. Even most of our own undergraduates, we suspect, could master the left–right discrimination in a single trial; a great many of them, for instance, are able to read, which proves their proficiency in mirror-image discrimination. What is required is a more sensitive index of the ease or difficulty of a discrimination. One such index that has become increasingly popular in the human experimental laboratory is the time, measured down to fractions of a second, that it takes a person to perform the discrimination.

William S. Farrell of Stanford University timed people as they reacted to an arrow, flashed on a screen for a tenth of a second.[22] The arrow could point up, down, left, or right. Under one condition, the undergraduate subjects had to move a lever in the direction indicated by the arrow, and the speed with which they did so was about the same regardless of the direction. Observe that this task does *not* require the ability to tell left from right, since any left–right asymmetry in the stimulus is simply copied in the response. Under another condition, however, the subjects had to call out the directions, ''up,'' ''down,'' ''left,'' or ''right,'' as indicated by the arrows. The discrimination of left and right in this case is a genuine mirror-image discrimination, and therefore *does* test the ability to tell left from right. In this case the left–right discrimination was more difficult than the up–down one. In fact, it took the subjects on average about 30 thousandths of a second longer to respond ''left'' or ''right'' than to respond ''up'' or ''down.'' Although this was but a slight difference, it was a reliable one, and it could not be attributed to differences in the time taken merely to articulate the words. We may suppose that it is a residual effect of a more pronounced difficulty experienced in childhood. Farrell recorded similar effects with respect to judgments about the position of a circle that could appear above, below, to the left of, or to the right of a fixation point.

Ruth H. Maki and her colleagues at North Dakota University have studied some interesting variations on this theme, with similar results.[23] For instance, they showed people a star and a circle which could be either side by side or one above the other. The subjects had to judge the truth or falsity of sentences like "The star is above the circle," or "The circle is to the left of the star." The judgments took slightly but reliably longer when the pairs were side by side, in which event the task was effectively a left–right mirror-image discrimination, than when they were one above the other. Maki and her colleagues also had their subjects judge the relative locations of states in the United States, with sentences like "Oregon is east of Illinois," or "Maine is north of Florida," and they discovered that judgments about east and west were slower than judgments about north and south. This was also true when the labels "right," "left," "above," and "below" were substituted for "east," "west," "north," and "south," respectively. This test is not strictly one of mirror-image discrimination since the subjects were not actually confronted with mirror-image stimuli, but it seems reasonable to suppose that it did draw on the subjects' internal knowledge of the spatial dimensions of the United States, and therefore did reflect the added difficulty imposed by telling left from right as compared with up from down. It appears that "east" and "west" are treated as equivalent to "right" and "left," respectively, probably because that is how they are usually located on maps.

Curiously enough, the difficulty with left–right mirror-image discriminations occurred only when the subject used the labels "left" and "right" or "east" and "west." There was no difference between left–right and up–down discriminations when arbitrarily chosen letters were used to designate the different directions. It is possible that the difficulty with "left" and "right" is a leftover from childhood, when telling left from right was a severe problem, but that with new labels the adult is freed from the shackles of the past.

Be that as it may, one can still demonstrate a left–right equivalence in adults which suggests a tendency to encode left–right mirror images in the same way. People may easily be able to discriminate mirror images, but they still treat them as somewhat alike, and they may unwittingly confuse them if they are not explicitly instructed to discriminate them. In one experiment carried out at the University of Rochester, for example, people were shown 2,500 pictures, mostly of everyday scenes, and then were tested for recognition.[24] What was chiefly remarkable about this experiment was the high levels of recognition that the subjects were able to achieve, after what was effectively a very long and boring slide show. However, the interesting thing from our point of view was that they were just as likely to recognize a picture as familiar if it was the left–right mirror image of the original as if it was the original itself. Indeed they were usually unable to say whether a test picture had been reversed, indicating a failure of mirror-image discrimination.

This mirror-image generalization, as we may call it, is not confined to recognition of everyday scenes. In his book *Orientation and Form,* Irvin Rock[25] describes an experiment by Olshansky in which subjects were shown novel shapes then tested two minutes later for recognition. Recognition was almost as accurate when the shapes were left–right reversed as when they were in their original orientations, and was significantly less accurate when they were up–down reversed. Accuracy of recognition was also impaired by rotation of the shapes through 45°, 90°, or 180° in their own planes, even though the subjects' heads were correspondingly rotated to preserve the same orientations with respect to the eyes. These two experiments demonstrate the near equivalence of left–right mirror images in memory, at least under conditions in which the left–right orientation of an event is relatively unimportant.

LEFT—RIGHT RESPONSE DIFFERENTIATION

Left–right response differentiation requires an animal to give consistently asymmetrical responses in the absence of consistently asymmetrical stimulus cues. The simplest case is that in which the animal persists in giving simple asymmetrical responses, such as turning right in a T-maze, or lifting the left paw. The more interesting and complex case is that in which the animal gives a left response to one stimulus and a right response to another, where the stimuli themselves convey no extrinsic left–right information. An example would be a rat in a jumping stand jumping to the left door when two squares are displayed and to the right door when triangles are displayed.

As we shall see, the evidence is scant compared with that on mirror-image discrimination, and appropriate controls, such as testing whether the animal can make up versus down responses, typically have not been used.

Rats

It is well know that rats can easily learn the simple left–right differentiations involved in always turning into the same arm (left or right) of a symmetrical maze shaped like a T. However they have considerable difficulty with more complex mazes involving several left–right choices unless there are external left–right cues, and they also learn the simple T-maze more easily if such cues are available.[26]

Rats often exhibit so-called spontaneous alternation in a T-maze, choosing to alternate left and right turns on successive runs. This implies an ability to differentiate left and right responses, at least insofar as there are no external left–right cues. Subtle cues may exist, however. One investigator has reported that spontaneous alternation may depend at least partly on an odor trail left over in one arm of the maze from the previous run, although the rats apparently do have a tendency to alternate independently of such external cues.[27] Rats can also learn quite readily to alternate turns in a T-maze in order to obtain food in alternate arms, although their ability to do so declines as the interval between successive trials increases.

As we shall see, studies of spontaneous alternation reveal something of the mechanisms involved in left–right differentiation, and the subject will be considered in more detail when we discuss experiments with woodlice later in this chapter.

In 1948, David H. Lawrence reported an experiment which can be taken to reveal the difficulty of the more complex kind of left–right response differentiation.[28] He taught rats to turn left in a white T-maze and right in a black T-maze, a task which meets our criterion of left–right response differentiation. This was contrasted with a task in which the rats had to choose one or other alley of a T-maze according to which alley was white and which was black. In the first task, the rats needed to distinguish black from white, but in the second task they did not need to be able to tell left from right. The first task proved much the more difficult. It is conceivable that the second task was the easier simply because it is easier for rats to discriminate black and white when they are presented at the same time than when they are presented on different trials. We suspect, however, that the main reason why the first task proved the more difficult was that it taxed the rats' ability to tell left from right.

Guinea Pigs

A simple experiment by Grindley[29] in 1932 showed that guinea pigs could be taught quite readily to turn their heads consistently to one side when a buzzer sounded directly beneath them. This is a task of the same order as that in which a rat learns to turn always into one arm of a T-maze. It seems that this simplest kind of left–right response differentiation seldom causes serious difficulty in any species.

Dogs

In 1964, the Polish psychologist Jerzy Konorski described a study in which it proved impossible to teach dogs to lift the right foreleg in response to a metronome and the left foreleg in response to a buzzer when the sounds emanated from the same location.[30] In another experiment dogs were unable to learn to approach a food tray on the left or right, depending on which of two tones was sounded from a speaker. The difficulty of these tasks clearly did not lie in discriminating the stimuli because the dogs were easily able to discriminate them when other training procedures were used. The problem therefore seems to have been one of differentiating the left and right responses. Both of the above tasks also proved quite easy when the sounds emanated from different spatial locations, probably because the locations provided the left–right cue. Without this cue, the dogs would have had to rely on their own ability to tell left from right, and the task was then impossibly difficult.

Human Adults

As we observed in Chapter 2, recall of the specific left–right orientation of an event can be regarded as a test of left–right response differentiation. Information on human ability on such a task is provided by an early experiment by the British psychologist Frederic C. Bartlett.[31] He showed people pictures of faces in various profiles and tested recall of these pictures half an hour later. There was a marked tendency to recall particular pictures as having been in the opposite profile to the originals, even though other details were correct. This adds to the evidence that we reviewed earlier, in discussing mirror-image discrimination, that even humans exhibit a strong tendency toward mirror-image equivalence in their memory for objects or scenes.

Woodlice

Experiments on alternation of turns in woodlice have been saved until last not on account of any idea of the lowly status of crustacea, but because these experiments reveal more than those on vertebrate species of the possible mechanism of left–right differentiation. Moreover the experiments are cheap and fun to carry out, which might tempt some of our readers to try them out for themselves.

Field observation of many invertebrates, including woodlice, mealworms, and pill-bugs, has shown that these small animals tend systematically to alternate left and right turns to avoid successive obstructions in their path. This is usually regarded as an inborn, rather than a learned, response connected with survival in the natural environment. However, it implies ability to perform left–right response differentiation, since the animal turns left or right in the absence of any external left–right cues.

This interesting behavior has been studied in the laboratory by having the animals walk in a narrow runway which contains sharp bends forcing a turn to left or right and T-shaped intersections allowing choice of left or right turns. It is found that when woodlice are forced to turn through 90° and then given a free choice to turn left or right, they tend to turn in the direction opposite to the forced turn.[32] A New Zealand psychologist, Robert N. Hughes, showed that alternation is more likely to occur when the time between forced and free turns is short.[33] He has suggested that the short-term memory involved may be peripheral, consisting of greater inhibition of neural components of the limbs adjacent to the outer walls of a maze turn—that is, the limbs that have to walk further. Moreover, alternation of turns by pill-bugs is not influenced by postural or external directional cues, which supports the idea that the critical cues determining choice of direction arise from something as simple as the differential distance moved by the right and left legs during a turn. Together with Donald M. Webster, one of us (I.L.B.) has tested this assumption in two experiments designed to separate cues related to leg movement from other cues that occur during a forced turn.[34]

In the first experiment we investigated the effect of turning woodlice on a turntable, so that there was no differential movement of the legs on the two sides of the body. We used four different runways, as shown in Figure 3.9. When the woodlice ran down Runway 1, which is the usual type of runway for demonstrating the alternation of turns, 80 percent of them in fact exhibited alternation, as expected. On Runway 2, however, the woodlice were rotated on a turntable when they reached the center of the runway. However, this turn did not influence their choice on the next free turn; half of the woodlice turned one way and half the other way. On Runways 3 and 4, the woodlice were turned on the turntable after making a forced turn. On the next turn, 80 percent of them turned in the direction opposite the original forced turn and were apparently not influenced by the direction of the turn on the turntable. These results demonstrate that turns on a turntable have no influence on the alternation of turns, suggesting that differential movements of the legs provide the critical cue.

In the next experiment we tested this directly by forcing the woodlice

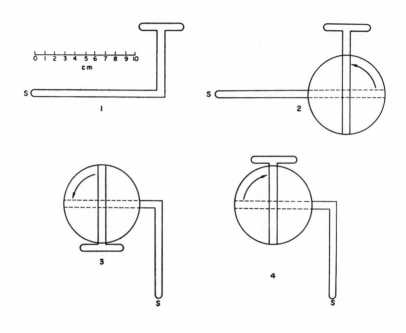

FIGURE 3.9.

We used four different runways to test observe movement patterns of woodlice after turning the insects on a turntable.

to make differential leg movements without turning! We did this by having the woodlice run down a straight section of runway in which a section of the floor on one or other side moved opposite the direction of the run. This is illustrated in Figure 3.10. When the moving part of the track was on the left, causing the left legs to work harder, most of the woodlice turned left at a choice point, but when the moving track was on the right they subsequently turned right. This result confirms Hughes's theory that differential leg movements provide the critical cue. The neuromuscular changes that signal this cue are evidently short-lived, however, since alternation breaks down if there are long delays between turns. We suspect that a similar explanation may hold for spontaneous alternation of turns in other animals.

In the course of the experiments on woodlice, we (the experimenters)

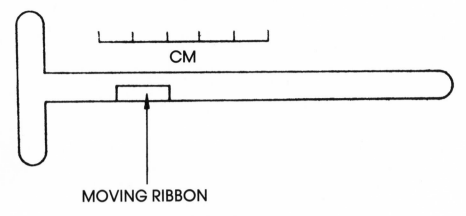

CM

MOVING RIBBON

FIGURE 3.10.

This runway with the moving walkway on one side makes one half
of the woodlouse work harder than the other half.

acquired a sneaking regard for these lowly creatures, who revealed
more "spine" than one might expect from their invertebrate status.
While developing the moving runway for the second experiment we
first tried a version in which the tape moved in the same direction as the
woodlouse was moving. Our purpose was to allow the legs on one side
to rest completely while the woodlouse traversed the tape. However we
found that the woodlice would not accept the free ride, but immediately
backed off the tape. We then tried the tape in the other direction, working against the woodlouse, and this worked splendidly. The woodlouse,
it seems, thrives on challenge, and is too proud to accept charity from
mere humans.

Summary and Conclusions

We found considerable evidence that animals find it difficult, sometimes apparently impossible, to discriminate left–right mirror-image
stimuli. We also cited evidence that dogs, at least, find it virtually impossible to choose a left or right response according to stimuli which
convey no left–right cues, and that rats also find this kind of task difficult. However, we found no evidence that animals find it particularly
difficult to learn the simplest kind of left–right response differentiation
in which all that is required is a consistent response asymmetry.

The difficulty with left–right mirror images does not seem to be perceptual. That is, animals seem to be able to perceive which way round things are if the task simply requires them to match one stimulus pattern to another, or to orient in the direction indicated by a stimulus. We saw, for instance, that rats can choose which set of mirror-image oblique lines matches a standard set about as easily as they can choose whether horizontal or vertical lines match a standard set. And when human subjects must push a lever in the direction indicated by an arrow, they are just as fast when the arrow points left or right as when it points up or down. It is only when the task requires the subject to *label* the stimuli with non-mirror-image labels that the difficulty arises.

If mirror-image discrimination is not basically a perceptual problem, then we might argue analogously that left–right response differentiation is not primarily a motor one. Animals presumably have no difficulty deciding in which direction to move in order to escape from predators or to hunt prey, or which paw to lift to lick a wound or reach for food. The problem only arises when an animal must choose which response to make on the basis of a cue which conveys no left–right information; again, this is a problem of coding or of remembering which response goes with which stimulus. The Canadian psychologist Donald O. Hebb made this point when he wrote of

> . . .the notorious difficulty of choosing between *left* and *right*, to be observed by anyone who tries to teach twelve-year-old children to "right turn" promptly on command. . .The child can very readily learn at the age of three that "left" and "right" each refers to a side of the body—but ah me, which one?[35]

Let us now turn briefly to the possible role of response asymmetries in mirror-image discrimination. We described evidence that pigeons may solve visual mirror-image discrimination by adopting asymmetrical postures or response strategies. Since most species appear to have little difficulty acquiring simple response asymmetries, it would not be surprising if these were to play a rather general role in helping animals solve more complex problems of telling left from right.

We suggested that pigeons may learn to discriminate mirror-image obliques by cocking their heads to one side so that 45° and 135° lines, for example, might be seen as though horizontal and vertical. Perhaps oblique lines may naturally induce a strategy of tilting the head. Indeed, there was some suggestion throughout our review of mirror-image discrimination that mirror-image obliques may be the easiest of mirror-image stimuli to discriminate, despite the suggestion that oblique lines may create perceptual as well as labeling difficulties. Thus, pigeons and cats appear to have no particular difficulty with mirror-image obliques while cats, at least, do have trouble with other mirror-image pairs. The octopus, on the other hand, apparently finds the discrimination of obliques to be as impossibly difficult as that of any other mirror-image pair. There is a ready interpretation for this. A head-tilting strategy would be of little avail to the octopus because its eyes are automatically maintained in a horizontal position regardless of the orientation of head or body.[36]

Postural asymmetries are effective because they provide asymmetrical cues in place of symmetrical ones. A similar role may be served by sensory asymmetries residing in the body rather than in the external environment. This was most clearly shown by the experiments with woodlice in which it seemed that woodlice remembered the direction of a previous turn in terms of a sensory asymmetry arising from different movements of the left and right legs. The idea that left and right cues may be encoded in terms of some difference in the sensory input from the two sides of the body is further explored in Chapter 10, in relation to evidence on the development of the left–right sense in children.

We may summarize this chapter by observing that the experimental evidence is for the most part consistent with our proposition that left–right confusion is a fundamental consequence of bilateral symmetry. Animals are generally confused on precisely those tasks which a perfectly symmetrical organism would find impossible: namely, those which meet our criteria of telling left from right. They are not confused on those tasks which simply require differential perception of mirror-image stimuli. We have suggested therefore that the confusion of mirror-image stimuli has to do with the processes of *labelling* and *memory* rather than with *perception*. In the next chapter, we develop a theory that explicitly relates left–right equivalence to symmetrical processes involved in learning and memory.

Chapter 4

Left–Right Equivalence and the Symmetry of the Brain

"Now, if you'll only attend, Kitty, and not talk so much, I'll tell you all my ideas about Looking-glass House." [Lewis Carroll, *Through the Looking-Glass*]

In this chapter we shall elaborate our theme that left–right confusion—or left–right equivalence, to emphasize its more positive aspect—is related to the bilateral symmetry of the brain. Specifically, we shall develop a neurological theory about how the brain might preserve its structural symmetry despite asymmetrical experience and so tend to record the memory of that experience independently of its left–right orientation. But before we discuss the problem in neurological terms, we need to set it in evolutionary context. We begin by discussing the evolution of bilateral symmetry.

THE EVOLUTION OF SYMMETRY

In his book, *Symmetry,* Hermann Weyl gives a succinct account of the evolution of bilateral symmetry.[1] The earliest forms of animals, he notes, were small creatures suspended in water where stimulation could impinge from any direction. These creatures were therefore more or less spherical. For those forms fixed at the bottom of the ocean, however, gravity would have provided a consistent directional influence, narrowing the set of symmetrical influences to those about the vertical axis. These creatures therefore tended to be radially symmetrical; they were asymmetrical with respect to up and down, but had no distinctive front or back, and no left or right. Animals capable of propelling themselves, whether through water, air or on land, created for themselves another directional influence along the axis of motion itself. The front-back axis was combined with the up–down one to form a sagittal plane. The environmental influences were then indifferent only with respect to left and right. The freely moving animal is therefore characterized by bilateral symmetry.

Bilateral symmetry is presumably an active rather than a passive adaptation to the lack of left–right bias in the environment, since it is achieved in the face of consistent left–right asymmetries at the molecular level. Indeed, the biologist Jacques Monod was rather contemptuous of the bilateral symmetry that seems to pervade the structure of animals.

> . . .these morphological, macroscopic asymmetries are superficial, and do not reflect the fundamental order *within* living things. I am not even referring now to the fact that we possess only one heart, on one side, and a single liver, on the other, although this is enough to show that our outwardly "bilateral" appearance is something of a fake. I am referring to the microscopic structures which are responsible . . .for all the properties of living things, namely proteins and nucleic acids.[2]

Since bilateral symmetry is not a characteristic of living tissue at the molecular level, its appearance at the more gross morphological level must be a consequence of special adaptation to the lack of consistent left–right biases in the environment. Indeed, bilateral symmetry applies most obviously to precisely those parts of the body and nervous system that are subject to environmental influences, including the limbs, the sense organs, and external bodily shape. Departures from symmetry are common in the internal organs, including the heart, stomach, and liver, which are relatively remote from the external environment. But any asymmetry in the limbs would tend to result in undesirable deviations from the straight and narrow path—the animal would be continually side-tracked. Moreover, in a world without systematic left–right biases, a well adjusted animal should be equally capable of turning in either direction, whether to pursue some prey or to flee from a predator, and equally adept at reaching or striking in either direction. Considerations such as these, as Weyl observes, ". . .may help explain why our limbs obey the laws of symmetry more strictly than (do) our inner organs."[3]

The advantages of symmetry apply as well to our sensory systems as to our limbs and muscles. Since danger or prey may lurk on either side, animals need to be equally sensitive to the environment on left and right. Martin Gardner, in *The Ambidextrous Universe,* puts it this way: "The slightest loss of symmetry, such as the loss of a right eye, would have immediate negative value for the survival of any animal. An enemy could sneak up unobserved on the right!"[4]

Symmetry of the limbs and sense organs in turn predisposes certain parts of the brain and central nervous system to be symmetrical—specifically, those parts that are concerned with the coordination of action, the interpretation of sensory information, and the integration of one with the other. Tests of telling left from right typically involve these very components. The most conspicuous exceptions to symmetry are to be found in the brains of humans, where structural asymmetries appear to be roughly correlated with the fact that in most people it is primarily the left cerebral hemisphere that is responsible for language.[5] The general preference for the right hand also appears to be more or less uniquely human.[6] These two asymmetries may at least partially explain why humans appear to have less difficulty in telling left from right than do other species. We shall discuss handedness and cerebral asymmetry in more detail in Part II of this book. For the present, we may observe that even in the human brain the impression of structural symmetry overrides the rather localized and inconsistent asymmetries. Even though most adult humans do not as a rule confuse left and right they nevertheless do show a tendency to treat them as equivalent.

The advantages of symmetry extend beyond perception and action, however, to learning and memory. The animal that is learning about the world must cope with the fact that a particular face or body is the *same* face or body whether it is in left or right profile. Similarly, if an animal is attacked from the left, it does not follow that all future attacks will occur from the left. To the extent that the animal learns from the experience of being attacked, it should be able to cope with future attacks whether from the left *or* right. Consequently, one might expect learning and memory to be characterized by *left–right equivalence.* Most events in the natural world could have occurred with the opposite orientation, so there is more to be gained by treating left–right mirror images as equivalent than by treating them as distinct.

LEFT–RIGHT EQUIVALENCE AS AN INBORN DISPOSITION

It might be argued that left–right equivalence is itself discovered only by experience. That is, an animal might initially register that mirror-image shapes are different, but then discover that they are in fact the same shape viewed from opposite sides. A child might at first suppose that her mother in left profile is a different person from her mother in right profile, and only gradually learn that they are the same helpful person. We think, though, that the truth is just the reverse of this: there is an inborn tendency to treat left–right mirror images as equivalent, and this makes it difficult to learn to tell them apart. We think that this tendency to treat left and right as equivalent is a product of evolution in a natural environment in which left–right mirror-image events nearly always are equivalent.

One reason for supposing that left–right equivalence in learning and memory is a product of evolution rather than of experience is simply that an animal that exhibited left–right equivalence from the start would be more likely to survive than one that did not. Suppose an animal were attacked from the right and managed to survive this experience. If it learned only to be wary of future attacks from that same side, and if it remembers only its strategies for dealing with a right-sided attack, it would remain vulnerable to an unexpected attack from the left side. But if its learning were generalized to include wariness about potential attacks from the left, and strategies to deal with left-sided as well as right-sided attacks, then the animal is better able to deal with the real world, in which attacks can occur from either side. Such an animal may be unable to remember which side the attack *did* occur on, but this is a small price to pay for the added survival value to be gained from left–right equivalence in learning and memory.

Observations of children learning to read and write also suggest that they begin with a strong predisposition to treat left–right mirror images as equivalent, and that this predisposition has nothing to do with experience. Most children have initial difficulty learning to discriminate letters of the alphabet from their mirror images, and they quite commonly write backwards; we shall discuss this in more detail in Chapter 10. Yet children are hardly ever exposed to reversed letters or backward script (except of their own making), so these reversal tendencies can scarcely be attributed to experience.

Even more convincing evidence that left–right equivalence is an inborn characteristic of memory comes from experiments carried out at Princeton University on infants aged from three to four months.[7] In one experiment infants were shown a picture of a man's face in right profile for one minute, followed by several ten-second exposures of three different pictures. One of these test pictures was the original right profile, another was the same man's face in left profile, and the third was a different man's face in right profile. The experimenters recorded the amount of time the infants spent looking at each of the pictures. During the test exposures, the infants spent more time looking at the new face in right profile than they spent looking at the original right profile, presumably because it was novel. But they spent no more time looking at the original face in left profile, which they evidently regarded as the "same" as the right profile. Using the same technique, the experimenters also found that mirror-image oblique lines were treated as equivalent, as were mirror-image U-shapes. Thus mirror-image equivalence is demonstrable in infants as early as three months of age.

Left–Right Equivalence and Pattern Recognition

Technically, left–right equivalence is part of the more general problem of *pattern recognition*. Objects, shapes, and other patterns can be recognized as the same despite the fact that they occur in different contexts or with different surface characteristics. We can recognize letters of the alphabet, for instance, in different locations, sizes, colors, typescripts, and, to some extent at least, orientations. Particular tunes can be identified even though played by different instruments, in different keys, or at different tempos. You can easily recognize a friend regardless of the clothes he or she is wearing, whether he or she is sitting or standing, smiling, or frowning. The problem of how we accomplish these acts of recognition is deceptively complex, probably because we take them for granted. Computer scientists have been unable to simulate on computers even quite commonplace human capacities, such as the ability to pick out the individual words in ordinary conversational speech, or the ability to recognize everyday objects in their natural settings. Even the lowly pigeon appears to exhibit a capacity for pattern recognition that is well beyond that of the most sophisticated present-day computer.[8]

The varying contexts or surface manifestations of a pattern may be described as merely *circumstantial;* they depend on the circumstances under which the pattern is perceived, but they are not critical to the pattern itself. In the natural world, left–right orientation is usually circumstantial, because it does not matter which way round a pattern is; it is still the same pattern. However this is not always true of people's artificial environment. For instance, left–right orientation *is* important in distinguishing a *b* from a *d*; these are not the same patterns, at least in the context of reading. But it is precisely because children have a tendency to treat left–right orientation as a circumstantial attribute, unimportant in the identification of a pattern, that they have difficulty learning to discriminate mirror-image letters.

Now, recognition of a pattern is presumed to involve matching that pattern against some representation that is stored in memory. That representation must itself be independent of circumstantial characteristics if we are to recognize the pattern as such. That is, if we can recognize a pattern independently of its left–right orientation, we must match it against a stored representation that is independent of left–right orientation. The nature of the memory storage that underlies the ability to recognize things is little understood; indeed, cracking the memory code is one of the great unsolved problems of our time. One thing that is reasonably certain, however, is that memory storage involves a structural change in the brain. In other words, the brain is *physically* altered by the very process of storing new information. The reader who understands this point, we regret to say, will never be quite the same again.

The brain and nervous system are made up of *neurons* that relay information from one part to another. When a neural impulse travels from one neuron to the next, it must cross a junction known as a *synapse*. It is generally believed that the structural changes that occur in memory take place at certain synapses in such a way that an impulse is more likely (or in certain circumstances, perhaps less likely) to cross these synapses.[9] These synaptic changes would then alter the pattern of neural firing that occurs in the brain, in such a way that the particular input that caused the changes would then be "recognized" if that input were repeated. The precise nature of these synaptic changes, and of the pattern of changes induced by specific inputs, are not known.

The next question, and indeed the critical one, is how the brain stores information about a pattern in such a way that the structural memory trace is independent of the left–right orientation of that pattern. We have a simple theory about this, a theory that does not depend upon the precise nature of the physical basis of memory.

A THEORY OF INTERHEMISPHERIC REVERSAL

The reader will recall from Chapter 2, we hope, that a bilaterally symmetrical device, such as a brain, could not tell left from right. Such a brain would exhibit left–right equivalence. One way to guarantee left–right equivalence in *memory*, then, would be through some mechanism that ensures that the structural changes that occur in memory are themselves symmetrical. In other words, we suspect that the brain tends to preserve its bilateral symmetry despite asymmetrical experience.

One way in which it might do this is through the commissures, tracts of nerve fibres, that interconnect the two sides of the brain. In man and most mammals the largest commissure is the *corpus callosum,* but from the point of view of memory storage and its structural symmetry we suspect that a smaller commissural tract, the *anterior commissure,* may be at least as important. These commissures relay information from one side of the brain to the other. In some parts of the brain it is known that the commissures connect mirror-image points, as shown schematically in Figure 4.1.[10] To the extent that this is so, the commissures would act as a kind of neural mirror, reflecting the pattern of neural excitation across the midline of the brain and so preserving an overall bilateral symmetry.

Our theory is that this interhemispheric mirroring effect occurs in the formation of memory traces in the brain.[11] If a particular input causes a structural change at a particular synapse on one side of the brain, then the commissures ensure that a change also occurs at the mirror-image synapse on the other side of the brain. This is sufficient to ensure that the brain remains structurally symmetrical. The principle is illustrated schematically in Figure 4.2. Suppose we represent memory-storage locations in the brain as little boxes, symmetrically located. We can represent storage, or structural change, by filling in a box. If a particular box is filled in, we simulate the effect of commissural transmission by also filling in the symmetrically located box on the other side. The ensuing pattern of filled and unfilled boxes must always remain bilaterally symmetrical, and the brain therefore remains unable to tell left from right even with respect to its own memories. It also follows that the memory record laid down by a particular spatial pattern is exactly the same as the record that would have been laid down by the left–right mirror image of that pattern.

We still lack the detailed neurophysical evidence that would unequiv-

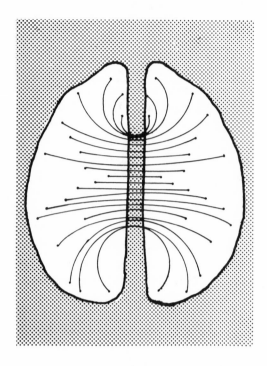

FIGURE 4.1.

Schematic drawing shows how the commissures might link mirror-image points in the two halves of the brain. (From R. W. Sperry, "Some General Aspects of Interhemispheric Integration," in U. B. Mountcastle, ed., **Interhemispheric Relations and Cerebral Dominance** [Baltimore: Johns Hopkins University Press, 1962], p.47. Reprinted with the permission of the author and publisher.)

ocally confirm or deny our theory. There is one result, however, which does lend some support. By applying some chemical substances, such as potassium chloride, directly to the brain surface of an animal, it is possible to create an epileptic focus at that place, and so induce epileptic seizures. Sometimes, an epileptic focus forms spontaneously at the mirror-image location on the other side of the brain, suggesting a mirror-image transfer of structural changes.[12] This observation does not of course prove that such a process occurs in the formation of normal memory records, but it is at least consistent with our theory.

For the most part, however, the evidence for our theory comes from

BEFORE INTERHEMISPHERIC TRANSFER

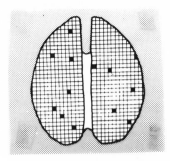

AFTER INTERHEMISPHERIC TRANSFER

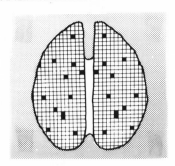

FIGURE 4.2.

Schematic drawing illustrates how commissural transfer would bring about mirror-image equivalence. On the left, we illustrate how a particular experience might bring about structural changes in the brain, shown by filled squares. On the right, the effects of mirror-image transfer result in changes at mirror-image points, preserving the structural symmetry of the brain. The "memory" is exactly the same as it would have been had the original experience been left–right reversed, so the brain is in effect unable to remember the original orientation of the experience.

psychological or neuropsychological observations, and is indirect rather than direct. One line of evidence has to do with a curious affliction known as mirror writing.

Mirror Writing

Since the emergence of scripts that are written laterally, there have always been eccentric individuals who have preferred to write in the direction opposite to the conventional one, so that their writing can be easily discerned only if it is held up to a mirror. The most famous mirror writer of all time was undoubtedly Leonardo da Vinci (1452–1519), the great Italian painter and inventor. His notebooks are crammed with script that runs from right to left instead of from left to right. Only very occasionally did he write in the conventional direction, as in rare communications that were intended for others. But even in the case of the elegant capital letters shown in Figure 4.3, which were clearly intended

FIGURE 4.3.

These mirror-imaged capital letters were designed by Leonardo da Vinci.

for public display, the letters are mirror-reversed. It has been suggested that Leonardo wrote backwards in order to conceal his ideas from the Church, but this can scarcely have been the case in this particular example.[13]

Leonardo was left-handed, and this was probably a factor in his mirror writing. Left-handers do seem to be more prone to this habit than right-handers. In 1698, Rosinus Lentilus described the case of a left-handed epileptic girl whose writing could be read only if viewed in a mirror. Later, he also described a soldier who had lost his right arm and subsequently wrote backwards with his left arm.[14] A modern survey shows that most people, whether left- or right-handed, can write backwards quite easily with the left hand.[15] It seems to be easier to write backwards with the left hand if one simultaneously writes forwards with the right hand. In one study, eleven and twelve-year-old children were asked to write down digits with both hands at once, and most of them, left- and right-handers, wrote them forwards with the preferred hand the backwards with the nonpreferred hand.[16]

However left–handedness cannot entirely explain mirror writing. After all, most left handers do not write backwards. It is sometimes suggested that it is natural for right-handers to write from left to right, but for left-handers to write from right to left. Yet many scripts, such as Hebrew, are written from right to left, even though the populations that write them are predominantly right-handed. Indeed, until about 1500 A.D., right-to-left scripts were about as numerous as left-to-right ones, and the gradual predominance of left-to-right scripts is probably due to historical factors rather than to any intrinsic superiority associated with right handedness.[17] Normal right-handers will spontaneously produce mirrored script if asked to trace out letters on their own foreheads. We also suggest the following experiment: hold a piece of paper on the underside of a table or desk, and try to write on it, with the pen held underneath the table pointing upwards. We predict that the writing will be backwards. This shows that the direction or script is not linked to handedness so much as to a spatial sense of which way round script is supposed to be.

There is evidence that mirror writing may occur as a result of injury to the brain, and specifically of injury on the left side. For instance, in 1881 the English neurologist W. W. Ireland described a patient suffering from aphasia (impairment of language) and from paralysis of the right side, both symptoms of damage to the left side of the brain. The patient exhibited mirror writing, which persisted even when recovery was sufficient to enable the patient to write with the right hand. Ireland anticipated an explanation in terms of interhemispheric reversal.

> It may be asked, is the image or impression, or change in the brain tissue from which the image is formed in the mind of the mirror writer, reversed like the negative of a photograph; or if a double image be formed in the visual center, one in the right hemisphere of the brain and the other in the left, do the images lie to each other in opposite direction. . . ? We can conceive that the image on the left side being effaced through disease, the inverse would remain in the right hemisphere which would render the patient apt to trace the letters from right to left. . .[18]

In his monograph *Mirror Writing,* published in 1928, the British neurologist Macdonald Critchley recorded many other cases of mirror writing as a consequence of damage to the left hemisphere of the brain.[19] Might this also explain Leonardo's mirror writing? Cardinal Luis of Aragon is said to have observed that Leonardo, when an old man of 65 years, was afflicted with a paralysis of the right arm, suggesting a pathology of the left side of the brain. Yet there appears to be no other evidence of paralysis or other symptoms of brain injury from Leonardo's earlier years, and he was left-handed and a mirror writer at least from the age of twenty years.[20] The mystery is therefore by no means resolved.

Another celebrated mirror writer was Lewis Carroll, although he only indulged in it occasionally to amuse his young friends. Nevertheless one of Carroll's biographers, Florence Becker Lennon, has argued that Carroll was born left-handed but forced to use his right hand, and so "took his revenge by doing a little reversing himself."[21] A change in handedness might conceivably have induced a change in cerebral control from one side of the brain to the other, so the tendency to mirror writing might have been less a question of revenge than of neurological disposition. But the point is probably academic, since according to Martin Gardner there is "only the flimsiest evidence that Carroll was born left handed."[22]

Macdonald Critchley noted that mirror writing sometimes occurs spontaneously in so-called states of dissociation, including hypnosis, intoxication, light anaesthesia, fatigue, and daydreaming.[23] It has been suggested that different states of awareness may be related to different modes of functioning in the two sides of the brain. Although we are sceptical of some of the claims made about the dual nature of consciousness, as we shall make clear in Chapter 7, it is not inconceivable that these states of dissociation may reflect a switch in control from the left cerebral hemisphere to the right. Since it is the left hemisphere that normally controls writing, at least among right-handers, this switch may well induce a tendency toward mirror writing.

In summary, mirror writing can sometimes be understood in terms of interhemispheric reversal. In most people, writing is a strongly lateralized skill, largely restricted to the right hand and left cerebral hemisphere. But given that the original learning is mainly restricted to the left hemisphere, we might expect the reversing influence of the commissures to be confined largely to the right hemisphere. Mirror writing may then occur if the right hemisphere assumes control—whether because of injury to the left, or because the person used the left hand, or because of some unusual state of awareness causing a switch in cerebral control.

Other Reversals

There is other evidence that motor skills may show a left–right reversal if control is shifted from one cerebral hemisphere to the other. In one study, for instance, people were taught to move a stylus rapidly round a slot, shaped rather like a clover leaf, using their right hands. When they were later tested with their left hands, they were faster at moving the stylus in the opposite direction to that which they had originally learned.[24] In other words, the skill they had learned was left–right reversed when the people switched hands, and thus cerebral hemispheres. In another experiment, rats were taught to turn into one arm of a T-maze when a light was on and into the other arm when the light was off—a left–right response differentiation. During training, saline solution was placed on one cerebral hemisphere, depressing its function. When the rats were tested with the *opposite* hemisphere depressed, the great majority reversed the response; that is, they turned into the arm of the maze opposite the one they had learned to turn into for the appropriate condition.[25] This result again suggests a left–right reversal of a memory representation between the two halves of the brain.

Spatial skills may also show interhemispheric reversal. The Russian neuropsychologist, Alexander Luria, described a patient with injury to the right side of the brain who drew a reversed map of Russia (see Figure 4.4).[26] The explanation of this could be the reverse of that proposed

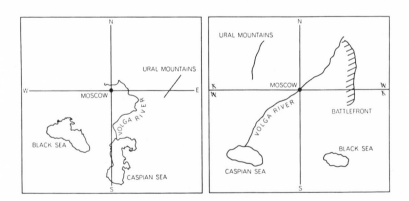

FIGURE 4.4.

On the left is a portion of the map of Russia, and on the right is a reversed version drawn by a patient with injury to the right parietal lobe of the brain. (From A. R. Luria, "The Functional Organization of the Brain," **Scientific American** [March 1970]: 69. Reprinted with the permission of W. H. Freeman and Company.)

by Ireland to explain mirror writing. In most people, the left cerebral hemisphere is dominant for speaking, writing, and other verbal skills, while the right cerebral hemisphere is dominant for nonverbal, spatial skills. Memory for maps and spatial locations may therefore be established primarily in the right hemisphere, but may undergo left–right reversal in the left hemisphere due to the effect of the commissures. Injury to the right hemisphere might therefore "release" the reversed information.

There have been a number of experiments with pigeons, cats, and monkeys in which attempts were made to teach one cerebral hemisphere a mirror-image discrimination, and then to test the other hemisphere in order to determine whether the discrimination was reversed. In the pigeon, each eye projects to the opposite side of the brain, so that covering one eye allows input to be transmitted only to one side of the brain—the same side as the covered eye. Nancy K. Mello taught pigeons with one eye covered to peck a key displaying a 45° line. When she switched the cover to the other eye, she found that the pigeons now pecked most often at a key displaying a 135° line, the left–right mirror image of the original.[27] She also taught pigeons various mirror-image discriminations with one eye covered, and found that the birds generally reversed their choices when the cover was switched.[28] These experiments are consistent with the notion of interhemispheric reversal.

In cats and monkeys (and humans, for that matter), the anatomy of the visual pathways is more complicated, since each eye projects to *both* sides of the brain. Simple tests in which a cover is switched from one eye to the other are therefore not equivalent to tests of interhemispheric transfer. In fact, the inside (or nasal) portion of the retina of each eye projects to the opposite side of the brain, while the outside (or temporal) portion projects to the same side. This division occurs in a region of the optic nerve known as the *optic chiasm* (see Figure 4.5). By cutting the optic chiasm through the middle, from front to back, it is possible to sever the crossed connections, so that the remaining projections from each eye are to the same side of the brain. The chiasm-sectioned cat or monkey is therefore functionally equivalent to a pigeon in that covering one eye restricts input to one cerebral hemisphere.

John Noble of the University of London was the first to try teaching chiasm-sectioned monkeys mirror-image discriminations through one eye, then testing them through the other. He did in fact record what he termed "paradoxical transfer"—the monkeys showed a reversed pref-

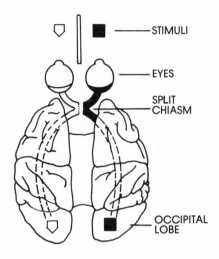

FIGURE 4.5.

Schematic representation of the visual system of the monkey shows that a cut through the optic chiasm means that information presented to the left eye is projected only to the left side of the brain, and information presented to the right eye only to the right side.

erence when tested with the untrained eye open.[29] This is again consistent with interhemispheric reversal. Two Italian investigators, G. Berlucchi and C. A. Marzi, found no evidence for reversal in chiasm-sectioned cats.[30] When tested with the untrained eye, the cats either showed a weak tendency to persist with the same choice they had learned with the trained eye, or else they responded randomly. Charles R. Hamilton and Susan B. Tieman obtained similar results with split-chiasm monkeys, using slightly different procedures from those used by Noble.[31] We have ourselves found inconsistent evidence for reversal in pigeons. We have also discovered that a pigeon viewing with only one eye tends to attend only to that part of a key on the side of the viewing eye, and this alone can explain the reversal without recourse to interhemispheric effects.[32] For instance, a pigeon viewing a 135° line on a circular key with only its left eye uncovered would see that part of the line that is in the left half of the key, and thus occupies the upper half of the key. But when the pigeon views with its *right* eye, it is the 45° line that is now seen to occupy the upper half of the key, and so the pigeon prefers that line to the 135° one. Hamilton and his colleagues have documented similar attentional switches, depending upon which eye is covered, in split-chiasm monkeys. There seems no need to suppose that the reversal has anything to do with a reversed memory record at all; it may be a simple consequence of attentional shifts.

We need not pursue this issue here. We have reviewed it in detail elsewhere,[33] and we do not in any case consider the technique of interocular transfer to be critical to the theory of interhemispheric reversal. Presenting information to one eye of a pigeon or of a split-chiasm cat or monkey may restrict the initial input to one cerebral hemisphere, but it does not prevent the hemispheres from sharing information via the commissures. We suspect that *perceptual* transfer across the commissures preserves the left–right orientation of the perceived pattern, and does not reverse it; that is, perceptual transfer is veridical, not reversed. Recall that our theory about mirror-image reversal across the commissures applies to the formation of structural *memory* records, and not to the routine transfer of perceptual information that occurs whenever we integrate spatial scenes across the visual field.

Suppose we project an asymmetrical pattern to one hemisphere of a pigeon or a split-chiasm cat or monkey. Call this hemisphere the direct hemisphere. Veridical information may be relayed to the other, or indirect hemisphere, and indeed establish a veridical memory record there. However the original input may establish a veridical record in the direct hemisphere, and thus a reversed record in the indirect one. The indirect hemisphere may therefore establish two records, one veridical, one reversed—which can perhaps explain the rather inconsistent results.

Split-brain Tests

A more direct test of our theory is simply to sever the commissures, an operation popularly known as splitting the brain. An animal should then have no difficulty learning to discriminate left–right mirror images, since the mechanism whereby memory records are left–right reversed would be abolished. The animal would also be incapable of establishing left–right equivalence—of recognizing a previously encountered pattern if it is left–right reversed.

In Chapter 3, we referred to an experiment described by Pavlov, in which a dog was unable to discriminate mirror-image touches when its commissures were intact, but easily able to do so when the commissures were cut.[34] We also described an experiment of our own, in which left–right equivalence in pigeons was abolished when their commissures were sectioned. When intact birds were taught to peck a key displaying a 60° line, they subsequently pecked almost as much to the mirror-image of that line (namely, a 120° line) as to the original, thus demonstrating mirror-image equivalence. Birds with sectioned commissures did not do so, however, but essentially treated the 120° line as though it were relatively unfamiliar.[35]

More revealing evidence on the role of the commissures in creating mirror-image equivalences comes from a re-analysis of John Noble's data on mirror-image discrimination in the monkey. We described above how Noble tested for interocular transfer of mirror-image discriminations, and indeed found some evidence for reversal. For reasons that we need not go into, Noble performed a variety of surgical operations on his monkeys, including cutting the optic chiasm, the corpus callosum, and the anterior commissure. André Achim, a graduate student at McGill University, noticed that those animals with their anterior commissures cut had no difficulty learning the left–right mirror-image discriminations, whereas the other animals did have difficulty.[36] This difference was not apparent on discrimination of up–down mirror images, or on discrimination of non-mirror-image pairs. The evidence is summarized in Figure 4.6.

This result was essentially serendipitous, and should be repeated before it is accepted as firm evidence. Moreover, there were a number of procedural variations that were irrelevant to the comparison we are making. For instance, all of the monkeys were trained with one eye covered, and this may conceivably have biased the comparison. Nevertheless, we think it does make reasonable sense to suppose that the anterior commissure might be critical to the formation of structural memory records across the two sides of the brain. This commissure interconnects the so-called inferotemporal cortices on the two sides, regions thought to be critically involved in memory.[37] There is additional evidence that damage to the inferotemporal cortex on both sides impairs the ability of monkeys to learn visual discrimination, with the striking exception of mirror-image discrimination, which is not impaired.[38] If the inferotemporal cortices are involved with the process of mirror-image *equivalence,* then bilateral damage to these areas might actually enhance

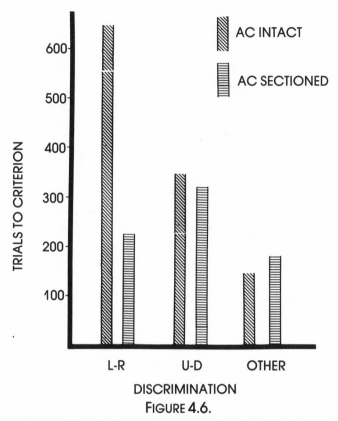

FIGURE 4.6.

This figure shows the number of trials it took monkeys to learn to discriminate left–right mirror images (L–R), up-down mirror images
(U–D), and other pairs of shapes. Monkeys with the anterior commissure (AC) intact took much longer to discriminate the left–right
pairs than the other pairs, but this difficulty was evidently removed
by section of the commissure (after Achim and Corballis, 1977).

mirror-image discrimination, although the enhancement would be off-
set by the loss of neural tissue dedicated to high-level coding and memory.

CONCLUSIONS

In this chapter we have argued that there is a built-in mechanism in the
brain for establishing left–right equivalence. This mechanism serves an
adaptive function in the natural environment, where left–right mirror-
image events or patterns usually *are* equivalent. We suggested that the
mechanism is such that structural memory records are formed corre-

sponding to both the actual event and to its mirror image. This has the effect of making it difficult to learn to discriminate mirror images, but it also has the advantage of making it easier to recognize patterns or events if they later occur with the opposite orientation. We also suggested that this reversal is accomplished by means of the interhemispheric commissures. In monkeys, and perhaps also in humans, the critical commissure may be the anterior commissure.

Of course we do not dare suggest that human infants should have their anterior commissures cut in order to help them learn to discriminate mirror images, and thus perhaps learn to read more easily—although that is exactly what we would predict. If God had intended us not to confuse mirror images, He would not have given us an anterior commissure. In fact, mirror-image equivalence possibly plays a critical role in the recognition and identification of real-world objects, and its advantages outweigh the disadvantages associated with the difficulty of telling left from right.

Even so, most animals *do* seem able to learn to tell left from right, albeit with difficulty. We suspect therefore that the interhemispheric reversal process that we have described may be somewhat attenuated, so that the reversed memory is in some sense weaker than the veridical one. This means that the animal exhibits some degree of left–right equivalence with respect to learning and memory, but is also to discriminate mirror images if this becomes necessary.

The ability to tell left from right is more important to humans than to other species, since the human environment does contain consistent asymmetries, most of them the products of our own asymmetry. Everyday objects, such as scissors, door handles, books and magazines and golf clubs bear the asymmetrical imprint of our own handedness. We have already observed that reading and writing of Western scripts require, respectively, mirror-image discrimination and left–right response differentiation. We do not know whether the mechanism for left–right equivalence is less pronounced in humans than in other species, or whether humans achieve their distinctive left–right sense with reference to the functional asymmetry of the human brain. We shall discuss this matter further in Part II, where our emphasis is on asymmetry rather than on symmetry.

Chapter 5

The Perception of Symmetry

We have already made much of the fact that the natural world, at least as it impinges on our senses of vision, touch, and hearing, is without systematic left–right bias. This lack of bias applies in the *overall* sense however, and not to *particular* manifestations of the world. We are seldom confronted with scenes or events that are perfectly symmetrical, even though the asymmetry of a given event is usually arbitrary and may be reversed on another occasion. Sometimes we *are* presented with near-perfect symmetry: the reflection of a landscape in a still pond may exhibit up–down symmetry, or the frontal view of another person or animal may display left–right symmetry. But such instances are rare. The pond is seldom perfectly still, and in any case may yield a reflection that is discolored or blurred. People or animals seldom reveal themselves in full frontal symmetry, but usually display some asymmetry of stance or expression, such as a hand on the hip or the head tilted, perhaps quizzically to the left or aggressively to the right.

In spite of the lack of symmetry in our natural surroundings, people often impose a rigid symmetry, especially left–right symmetry, on works of art, design, or architecture. In so doing, they may express their own internal symmetry rather than any symmetry in the world about them. Figure 5.1 illustrates a highly artificial symmetry in a design segment from the silver vase of the Egyptian King Entemena, dating from

FIGURE 5.1.

A design segment from the silver vase of King Entemena (c. 2700 B.C.) illustrates left–right symmetry. (Reproduced with the permission of Musée du Louvre, Paris, France.)

about 2700 B.C. The bilateral symmetry of the lion-headed eagle in the center of the segment is carried through the rest of the design so that the other animals are duplicated in mirror-image profiles. This example is of some historical interest because it is the precursor of the two-headed eagle that can be traced through Persian, Syrian, and Byzantine cultures, appearing most recently in the coats-of-arms of Czarist Russia and the Austro–Hungarian Empire.[1] The two-headed eagle, with its two heads in opposite profiles, illustrates how the principle of symmetry may be so powerful as to distort the representation of reality.

By the same token, however, symmetry may also be seen as a repressive force, limiting creative expression. The English art critic John Ruskin (1819–1900) wrote about the appreciation of architecture: "I found the love of largeness, and especially of symmetry, invariably associated with vulgarity and narrowness of mind."[2] Ruskin also quoted one Madame de Maintenon, who was even more severe. Of a particular Renaissance monarch she wrote: "He prefers to endure all the drafts from the doors, in order that they may be opposite one another—*you must perish in symmetry.* "[3] These pronouncements find some support in the modern work in experimental aesthetics. Most people, the vulgar hordes, as Ruskin might have said, judge symmetrical shapes to be more interesting and pleasing than asymmetrical ones,[4] but artists or those deemed especially creative tend to prefer asymmetrical shapes.[5]

The choice between symmetry and asymmetry is rarely an absolute one, however. Hermann Weyl remarks that ". . .seldom is asymmetry merely the absence of symmetry. Even in asymmetric designs one feels symmetry as the norm from which one deviates under the influence of forces of a non-formal character." The tug-of-war between symmetry and asymmetry is well captured by Dagobert Frey: "Symmetry signifies rest and binding, asymmetry motion and loosening, the one law and order, the other arbitrariness and accident, the one formal rigidity and constraint, the other life, play and freedom."[6] The modern British art critic Sir Kenneth Clark makes the same point: "One realises that symmetry and consistency, whatever their merits, are the enemies of movement."[7]

Another point of view however is that symmetry is too perfect a condition to be associated with mere mortals. This seems to be the message of William Blake's famous poem that we quoted at the beginning of the book.

> Tyger! Tyger! burning bright,
> In the forests of the night,
> What immortal hand or eye
> Could frame thy fearful symmetry?

Martin Gardner in his book, *The Ambidextrous Universe,* reminds us that H.S.M. Coxeter, in his *Introduction to Geometry,* reminds us (how could we forget?) that the reference here is to bilateral symmetry.[8] The Australian poet Anna Wickham, in her poem "Envoi," appeals more directly to God as the source of symmetry.

> God, Thou great symmetry
> Who put a biting lust in me
> From whence my sorrows spring,
> For all the frittered days
> That I have spent in shapeless ways
> Give me one perfect thing.[9]

In the *Feynman Lectures on Physics,* Richard P. Feynman describes a gate in Neiko, Japan, that is intricately and elaborately carved, with princes and dragon heads worked into its gables and pillars. It was built at a time of great influence from Chinese art and is sometimes said to be the most beautiful gate in all of Japan. For all its intricacy, the gate is very nearly symmetrical. The only deviation from symmetry is that one small design element on one of the pillars is upside down. Feynman writes: "If one asks why this is, the story is that it was carved upside down so that the gods will not be jealous of the perfection of man. So they purposely put the error in there, so that the gods would not be jealous and get angry with human beings."[10]

THE PERCEPTUAL SALIENCE OF SYMMETRY

When left–right symmetry is present in a design, it is immediately apparent. "Symmetry," wrote Blaise Pascal (1623–1662) in his *Pensées,* "is what you see at a glance."[11] The perceptual salience of left–right symmetry over other comparable kinds of regularity can be illustrated with reference to so-called random-dot patterns. These are generated by computer to exhibit certain regularities, such as symmetry or repetition about an axis, but they are otherwise random and without coherent shape or form. The examples in Figure 5.2. show symmetry about the vertical, or left–right symmetry, and symmetry about the horizontal, or up–down symmetry. Left–right symmetry is the more immediately obvious, as we trust the reader may verify. It is also more noticeable than repetition about the vertical; indeed, observers seldom even notice at all if the right half of a pattern is the same as the left half, whereas it is immediately obvious if the right half is the mirror-image of the left half, producing left–right symmetry. Bela Julesz of the Bell

FIGURE 5.2.

Random-dot patterns illustrate a left–right symmetry (**left**) and up–down symmetry (**right**). The left–right symmetry is the more immediately noticeable. (Figure constructed by Ernst Mach in 1886 and reproduced in B. Julesz, **Foundations of Cyclopean Perception** [Chicago: University of Chicago Press, 1971].)

Telephone Laboratories, who pioneered research on these patterns, has found that left–right symmetry in random-dot patterns can be detected even when exposure is as short as one twenty-fifth of a second.[12]

The salience of left–right over up–down symmetry was also observed by the Austrian scientist Ernest Mach.

> The vertical symmetry of a Gothic Cathedral strikes us at once, whereas we can travel up and down the whole length of the Rhine or Hudson without becoming aware of the symmetry between objects and their reflections in the water. Vertical symmetry is indifferent, and is noticed only by the experienced eye.[13]

The point is further underlined by an elegant technique devised in the 1930s by the German psychologist Erich Goldmeier.[14] Observers are shown a shape that is symmetrical about both the horizontal and vertical axes and asked to compare it with two modified versions, one symmetrical about the horizontal only and the other symmetrical about the vertical only; examples are shown in Figure 5.3. The observers nearly always choose the doubly symmetrical shape to be more like the vertically symmetrical one than the horizontally symmetrical one. This shows that the left–right symmetry is perceptually dominant over the up–down symmetry.

FIGURE 5.3.

Which of the bottom two shapes looks more like the top one? Most observers choose the one on the left, which is left–right symmetrical, rather than the one on the right, which is up–down symmetrical (after Goldmeier, 1935).

Children notice left–right symmetry at an earlier age than they notice up–down symmetry or symmetry about a diagonal. For instance, Susan F. Chipman of the National Institute of Education and Morton J. Mendelson of McGill University had children judge the complexity of various patterns. They observe that, other things being equal, the children generally judged patterns to be simpler if they were symmetrical than if they were not. However, kindergarten children were influenced only by left–right symmetry and double symmetry (i.e., symmetry about both horizontal and vertical), and not by up–down symmetry or symmetry about a diagonal. Up–down symmetry influenced the judgements of children in Grade 2, whereas symmetry about a diagonal did not seem to exert a stable influence until Grade 6.[15]

Experiments also show that, when timed, human adults react more quickly in identifying patterns that exhibit left–right symmetry than in identifying up–down symmetry or left–right repetition. Our own studies show that this effect may depend to some extent on how the patterns are perceived. For instance if people must decide whether two left- or right-pointing arrowheads are pointing in the same or opposite directions, they are actually faster at making "same" than at making "opposite" (or "different") decisions, implying an advantage of repetition over symmetry. But if they have to judge the same pairs "symmetrical" or "asymmetrical" (or "repeated"), the advantage lies with symmetry. In another experiment, people judged whether dot patterns were symmetrical or repeated across a vertical line. Regardless of whether the judgements were of "same" versus "opposite," or of "symmetrical" versus "repeated," the symmetrical patterns were detected more quickly than the asymmetrical ones when the two halves of the patterns were close together. The advantage of symmetry was lost when the halves of the pattern were separated.[16] What these experiments show is that the symmetry of a pattern is especially salient when the pattern is perceived as a unitary whole. It is not so apparent when the two halves of the pattern are seen as separate entities to be compared.

The left–right symmetry of a figure is therefore one of the first things we notice about it. This rapid detection of symmetry may serve to cut down the subsequent perceptual analysis that must be carried out in order to identify the shape. For instance, if people are shown shapes that are symmetrical but otherwise meaningless, they usually move their eyes over only one side of the shapes.[17] This suggests that a person can tell that a shape is symmetrical before looking at it in detail, so that it is then unnecessary to explore the details of both sides. Given the knowledge that a shape is symmetrical, one need only examine one side in order to extract information about the shape as a whole.

Perception of symmetry is not restricted to humans. Even pigeons can learn to peck a key when it displays a pattern that is left–right symmetrical but not when it displays an asymmetrical pattern, or, conversely, to peck to asymmetrical patterns but not to symmetrical ones. After they have been trained with specific symmetrical and asymmetrical patterns, they can then correctly classify as symmetrical or asymmetrical patterns that they have never seen before.[18] In other words, pigeons can be taught the *concept* of left–right symmetry. It is not yet known whether they can be taught the concept of up–down symmetry, or whether this is more difficult than left–right symmetry.

PERCEPTION OF SYMMETRY
AND THE SYMMETRY OF THE BRAIN

It seems natural to relate the perceptual salience of left–right symmetry to the bilateral symmetry of the body. Sir Kenneth Clark, in his lectures on *Civilization,* said, "Symmetry is a human concept, because with all our irregularities we are more or less symmetrical and the balance of a mantlepiece by Adam or a phrase by Mozart reflects our satisfaction with our two eyes, two arms, and two legs."[19] Pascal, in *Pensées,* was more impressed with the role of the human face. The immediacy with which we perceive left–right symmetry, he said "is founded on the fact that there is no reason for any difference, and likewise on the shape of the human face. Whence it comes that we do not ask for symmetry in height or depth, but only in breadth."[20]

Ernst Mach was even more explicit, relating the perceptual salience of left–right symmetry to the bilateral symmetry of the visual system itself. Indeed, he thought that the salience of symmetry was essentially a manifestation of the confusion of left–right mirror images.

> It is a fact, then, that the two halves of a vertically symmetrical figure are easily confounded and that they therefore probably produce very nearly the same sensations. The question, accordingly, arises, *why* do the two halves of a vertically symmetrical figure produce the same or similar sensations? The answer is: because our apparatus of vision which consists of our eyes and of the accompanying muscular apparatus is itself vertically symmetrical.[21]

In other words, left–right symmetry produces an effect much like that of repetition: "The right half of the figure stands in the same relation to the right half of the visual apparatus as the left half of the figure does to the left half of the visual apparatus."[22]

But we must tread carefully here. In Chapter 2 we carefully explained what it means to be able to tell left from right, and we pointed out that a symmetrical system could not tell left from right. However, the perceptual salience of left–right symmetry has nothing directly to do with telling left from right. There is no reason in principle to expect a symmetrical system to be confused about the left–right orientations of the two halves of a symmetrical figure. It might be unable to *label* the two halves distinctly if they are displayed one at a time, but it need have no difficulty telling that the two halves are pointing in opposite directions. Left–right confusion is a problem of labeling, not of perception, whereas the salience of left–right symmetry is an immediate, holistic perceptual experience. In other words, we think that Mach was incorrect in linking the perception of symmetry directly to the confusion of left and right, although both may ultimately depend on the bilateral symmetry of the nervous system.

Mach was confused about another point. He found it difficult to understand why people with only one eye would still be able to perceive symmetry.

> The presence of a sense of symmetry in people possessing only one eye from birth is indeed a riddle. Of course the sense of symmetry, although primarily acquired by means of the eyes, cannot be wholly limited to the visual organs. It must also be deeply rooted in other parts of the organism by ages of practice and can thus not be eliminated forthwith by the loss of one eye. Also when an eye is lost, the symmetrical muscular apparatus is left, as is also the symmetrical apparatus of innervation.[23]

The last phrase contains the key, since it is the visual *fields* rather than the eyes that are mapped symmetrically in the two halves of the brain. The part of the visual field to the left of where one is looking is projected to the right side of the brain, just as the part of the visual field to the right is projected to the left side of the brain. This is so regardless of which eye is viewing and remains true if one loses an eye.

The theory relating perception of symmetry to the symmetry of the visual system of the brain was clearly stated by Bela Julesz of the Bell Telephone Laboratories. Julesz found that observers could not detect left-right symmetry in briefly presented random-dot displays unless they were fixating on the axis of asymmetry. That is, the patterns had to be presented symmetrically with respect to the visual system itself. Julesz argued that symmetry was detected by means of point-to-point comparisons between symmetrical regions of the brain.[24] With symmetrical projection of a pattern, a given part of the left side of the pattern would project to a particular region in the right cerebral cortex, while the corresponding part of the right side of the pattern would project to the symmetrical location in the left cerebral cortex. A built-in comparison process linking these symmetrical regions would then enable the brain to detect the symmetry of the pattern itself.

In Chapter 4, we suggested that a commissural system linking mirror-image points across the two halves of the brain might explain left-right equivalence in the formation of memory records. We suggested further that the anterior commissure might play the critical role there. However, we doubt that the same system explains the perception of symmetry, which involved *perceptual* comparison rather than the formation of *memory* traces. In general, the transfer of perceptual information from one side of the brain to the other does not seem to involve mirror-image reversal. For instance, the main cerebral commissure, the corpus callosum, does not connect mirror-image points in the occipital lobes of the brain, which are the lobes that are primarily involved in visual perception. Rather, the fibers of the corpus callosum seem primarily concerned with maintaining perceptual continuity and with preserving left-right orientation across the two halves of the visual field.[25]

Even so, there is evidence for mirror-image mapping at some level in the visual system. Julesz cites the case of a blind woman subjected to electrical stimulation applied directly to the surface of her visual cortex. This induced what are known as *phosphenes,* or phantom images corresponding in location to the stimulated region of the cortex. When stimulation of a particular region on one side of the cortex exceeded a certain value, the woman sometimes saw a new phosphene at a point in the visual field symmetrically located with respect to the original phosphene.[26] This implies transmission between mirror-image points in the two sides of the brain.

Some people seem to have a natural capacity to perceptually reverse what they see. The *New York Times* of April 14, 1978 describes the case of a woman who can read, write and speak as easily backwards as forwards. She is quoted as saying, ''It's like I have a screen in my head. I can just flip it backward. It's just so easy. To me, it's like doing everything.'' She developed the skill, she claimed, by reversing road signs in her mind to pass the time. After discussing her anomaly with experts, she seemed of the opinion that her brain developed in an unusual way, yet she disclaimed any suggestion that it was unnatural: ''You know some people smoke marijuana and stuff. I never smoke that stuff. I call myself a natural head.''

Mirror-image mapping across the two halves of the visual cortex may be a rather primitive mechanism, perhaps involving connections that are lower down in the brain than the corpus callosum. For instance, Colwyn Trevarthen, in his studies of patients with split corpus callosums, has observed that these patients tend to interpret diagonal lines in each visual half-field as being "in-line" when in fact they form a symmetrical, V-shaped configuration.[27] In these so-called "split-brained" patients, the two half-fields are effectively disconnected from one another; for instance, if the patient fixates the center of a word like "teapot," he will react as though he has seen separate words, "tea" and "pot," each projected to a different cerebral hemisphere. Yet there is some primitive awareness of integration across the field, and the patients appear to be more aware of symmetry between the fields than of continuity or alignment across them. Moreover, split-brain patients show a tendency to accomplish perceptual completions of half-pictures of familiar symmetrical objects presented to a single half-field. For instance, a composite picture consisting of half a bee in the left visual field and half a rose in the right visual field is "interpreted" by the right cerebral hemisphere as a *whole* bee and by the left cerebral hemisphere as a *whole* rose.[28].

Julesz suggests that this primitive, mirror-imaging tendency in visual perception might be a throwback to a more primitive stage of evolution when the eyes were more laterally placed and movement across the field of an eye would be interpreted as movement in the front-back plane, rather than the left-right plane. Front–back equivalence between the two visual fields would be tantamount to a left-right *reversal*. For example, an object moving front to back past the animal would move left to right past the right eye but right to left past the left eye. This may have set the stage for a mapping process within the brain that establishes a mirror-image correspondence between the representations of the two visual fields, and thus creates a special sensitivity to symmetrical stimulation.

It is of course true that we *can* detect up–down symmetry. Moreover we can detect left-right symmetry even when we do not fixate the axis of symmetry and even though the experience of symmetry may not be so compelling as it is when the symmetry of the pattern is superimposed on the symmetry of the visual system. Julesz argued that symmetry is sometimes detected by a more cognitive appraisal of a pattern, and in this case does not require any resonance with the brain's own symmetry.[29] Mach, however, made a more interesting suggestion. He thought that we might detect up–down symmetry by turning the figure round so that it is aligned with the symmetry of the visual system. The figure might be turned around either physically, or else, in Mach's prophetic words, "by an *intellectual* act" (his italics).[30]

The idea that we might be able to mentally rotate patterns, and so imagine them in different orientations, has been explored recently by Roger N. Shepard and his colleagues at Stanford University. Shepard has argued that when we imagine a pattern in a different orientation, the neural representation at some level in the brain is the same as that induced by actually *seeing* the pattern in that orientation.[31] If this is so, then it is not entirely inconceivable that one might detect up–down symmetry by imagining the pattern rotated through 90°, and so aligning the neural representation with the symmetry of the brain.

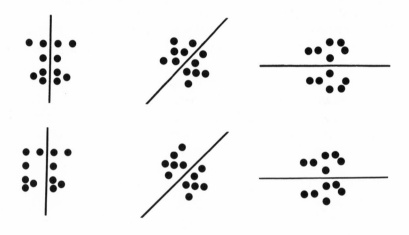

FIGURE 5.4.

Subjects were asked to judge whether patterns like these were symmetrical or repeated about the line. They were fastest when the line was vertical, slowest when it was horizontal (from Corballis and Roldan[32]).

One of us (M.C.C.), in conjunction with Carlos E. Roldan, has explored this possibility. We showed observers patterns of dots that were either symmetrical or repeated about a line: examples are shown in Figure 5.4. The line could be oriented vertically, horizontally or diagonally. We timed the observers as they judged whether the patterns were or were not symmetrical about the line, and discovered that the decisions were fastest when the line was vertical, slowest when it was horizontal, and intermediate when it was diagonal. This result is consistent with the interpretation that the observers were "mentally rotating" the patterns to the vertical before making their decisions; thus it took longer to rotate the patterns when they were horizontal than when they were diagonal. We also tested the observers with their heads tilted 45°, and discovered that the judgements were now fastest when the patterns were tilted by the same amount. In other words, the optimal condition for detecting symmetry occurs when the pattern is aligned with the *retinal* vertical.[32] These results therefore lend support to the theory that symmetry is detached in relation to the symmetry of the visual system itself, and that observers may actually mentally rotate patterns into alignment with the visual system before they make their judgment.

We do not know whether symmetry is *necessarily* detected with reference to the symmetry of the visual system itself. We think it quite likely, as Julesz suggests, that people *can* tell whether a pattern is symmetrical by means of a more deliberate, conscious act of comparing the two sides of a pattern—an act which does not rely on a point-to-point comparison between symmetrical locations in the visual system of the brain. For instance, Irvin Rock and Robyn Leaman, using the technique of Erich Goldmeier that we described earlier, found that left–right symmetry was more salient than up–down symmetry even when the observers tilted their heads 45°, so that both axes of symmetry were equally inclined on the retina.[33] In this case the salience of left-right symmetry did not depend on alignment with the symmetry of the visual system, which is contrary to our own results on the speed of judging symmetry. Even so, there may have been some factor in Rock and Leaman's experiment compensating for head tilt, so that the left–right symmetrical patterns, although not aligned with the symmetry of the visual system at the retinal level, were nevertheless aligned with the symmetry of the brain at some higher level of processing.

Rock and Leaman argue that the perceptual salience of symmetry is simply a result of sensitization to the fact that left–right symmetry is widespread among animal forms and manmade objects. They suggest that this sensitization could come about either through learning or through biological evolution. We began this chapter by pointing out that, despite the ubiquity of symmetrical forms, we are seldom exposed to perfectly symmetrical stimulation. This, perhaps, makes it unlikely that we learn to perceive symmetry simply through experience. Rather, sensitization to symmetry may well be the product of evolution and may have to do with the evolution of a symmetrical nervous system. We suspect, moreover, that sensitization to symmetry is not merely the passive outcome of exposure to symmetrical forms, but may involve active processes of mental imagery which enable us to detect the symmetry of a form even when the form is not displayed symmetrically. Through "mental rotation" we may be able to align a form with the symmetry of the brain and so detect its symmetry with reference to the point-to-point comparison process described by Julesz.

Is sensitivity to symmetry merely an evolutionary throwback to a more primitive stage when the eyes were laterally placed, as Julesz suggests? Its origins may well date from that early stage, but we suspect that the ability to detect symmetry is no mere evolutionary curiosity. Instead, it probably has considerable adaptive significance even to humans. Symmetry is a kind of redundancy, common to many biological forms, and the ability to detect it eases much of the burden of perception and pattern recognition. If one detects that a form is symmetrical, one effectively halves the amount of subsequent perceptual processing that must be carried out. Consequently, our considerable powers of mental imagery may have evolved partly to enable us to capitalize on a relatively primitive device for detecting symmetry.

PART TWO

The Emergence
of Asymmetry

At last, after much painful thought, Zeus had an idea. "I think," he said, "That I have found a way by which we can allow the human race to continue to exist and also put an end to their wickedness by making them weaker. I will cut each of them in two; in this way they will be weaker, and at the same time more profitable to us by being more numerous. They shall walk upright upon two legs. If there is any sign of wantonness in them after that, and they will not keep quiet, I will bisect them again, and they shall hop on one leg." With these words he cut the members of the human race in half, just like fruit which is to be dried and preserved, or like eggs which are cut with a hair. [Plato, *The Symposium*]

Chapter 6

The Origins of
Right Handedness

There can be few topics which have generated more superstition than that of human handedness. It may not be an exaggeration to claim that every human culture associates different properties or values with the terms *left* and *right*, and that the nature of these properties is related, either directly or metaphorically, to the functional differences between the left and right hands. Since the majority of humans prefer using their right hands to their left hands, and are more skilled with their right hands, positive values are generally assigned to the right and negative values to the left. Our very language expresses the virtue of being dextrous, adroit, or righteous, while there is something distinctly dubious about being sinister or gauche. A "right-hand man" is a trusted friend, while a "left-handed compliment" is an insult. The right hand is used for shaking hands, saluting, making the sign of the cross, laying on of hands, and for swearing on the Bible; the left hand is the "hand of the privy," and the hand that delivers the *coup de grâce* to a dying adversary.

The assignment of positive and negative values extends generally to the left and right sides of the body. The Maoris of New Zealand believed that if a person experienced a tremor during sleep the body had been seized by a spirit, and it was critically important to determine which side of the body was afflicted. A tremor on the right foretold good fortune and life, while a tremor on the left meant ill-fortune and even death.[1] In remarkably similar fashion, the native people of Morocco attach a great significance to the twitching of an eyelid. Twitching of the right eyelid signifies the return of a member of the family or some other good news, while twitching of the left is a warning of impending death in the family.[2]

According to the French social anthropologist Robert Hertz, whose classic essay on the subject was published in 1909,[3] the dominant polarity associated with right and left is that between the sacred and the profane. To the Maoris the right was the side of the gods, as well as the side of strength and life, while the left was associated with profanity, demons, weakness, and death. We need look no further than the Bible to discover the same theme (Matt. 5:25).

> And He will set the sheep upon His right hand and the goats upon His left. Then shall the King say to those upon his right, 'Come, ye blessed of my Father, and inherit the Kingdom prepared for you from the beginning of the world'. . . .Then shall He also say to those on the left, 'Depart from me, ye accursed, into everlasting fire prepared for the Devil and His angels.'

In the Pythagorean table of opposites, given by Aristotle,[4] the right was associated with the limited, the odd, the one, the male, the state of rest, the straight, the light, the good, and the square, while the left signified the unlimited, the even, the many, the female, the moving, the curved, the dark, the evil, and the oblong. Remarkably similar tables can be constructed from the symbolism of other quite unrelated cultures, such as the Nyoro of East Africa[5] and the Gogo of Tanzania.[6] It is noteworthy that the symbolism expresses the universality of male domination, with the male associated with the right and the female with the left. The Maori expression *tama tane*, literally "male side," referred to the right, while the *tama wahine*, "female side," referred to the left. Hertz[7] quoted a Maori proverb: "All evils, misery, and death come from the female element." According to the 19th century Swiss historian J. J. Bachofen, we may find a reversal of traditional values in matriarchal societies and a corresponding emphasis on the left. In the Isis cult of ancient Egypt, for instance, honor was given to Isis, the wife, over Osiris, the husband, and also to mother over son and to night over day, and the Isis procession was headed by a priest carrying an image of the left hand.[8]

Empedocles, the Sicilian philosopher of the 5th century B.C., thought that males were hotter than females and the right hotter than the left, so that the sex of a child was determined by rightward or leftward location in the womb. He is also said to have thrown himself into the crater of Mt. Etna, ostensibly to prove that he was a god; or perhaps he sought greater heat to restore his flagging masculinity, as this poet seems to suggest.

> Great Empedocles, that ardent soul
> Leapt into Etna, and was roasted whole.[9]

Curiously enough, something of his theory survives in modern biology. Ursula Mittwoch, in a recent article called "To be born right is to be born male," notes that in hermaphrodites with mixed sex organs, testes are more often found on the right and ovaries on the left. She suggests that the same lateralizing tendencies are present in normal males and females, though overridden by the influence of the sex chromosome.[10] We might perhaps see further confirmation of the Empedoclean principle in the report by Jerre Levy and Jerome Levy, daughter and father, that in most men the right foot is larger than the left, while in women the left is larger than the right. These tendencies are reversed among left handers.[11]

Superstition related to handedness is by no means an ancient or primitive phenomenon. For instance, the possibility of a link between handedness and sex was altogether too much for a certain element of the psychoanalytic school to resist. In 1923, Wilhelm Fliess, a friend and colleague of Sigmund Freud, wrote as follows:

> Where left handedness is present, the character pertaining to the opposite sex seems more pronounced. This sentence is not only invariably correct, but its converse is also true: where a woman resembles a man, or a man resembles a woman, we find the emphasis on the left side of the body. Once we know this we have the diviner's rod for the discovery of left handedness. This diagnosis is always correct.[12]

Freud himself did not accept this dogmatic theory. Indeed, he wrote a psychoanalytic study of Leonardo da Vinci without once suggesting that there might be a relation between Leonardo's left handedness and his homosexuality,[13] although in a letter to Fliess he did suggest Lenardo as a possible example.[14] Nevertheless Fliess's insistence on his wrong-headed theory eventually led to his estrangement from his more illustrious colleague.

The universality of left–right symbolism, with the right accorded the

superior status, is testimony to the universality of right handedness itself. There are no known cultures or societies, present or past, in which
right handers have not constituted the majority. Occasionally there has
been a suggestion that there may have been a society consisting predominantly of left handers, but the evidence is invariably flimsy and does not
stand up against the overwhelming evidence for the universality of right
handedness. For instance, at least one 19th century authority[15] claimed
that the ancient Hebrews must have been predominantly left handed, on
the grounds that Hebrew is written from right to left instead of from left
to right. As we pointed out in Chapter 4, however, the direction of script
does not seem to bear any strong relation to handedness. Until about
1500 A.D. right-to-left scripts were about as common as left-to-right
ones.[16] Indeed, it may have seemed more natural, especially in engrav-
ing hieroglyphics in clay or stone, to begin on the right precisely because that is where the right hand is located. Abram Blau, who wrote a
scholarly, but in some respects misguided, monograph on handedness
in 1946, also drew attention to the 700 left-handed men in the army of
Benjamin, referred to in the Old Testament (Judges 20:16), as further
evidence for a predominance of left handers among the ancient Hebrews.[17] He neglected to mention, however, that the 700 were but a fraction of the total army of 26,000.

It has been argued that the ancient Egyptians may have been predominantly left handed because they tended to depict humans and animals in
right profile in hieroglyphics and on the walls of monuments.[18] It is generally agreed that it is more natural for left handers to draw right profiles, just as the natural tendency for right handers is to draw left profiles. Sir Daniel Wilson, a 19th-century authority, thought that this
argument, at least as applied to the ancient Egyptians, was probably
misleading, because the choice of profile depended on other considerations. In columns of hieroglyphics, for instance, the profiles typically
face toward the center line. On monuments and buildings the direction
of profiles depended on overall design rather than on the whim or con-
venience of the sculptor.[19] Adolf Erman, another 19th-century expert on
the ancient Egyptians, made the more compelling point that it was a general law of art that figures should present their right sides to the specta-
tor, which might be taken as evidence that the ancient Egyptians were
actually *right* handed.[20]

Wilson himself, after discussing the evidence from the Egyptian and
other early civilizations in detail, came to the conclusion that the only

evidence for a left-handed people that could not be dismissed on the basis of other evidence was to be found in a passage in the Eclogues of Stobaeus, the Macedonian, written in about 600 A.D. ". . .Those on the southwest are sure-footed, and for the most part fight with the left hand; and as much force as others exert with their right side, they exert by application of their left."[21] A similar curiosity occurs in John H. Tooke's *Diversions of Purley, 1786–1805* published in 1840: "I remember to have read in a voyage of Da Gama's to Kalekut. . .that the people of Melinda, a polished and flourishing people, were all left handed."[22]

Such isolated anecdotes fade into insignificance when set against the considerable evidence from art, stories, and words themselves which overwhelmingly indicate a universal preference for the right hand. Moreover, evidence that the majority of humans are right handed goes back as far as the historical record takes us. Two Canadian psychologists, Stanley Coren and Clare Porac, examined over a thousand photographs and reproductions of drawings, paintings, and sculptures dating from about 15,000 B.C. to 1950 A.D., and tabulated unambiguous representations of handedness. Over the entire period the incidence of right handedness remained approximately constant at about 90 percent. Coren and Porac concluded that humans have been predominantly right handed, without significant variations in incidence, for at least 50 centuries.[23] Ancient stories also attest to the predominance of the right hand, not only in explicit references to handedness, but also in the attribution of positive values to the right and negative values to the left, as we have already seen. Linguistic terms reveal the same bias: "Even among the degraded Australians, and the Pacific Islanders," wrote Sir Daniel Wilson with arrogant ethnocentrism (some of our best friends are Australians), "terms for right, the right hand, or approximate expressions, show a familiarity with the distinction."[24]

Although history reveals a universal preference for the right hand, the prehistoric record is more equivocal. Some authors have argued that right handedness gradually emerged during the Stone Age, some 5000 years before Christ, but was not clearly established until the Bronze Age, between 3000 and 1000 B.C.[25] Writing in 1890, Gabriel de Mortillet suggested that *left* handedness may have been about twice as prevalent as right handedness in neolithic (late Stone Age) times. His excavations in France and Switzerland yielded 197 stone scrapers adapted to the left hand, 105 adapted to the right hand, and 52 usable by either.[26]

Some years earlier, however, de Mortillet had claimed that there was actually a slight bias toward the right hand, judging from Stone Age implements discovered in the Somme gravels.[27] Paul Sarasin, a more recent investigator, found about equal numbers of left-handed and right-handed implements around Moustier, in France, again with a slight bias favoring the right.[28] What is clear, however, is that these data are in marked contrast with those based on artifacts from the Bronze Age, when the bias in favor of the right hand was strikingly evident. The bronze sickle, for instance, was manufactured for the exclusive use of right handers.[29]

The apparent discontinuity between the Stone Age and the Bronze Age has been taken as evidence that the origins of right handedness are cultural rather than biological. Abram Blau, for instance, attributed right handedness in tools to the whim of the inventor.[30] Once established in tools, right handedness would effectively be imposed on the population, who had little choice in the matter. However, as Lauren J. Harris of Michigan State University has pointed out, the argument can easily be reversed. With the development of the more sophisticated tools during the Stone Age, the toolmaker may at last have had sufficient reason to match the tool to the already existing hand preferences among the potential users.[31] The fact that right handedness emerged in apparently quite unrelated cultures suggests, contrary to Blau, that its origins are biological rather than cultural.

There is other evidence, moreover, that right handedness may go back much further than the Stone Age. In 1925, Raymond A. Dart discovered in South Africa the fossil remains of a creature called *Australopithecus,* dating from the Pleistocene period about two million years ago.[32] This creature is the earliest on record to exhibit human-like as distinct from ape-like qualities, and was widely hailed as the "missing link" between ape and man. Among the most conspicuously human of its characteristics was its capacity for murder. Around the sites of fossil remains Dart also discovered many skulls of baboons, which had evidently been hunted and killed by *Australopithecus.* Although smaller than the baboon, *Australopithecus* had the decisive advantage of a weapon, possibly the thighbone or armbone of an antelope. Examination of the baboon skulls revealed that most had been struck from the front and on the left, indicating that the majority of attackers were right handed. Dart also examined the skull of an adolescent *Australopithecus,* which had been struck just to the left of the point of the jaw. It had evidently been murdered by a right-handed member of its own species.

HANDEDNESS IN OTHER SPECIES

We know of no evidence that bears on the handedness of our human ancestors prior to *Australopithecus;* indeed, there is a hiatus in the prehistoric record between this hominoid creature and the apes of the Miocene and Pliocene eras of more than three million years ago.[33] It is pertinent to enquire whether consistent handedness is to be observed in present-day species, especially those closest to humans. It is therefore of interest that G. B. Schaller, in his book *The Mountain Gorilla,* writes that he saw eight of these gorillas giving displays of chest-beating, and all favored the right hand.[34] Anecdotal evidence of this sort is notoriously subject to error and artifact, however, and we shall need more controlled tests to confirm that the mountain gorilla is truly right handed.

Chimpanzees do not, as a species, display an overall preference for one or other hand, even though observations in the wild suggest that they use primitive tools in a variety of ways. For instance, they use twigs or sticks to extract termites from their holes, an activity known as "termiting." In her observations, Jane Goodall noted no overall preference for the left or right hand in termiting.[35] Individuals often showed a consistent preference, but about as many preferred the left hand as preferred the right. This has been confirmed in laboratory studies of hand preference, not only in chimpanzees,[36] but also in monkeys,[37] rats,[38] and mice.[39] Even the lowly mouse has a preferred paw in reaching for food, and the preferred paw is usually the one with the stronger grip, but left-pawed and right-pawed mice exist in equal proportions.

There have been a few claims of biased overall preferences in other species. In one study of paw preferences in cats, about twice as many preferred the left paw as preferred the right, although nearly half showed no consistent preference at all.[40] According to another report, parrots generally prefer the left foot in picking up bits of food.[41] At a recent conference on handedness, a member of the audience announced that the great majority of raccoons around his home reached for food with their right paws.[42] These claims must await confirmation, since some previous assertions about biased preferences in animals have not survived more rigorous testing. There are many traps for the unwary in testing the pawedness of animals. For instance the animal may be housed in a cage with some marked asymmetry, such as a food dispenser set closer to a wall on one side than on the other; it has been shown that the paw preferences of mice are markedly influenced by making a food source more accessible to one paw than to the other.[43] Again, in offering food to animals in the wild, the would-be investigator may unwittingly impose his own handedness on the recipient, perhaps in his gestures or in the way he places the food.

This is perhaps an appropriate place to gather the threads of evidence we have discussed so far. By and large, it appears that the predominance of right handedness is uniquely but universally human. We do not know precisely when it emerged in human evolution, but we suspect it goes back beyond the Stone Age at least to *Australopithecus*. It may transpire that other primates, such as the mountain gorilla, exhibit an overall preference for the right hand, but the primates so far tested in the laboratory do not display any such preference. The fact that right handedness is very largely if not entirely restricted to humans suggests that it evolved in relation to specifically human skills, such as the use of sophisticated tools or the development of language. We shall develop this theme in Chapter 9. Finally, the fact that right handedness emerged in geographically distinct and unrelated cultures suggests that its origins were fundamentally biological rather than cultural.

THE DEVELOPMENT OF HANDEDNESS

Another perspective on the question of whether handedness is fundamentally biological or cultural can be gained by studying the development of handedness in human children. Until fairly recently, however, the child has been the vehicle rather than the source of theories of handedness; that is, most authorities have simply asserted how handedness develops without bothering to check the facts. The fundamental debate actually goes back at least to Plato and Aristotle. Plato attributed right handedness to "the folly of nurses and mothers,"[44] while Aristotle believed that it was fundamentally organic.[45]

Associated with the view that handedness is a product of experience rather than any biological predisposition, there have been movements throughout history to restore in people their natural ambidexterity. For instance, in the *Dialogues* Plato has the Athenian say that "those who make the left side weaker than the right act contrary to nature."[46] Another champion of ambidexterity was the 18th-century French philosopher Jean Jacques Rousseau (1712–78). In *Émile* he wrote:

> The only habit the child should be allowed to contract is that of having no habits; let him be carried on either arm, let him be accustomed to offer either hand to use one or other indifferently. . .[47]

Movements to foster ambidexterity may have reached their peak toward the end of the 19th century, largely through the efforts of the English novelist and propagandist Charles Reade. In a letter to *Harper's Weekly* in 1878, he made plain his views on the origins of handedness.

> . . .six thousand years of lop-armed, lop-legged savages, some barbarous, some civilized, have not created a single lop-legged, lop-armed child, and never will. Every child is even and either handed till some grown fool interferes and mutilates it.[48]

Another vigorous advocate of ambidexterity was Robert Hertz. "One of the signs which distinguish a well-brought-up child," he wrote, with studied irony, "is that its left hand has become incapable of independent action."[49] Around the turn of the century one John Jackson, author of an influential tract called *Ambidexterity or Two-Handedness or Two-Brainedness* (1905),[50] founded the Ambidextral Culture Society in England. Among its supporters was Lord Baden–Powell, founder of the Boy Scout movement. To this day, as part of a compensatory scheme introduced by Baden–Powell, the Boy Scouts shake hands with the left hand.

No amount of campaigning for the liberation of the left hand seems to have moved us any closer to ambidexterity. Right handers have remained solidly in the majority even, we suspect, among the Boy Scouts. This is not to say that there are no pressures toward right handedness. During this century the proportion of those writing with the left hand increased within about three generations from about 2 percent to nearly 12 percent, according to an English survey.[51] Even today, Chinese adolescents in Taiwan are much less likely to eat or write with their left hands than are adolescents of Chinese extraction in California, presumably because of cultural taboos in Taiwan that are not present in permissive California.[52] But the difference is confined to eating and writing; for other activities the two groups were comparable with respect to handedness. It seems unlikely that there is any significant environmental pressure to comb one's hair or clean one's teeth with the right hand, yet some 90 percent of the population do so. We do not think that cultural pressure to use the right hand for certain activities causes the majority to be right handed; rather the pressure simply represents the tyranny of the right-handed majority over the left-handed minority. We are all in favor of Gauche Liberation Movements, but we do not think that such movements will significantly alter the proportion of left handers in the human population.

But if the environmental theory of right handedness has lacked conviction, organic theories have not fared well either, at least historically. Perhaps the main reason for this is simply that the two hands *look* so much alike—there is no obvious anatomical basis for any asymmetry. It is no doubt this striking discrepancy between anatomical symmetry and functional asymmetry that is responsible for the symbolic potency of the left–right distinction, documented at the beginning of this chapter. "What resemblance more perfect than that between the two hands," exclaimed Robert Hertz, "and yet what a striking difference there is!"[53] No wonder people sought the intervention of gods and supernatural forces to explain the distinction between left and right.

Not all have sought refuge in the irrational, however. There have been many attempts to link right handedness to other asymmetries of the human body. The 17th-century English physician, Sir Thomas Browne (1605–1682) reviewed a number of early organic theories, and rejected them in favor of a cultural explanation.[54] For instance, the Italian, Gabriello Fallopio (1523–1612), after whom the Fallopian tubes are named, attributed right handedness to the Azygos vein, which emerges only from the right side of the heart. Browne pointed out that this vein does not branch into the arms or legs on either side, and so should have no influence on handedness or footedness.

The English philosopher, Sir Francis Bacon (1561–1626), emphasized the rightward displacement of the liver. He argued that the senses depend on the brain and are symmetrical because the brain is symmetrical—a false premise, as it turned out—but that movements are "somewhat holpen from the liver," and therefore exhibit a right-sided superiority.[55] A difficulty here is that the vast majority of left handers also display the usual rightward asymmetry of the liver. There is a condition known as *situs inversus viscerum* in which the internal organs are left–right reversed, but this is much too rare to explain left handedness.[56] Moreover, in 1788, Matthew Baillie published a description of a man with complete reversal of the heart and other visceral organs, but who was nonetheless clearly *right* handed.[57]

This critical case seems to have been overlooked by 19th-century theorists, who persisted in seeking a relation between handedness and the situs of the internal organs. For instance, one Samuel S. Fitch emphasized the rightward displacement of the lungs, which "give us the power of action," and went so far as to suggest that "in all cases where people are left handed the left lung will be found to be the larger."[58] Andrew Buchanan argued that the rightward displacement of the lungs and liver produced a shift in the center of gravity of the body, resulting in greater development of the right leg and foot, which in turn increased the precision of movements in the right arm.[59] Sir Daniel Wilson, in his scholarly review of 1872, dismissed all such theories, documenting further cases of right handers with congenital *situs inversus*. He also pointed out that many animals possess comparable internal asymmetries but do not display consistent handedness.[60]

Another theory that seems to have originated in the 19th century is that handedness depends on birth position. Some 96 percent of babies are born head first, and of these about 90 percent are born with their heads turned to the left and 10 percent with their heads turned to the right. In 1828, the French physiologist A. J. Comte pointed out that these percentages approximated those of right and left handers, respectively.[61] He further suggested that those born with their heads to the left were in fact twisted to the left in the uterus, so that the left arm would be pressed against the mother's back and right arm would be against the abdomen. Since the abdomen is the more yielding, there would be less pressure on the right arm than on the left, causing the child to become right handed. The reverse argument applies to those whose heads are twisted to the right. Conte did not actually observe whether there was a relation between birth presentation and subsequent handedness, but seems to have relied on evidence of an impressionistic sort. An abstract published in 1938 claimed that there is in fact no correlation between birth presentation and handedness, although no details were given.[62] We know of no other evidence on the matter. The theory does not of course explain how infants come to be in different asymmetrical fetal positions in the first place.

As early as 1646, Thomas Browne had called for systematic observations of children, in the hope that this might settle the issue of whether handedness was acquired or of organic origin.[63] Such observations were slow to appear, and are somewhat indecisive to this day. One observer was Charles Darwin, who wrote in 1877 that his own son had developed a preference for the right hand when about two and a half years old, but subsequently proved to be left handed.[64] He thought that the boy's left handedness was inherited, since his grandfather, mother, and brother were all left handed. In 1891, the psychologist G. Stanley Hall reported the opposite switch; two infants who initially showed a preference for the left hand later settled down to become right handed.[65] Yet again, Helen Woolley reported in 1910 that her daughter at eight months would only wave "bye-bye" with the left hand, which she attributed to the fact that nurse always carried the child on her left arm, leaving the child's left arm free. At about fifteen months, the child waved habitually with the right hand, and was by then clearly right handed in other activities as well.[66]

Later, more controlled studies have added support to the curious observation that infants show an initial preference for the hand opposite the one they ultimately prefer. One of the most extensive and well documented investigations was that carried out in the Yale Clinic of Child Development by Arnold Gesell and Louise B. Ames, and reported in 1947.[67] These investigators took records on moving film of groups of children ranging in age from eight weeks to ten years of age. The numbers in the groups ranged from twelve to forty-five. The children were filmed in situations contrived to secure responses to various objects, such as pencils, paper, cubes, and construction toys. The first clear preference, at sixteen to twenty weeks, was generally for the *left* hand. However there were frequent shifts between left handedness, bilaterality and right handedness during the first year of life. Cyclic fluctuations persisted until the age of about eight years, but the initial dominance of the left hand gave way after the first year to an increasing dominance of the right hand among the majority of children. George Seth of Queen's University, Belfast, observed the development of nine infants, and he also found that left handedness prevailed during the first nine months, but thereafter gave way to right handedness.[68] Oddly enough, the same phenomenon has also been observed in a baby chimpanzee, whose earliest preference was for the left arm and left foot, but who subsequently became right handed and right footed.[69] Perhaps we should not make too much of this, since it is but a single case and chimpanzees as a species do not display an overall preference for the left or right hand.[70]

Since right handedness emerges only gradually over the first year of life, it might at first seem reasonable to suppose that it is acquired by learning or imitation. However, it is not clear how this would explain the early preference for the left hand. Gesell and Ames themselves argued against such an interpretation. They were struck by the orderly way in which hand preferences fluctuate. Children of a given age were remarkably consistent in their preferences, especially at the younger ages. Gesell and Ames concluded that "handedness is a product of growth." In other words, it is programmed into the structure of the nervous system and unfolds as part of the process of physical maturation rather than as a response to environmentally or culturally imposed biases. Seth reached essentially the same conclusion.

A further reason for supposing that handedness is a product of maturation rather than learning is that children exhibit a striking postural asymmetry both before and shortly after birth, and this seems to be related to subsequent handedness. This asymmetry (not to be confused with the asymmetry of birth presentation) is the so-called tonic neck reflex, in which the head is turned to one side, the arm and leg on that side are extended, and the opposite arm and leg are flexed. Most children display a right tonic neck reflex, which is to say that they turn their heads to the right. Gesell and Ames followed up nineteen children, nine with a left tonic neck reflex, three who showed the reflex in both directions, and seven with a right tonic neck reflex.[71] Four of these children subsequently became left handed, and all had revealed a left tonic neck reflex in infancy. The five other children with the left tonic neck reflex were right handed at ten years, but had shown some ambilaterality or left handedness at one or five years of age. Those with bidirectional reflexes also showed some ambilaterality, but were predominantly right handed. The children with right tonic neck reflexes were exclusively right handed, with the exception of one who showed some ambilateral tendencies prior to age ten but was right handed at ten years.

These observations reveal some relation, albeit an imperfect one, between handedness and the tonic neck reflex. Those versed in statistical procedures may note, however, that the correlation is not statistically significant,[72] suggesting that it may be no more than a chance occurrence. But from our present point of view, the important aspect of the data is that the *right* tonic neck reflex strongly predicts *right* handedness; we shall argue in the following chapter that left handedness is a rather special condition, and actually arises from the lack of any biological predisposition to be either left or right handed. Consequently, we think that the relation described by Gesell and Ames is good evidence that right handedness is biologically predetermined, since it is predicted by an asymmetry that can be detected before birth. Let us for the moment reserve judgement about the nature of left handedness.

Gerald Turkewitz of the Albert Einstein College of Medicine in New York has also studied the tonic neck reflex in infants. The majority in any ward of healthy, full-term babies can be seen to lie with their heads to the right. Turkewitz and his colleagues have shown that newborn infants are also generally more sensitive to sounds on the right and to touches on the right side of the face than to comparable stimulation on the left, probably because they expose the right sides of their heads to the external environment more often than they expose the left sides.[73] However, we know of no data relating these asymmetries to subsequent handedness.

Finally, despite the failure of earlier theorists to convincingly relate handedness to the asymmetry of the internal organs, there is now clear evidence that handedness is related to the asymmetry of the human brain. As was the case with handedness and the tonic neck reflex, the relation is much more consistent among right handers than among left handers; more than 95 percent of right handers have speech and language represented primarily in the left side of the brain, whereas left handers show a much more variable pattern.[74] Moreover, some manifestations of cerebral asymmetry can be detected in early infancy, and even before birth.[75] These matters will be pursued in Chapter 9, but for the moment we may simply note that they confirm the biological origins of right handedness, and remove some of the mystery associated with the remarkable anatomical symmetry of the limbs. It appears that the organic basis for handedness resides, not in the heart, lungs, or liver, but in the brain.

SUMMARY AND CONCLUSIONS

Right handedness is a characteristic that appears to be exclusively but universally human. We have argued that it is biologically rather than culturally determined. One line of argument appeals to the very universality of right handedness across diverse and seemingly unrelated cultures. The other is that, although right handedness in not itself manifest until late in the first year of life, it is correlated with other asymmetries that are evident at or before birth. We do not deny that there are environmental pressures to be right handed, or that some naturally left-handed individuals may be compelled to use their right hands on certain tasks. We suspect however that these very pressures have their origins in the fundamental right handedness of most human beings.

So far we have very largely neglected that articulate and often talented group, the left handers, who have remained a persistent and approximately stable minority for thousands, perhaps tens of thousands, of years. The question of variations in handedness is somewhat distinct from that of why the majority of people are right handed. This is the subject of the next chapter.

Chapter 7

Variations in Handedness

"The left handed are precious;" says Jean Valjean in Victor Hugo's *Les Misérables*, "they take places which are inconvenient for the rest." And so they do for theories of handedness; although the human record suggests an overwhelming dominance of the right hand, it appears that there has always been a stable minority of left handers despite the pressures of our right-handed world. The main question is whether variations in handedness are due entirely to environmental (including pathological) influences or whether there is also some genetic effect. The reader should note that this question is logically distinct from the question of the origins of right handedness. We argued in the previous chapter that right handedness is a biological characteristic of humans, but it is entirely possible that variations from the general pattern of right handedness are due wholly to environmental influences. We shall argue, however, that this variation is at least partly under genetic control.

Before we pursue this theme, however, we must examine more closely how handedness is measured, since precise measurement can provide some clues about the underlying determinants of handedness.

MEASURING HANDEDNESS

Although people can generally classify themselves as right or left handed, with some perhaps better described as ambidextrous, it is fairly clear that there are *degrees* of handedness. That is, there is a more or less continuous range from extreme right handedness, through ambidexterity, to extreme left handedness. It is also useful to distinguish between *preference* for one or other hand, and difference in actual *performance* between the two hands. A person may prefer to use one hand for a certain task, but may be more skillful with the other hand—although this state of affairs is rare, at least among those who exhibit strong handedness.

In measuring *preference,* the usual method is to select a number of different manual activities and enquire as to which is the preferred hand in each case. One widely used test is the Edinburgh Inventory, developed by the late R. C. Oldfield at Edinburgh University.[1] The testee is simply asked to indicate the preferred hand in ten different activities, which were carefully culled from a larger set to provide a reliable overall index and to exclude activities with an obvious cultural bias. The inventory, together with instructions for scoring, is shown in Table 7.1. As explained there, it is possible to compute from the subject's preferences a so-called *laterality quotient,* ranging from + 100 for extreme right handedness, through 0 for complete ambidexterity, to –100 for extreme left handedness.

When this inventory was administered to 394 men and 734 women undergraduates at Edinburgh University, 10 percent of the men and 5.92 percent of the women were found to have quotients of less than zero, indicating at least some degree of left handedness.[2] These percentages may not be representative of the population as a whole, but they do illustrate the common observation that the proportion of left handers is higher among men than among women. It has been suggested that this difference may reflect a bias in reporting rather than in real difference in handedness;[3] nevertheless the same clear difference was apparent in the study of 4,143 Chinese adolescents in Taiwan that we refer to in Chapter 6.

Although the Edinburgh Inventory reveals a continuum of laterality quotients, most people are clearly left or right handed, and relatively few are ambidextrous or display even preference. That is, people tend to cluster towards the ends of the continuum, creating a distribution that is *bimodal* (see Figure 7.1). For instance, about 50 percent of right handers, defined as those with laterality quotients greater than zero, have laterality quotients above 80, while 50 percent of left handers have laterality quotients less than –76. It is also evident however that there is a

TABLE 7.1

EDINBURGH HANDEDNESS INVENTORY

The following is the short form of the inventory developed by R. C. Oldfield and standardized in Edinburgh. The instructions to the subject are as follows:

> Please indicate your preferences in the use of the hands in the following activities by *putting + in the appropriate column.* Where the preference is so strong that you would never try to use the other hand unless absolutely forced to, *put + +.* If in any case you are really indifferent *put + in both columns.*
>
> Some of these activities require both hands. In these cases the part of the task, or object, for which hand preference is wanted is indicated in brackets.
>
> Please try to answer all the questions, and only leave a blank if you have no experience at all of the object or task.

		LEFT	RIGHT
1.	Writing	☐	☐
2.	Drawing	☐	☐
3.	Throwing	☐	☐
4.	Scissors	☐	☐
5.	Toothbrush	☐	☐
6.	Knife (without fork)	☐	☐
7.	Spoon	☐	☐
8.	Broom (upper hand)	☐	☐
9.	Striking Match (match)	☐	☐
10.	Opening box (lid)	☐	☐

To find your *laterality quotient,* add up the number of +s in each column. Subtract the number under LEFT from the number under RIGHT, divide by the total number, and multiply by 100.

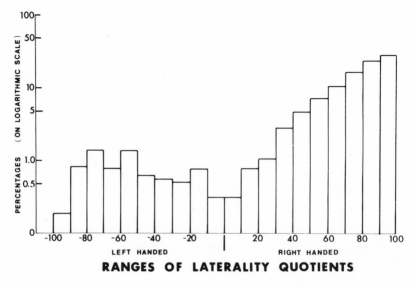

RANGES OF LATERALITY QUOTIENTS

FIGURE 7.1.

Graph showing the percentage of people with different laterality quotients was calculated from statistics gathered through the Edinburgh Handedness Inventory. Notice that people tend to fall near the extremes rather than in the middle of the range (after Oldfield, 1971).

rather more even distribution across the left-handed range than across the right-handed range. Right handers therefore seem to be more right handed than left handers are left handed. Because left handedness seems to be more diffuse, some authors have preferred the label "non-right handed" to "left handed."

Let us now consider differences in actual *performance* between the two hands. These probably provide a more reliable index of handedness since they do not rely on individual testimony. People are regrettably not always to be trusted in what they say they do, and some are of course confused as to which is left and which is right. A pioneer in the measurement of handedness by performance was the indefatigable British scientist Sir Francis Galton, who tested 7,000 men and boys at the Health exhibition of 1884 on their ability to squeeze a dynamometer with each hand in turn.[4] This device gives a reading of the strength of grip exerted by each hand. When the score for the left hand was subtracted from that for the right hand, the difference was in the majority of cases positive, indicating on overall advantage for the right hand. However these difference scores were not distributed bimodally like those based on tests of preference. Instead, the distribution was bell shaped. That is, most people fell near the middle of the range, although to the right of the point of neutrality, with relatively few clustered at the extremes. This distribution of differences in strength between the hands seems to have been approximately constant from age six to eighty.

Marian Annett, now at the Lanchester Polytechnic in Coventry, England, has developed a task which measures skill rather than strength.[5] Subjects are timed as they move pegs from one row of holes to another, using each hand in turn. Again, the distribution of differences between the hands in the time it takes to perform the task favors the right hand overall, is bell shaped rather than bimodal and remains approximately constant with age, at least between three-and-one-half and fifteen years. Because the difference does not change with age, Annett argues that the peg-moving task provides a measure of handedness that is relatively uncontaminated by the effects of learning or of environmental influences. This measure is highly consistent with stated preferences, and it is noteworthy that women are more often right handed than are men, suggesting again that this difference is not simply a matter of subjective bias.

One complication in using tests of skill to assess handedness is that many skills require unique contributions from each hand, and the difference between hands seems to be one of kind rather than one of degree. Jerome S. Bruner of Oxford University has argued that one hand can usually be described as the *operating* hand, while the other is specialized for *holding*.[6] One hand holds the wood while the other wields the hatchet, one holds the nail while the other swings the hammer, one holds the paper while the other manipulates the pen. The operating hand is usually identified as the preferred or dominant one; this indeed is implicit in three of the operations included in the Edinburgh Inventory. In some cases, such as in playing certain musical instruments, this characterization does not seem to apply quite so obviously; in playing a violin, for instance, can one truly say that the bowing hand is more skillful or "operative" than the hand that controls the strings? Perhaps so; Charles Chaplin, a left hander, had a "left handed" violin specially constructed for his own use,[7] suggesting that there may be a fundamental "handedness" even for playing the violin. However, there still seem to be some respects in which we lack an adequate description of the qualitative aspects of handedness.

In tasks performed with a single hand, however, both hands seem to operate in qualitatively much the same way. In a study carried out at McGill University, R. H. Barnsley and M. S. Rabinovitch tested people with each hand in turn on a wide range of unimanual skills, and used a technique called factor analysis to determine the number and nature of the dimensions underlying performance.[8] Performance seemed to be characterized by the same dimensions, or factors, regardless of which hand was used. The most important factors were identified as reaction time, speed of arm movement, wrist–finger speed, arm–hand steadiness, arm-movement steadiness, and aiming. These constitute independent aspects of unimanual skill, and in all except reaction time, the subjects performed better when they used their preferred rather than their unpreferred hands, indicating again that handedness is reasonably consistent whether measured in terms of skill or preference. Barnsley and Rabinovitch nevertheless argued that handedness should be assessed in terms of skill rather than preference, and that performance on each factor should be sampled in order to provide a balanced index.[9]

There are some simple operations which most self-avowed right handers can do better with their *left* hand.[10] For instance, try flexing a single finger at the middle joint to an angle of $90°$, as shown in Figure 7.2. Most right handers can do this more readily with the fingers of the left than of the right hand. Another example, also illustrated, is to hold the two outside and two inside fingers together, and to spread the two pairs as far apart as possible. Most people can achieve a wider separation with the left hand than with the right. It is not clear what explains these phenomena, but they do warn against assuming a universal superiority of one or other hand.

Of course, handedness is not the only manifestation of external asymmetry, although it is the most striking. Most people display a preference for one foot in kicking a ball, or for one eye in aiming a gun or looking through a telescope, or for one ear in listening to the telephone. In each of these examples, but in varying degrees, there is in overall preference for the right member. These preferences are also loosely correlated with each other so that, for instance, a person who is right handed is more likely than a left hander to be right footed, right eyed, and right eared, but the correlations are far from perfect.[11] Control over the facial muscles also apparently exhibits an asymmetry, but here the advantage appears to reside on the left. Most people can smile and grimace with greater flexibility on the left than on the right side of the face.[12] Our concern in this chapter is with handedness rather than with these other

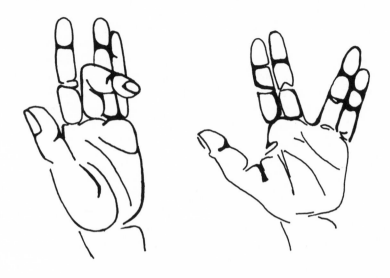

FIGURE 7.2.

Most people find these hand postures easier to adopt with the left than with the right hand (after Kimura and Vanderwolf, 1970).

asymmetries, partly because it has been more extensively studied and quantified, and partly because we think it is the most fundamental of the external asymmetries. Nevertheless, all of these asymmetries, including handedness, may reflect asymmetries of the brain, which are discussed in the following chapters.

Although we have stressed that handedness is a graded characteristic, most investigators have persisted in classifying people into separate categories, such as right, left and mixed handers. We shall ourselves do this in the remainder of this chapter. Questionnaires or test batteries, whether based on preference or on skill, are thus commonly used to provide criteria for classification rather than indices or quotients for use in their own right. This practice may reflect a lack of sophistication on the part of theories of handedness. Alternatively—and this is the version we prefer—it may be the case that there are categories at some fundamental biological level, but that the vagaries of culture and the environment superimpose a continuous range of possible manifestations of handedness. We shall develop this theme in the following sections.

THE INHERITANCE OF HANDEDNESS

Whether one believes that variations in handedness are due to environmental or to genetic variations, there is no disputing that handedness is inherited, at least to a degree. That is, a person is more likely to be left handed if one or other parent is left handed, and more likely still if both parents are left handed. Table 7.2. summarizes data on the handedness of children as a function of parental handedness. But as with the inheri-

---

TABLE 7.2

INHERITANCE OF HANDEDNESS

The table shows the percentage of left handers born to parent who are both right handed, of opposite handedness, and both left handed, in surveys taken at different points in time:

Survey	Parental Handedness		
	Both Right	Mixed	Both Left
Ramaley (1913)	12.2	32.4	85.7
Rife (1940)	7.6	19.5	54.5
Annett (1978)	9.2	20.5	22.2
Weighted Average	9.2	22.1	51.9

The data of Ramaley and Rife are summarized by Collins (see note 21). Annett's data are from two surveys conducted in the 1970s, and are summarized in her 1978 article (see note 37). The fluctuations between surveys are probably due as much to variations in the criterion for left handedness as to historical factors. The extreme fluctuations under "Both Left" can be attributed to the small samples. Across all samples, there were only 27 children in this category.

tance of money, the transmission from one generation to the next is not perfect. Even if both parents are left handed, there is only about an even chance that an offspring will also be left handed. Nevertheless, like madness or success on the Stock Exchange, handedness can be said to run in families.

The vast majority of families are of course predominantly right handed, so any evidence for a left-handed lineage is of special interest. There is an age-old tradition in Scotland and Ireland that people with the surname of Kerr (anglicized to Carr) tend to be left handed. The name is derived from the Gaelic *caerr,* meaning awkward, and the terms *car-handed, ker-handed,* and *carry-handed* are still in vernacular use to refer to a left-handed person. We hasten to add that any reputation for awkwardness seems to reside not in the Kerrs themselves, but in the problems they posed to the English, as the following anonymous poem makes clear.

> But the Kerrs were aye the deadliest foes
> That e'er to Englishmen were known,
> For they were all bred left-handed men
> And 'fence against them there was none.

According to *The Times* of London of 4 January 1972, a quick survey of Carrs and Kerrs listed in *Who's Who?* revealed that "rather more than half" were right handed.

To say that handedness is inherited is not necessarily to imply that it is *genetically* inherited. It may simply be the case that children imitate their parents, or that parents tend to teach their children to be like themselves in handedness. We have argued in the previous chapter that *right* handedness is probably not acquired in this way, but depends at least in part on some biological predisposition; however, *left* handedness might still be due to an environmental influence. This influence might be quite subtle. For instance, Abram Blau, in his 1946 monograph, argued that left handedness is merely a symptom of emotional negativism, a stubborn streak,[13] and perhaps it is this rather than left handedness itself that is inherited.

Paul Bakan of Simon Fraser University has proposed that left handedness may be the result of lack of oxygen at birth. He suggests that the tendency to birth stress may itself be inherited, although he also points out that some 85 percent of left handers have two right-handed parents. Bakan's argument is largely indirect, although based on a wide range of observations. He points out that left handedness is more frequent among males than among females, among twins than among the singly born, and among first borns than among younger siblings. Males, twins, and first borns are all supposedly prone to the higher incidence of birth stress. Bakan also cites evidence that left handedness is associated with epilepsy, mental retardation, speech problems, learning disabilities, schizophrenia, and a number of other pathological or abnormal conditions which we might expect to be related to brain damage. For those left handers who are alarmed by this woeful inventory, Bakan points out that in most cases the effects of lack of oxygen at birth are transitory, and he suggests that handedness may be affected without any other adverse complications.[14]

Yet not all of the evidence favors Bakan's view. Several authors have failed to confirm the relation between left handedness and birth order.[15] Although Bakan cites one follow-up study in which it was found that children who took longer to establish breathing were more likely to be left handed at the age of three years,[16] a large-scale follow-up study in England failed to reveal *any* clear relation between birth complications and subsequent handedness.[17] Our own view is that the association between birth stress and handedness is, if anything, slight, and that the majority of left handers are probably left handed for reasons unconnected with brain pathology. Bakan may well have a case, but he has almost certainly overstated it.

In general, theories which attribute variations in handedness wholly to environmental causes, including pathological ones, are difficult to prove, since one does not have access to, or control over, a child's total environment. By contrast, genetic theories are usually fairly explicit and make rather precise predictions about the inheritance of handedness. Let us therefore now explain some of the main characteristics of genetic theory, as it might be applied to handedness. We shall then consider some of the objections to genetic theory, before concluding with a particular theory that we think elegantly incorporates both genetic and environmental variation, and captures most of the characteristics of the inheritance of handedness.

GENETIC THEORY

The simplest kind of genetic theory would be one in which handedness is controlled by a single gene locus for which there are two alternative *alleles*, one coding right handedness which we shall call R, the other coding left handedness, L. Alleles are alternative forms of a gene that can occupy the same locus on the chromosomes. The chromosomes occur in pairs, one donated by each parent, so that individuals can be classified as *RR, RL,* or *LL,* depending upon whether they carry two *R* alleles, one of each, or two *L* alleles. *RR* and *LL* individuals are called *homozygotes* because each pair of alleles is the same, while *RL* individuals are called *heterozygotes.* It is plausible to assume that the R allele is *dominant* and the L allele *recessive,* which means that heterozygotes will generally be right handed. According to this classical kind of genetic theory, only *LL* individuals should be left handed.

A simple theory like this was proposed in 1913,[18] but must be ruled out because it implies that the children of two left-handed parents must *always* be left handed. Left-handed parents must be *LL,* and can therefore donate only *L* alleles to their children; consequently, the children themselves must also be left handed. In fact, as Table 7.2 illustrates, surveys generally show that just under 50 percent of the children of left-handed parents are themselves left handed. It is possible, however, to ''soften'' the theory in various ways to accommodate the observed correlation between parents and children. One could argue that some left-handed parents are left handed for pathological reasons, such as lack of oxygen at birth, rather than for genetic reasons, and that these parents may pass on an *R* allele. One could say that one or other allele has limited *penetrance,* so that, for instance, only a proportion of *LL* individuals will actually be left handed.[19] There are in fact a number of reasons why the *phenotype,* the characteristics actually exhibited by an individual, might not be fully determined by the *genotype,* the genetic make-up of the individual.[20]

The difficulty with modified genetic theories of this kind is not so much that they are demonstrably false, but rather that they tend to be arbitrary. It is easy enough to invent reasons why the observed facts do not fit a theory, but in so doing one tends to lower the credibility of the theory. For instance, it might well be argued that departures from the theory are due to pathological influences, but one might as well then follow Bakan and argue that left handedness is due *entirely* to pathological influence. The problem is in deciding where to draw the line. There are, however, a number of more specific arguments against genetic theories that we now consider.

ARGUMENTS AGAINST GENETIC THEORIES

One person who has argued against genetic theories of handedness is Robert L. Collins of the Jackson Laboratory in Bar Harbor, Maine.

Collins showed that mice usually exhibit consistent handedness (or pawedness) in reaching for food in a glass tube, and that the preferred paw is also usually the one with the stronger grip. As we saw in the previous chapter, however, individual mice are as likely to be left pawed as right pawed. Moreover, the proportions are unaltered by selective breeding for pawedness. Even after several generations of mating between left-pawed mice, the offspring remain equally divided between left and right pawers.[21] The same is true of rats.[22] These observations reveal that variations in the direction of pawedness in rats and mice are not under genetic control.

Collins also showed that pawedness in mice was strongly influenced by moving the glass tube toward the right of the cage, so that it was then more accessible to the right paw than to the left.[23] The majority of mice then reached with their right paws, although a stubborn minority of about 10 percent persisted in awkwardly reaching with their left paws—a proportion, as Collins points out, "not unlike the proportions of left handers in human societies." In one respect, however, the data failed to match those based on measurement of human handedness: the incidence of left pawedness was higher among female mice than among males, whereas the opposite is true of human handedness. Collins argues that genetic variation can affect the *degree* of pawedness, but that the *direction* of pawedness depends upon environmental biases and on a random process—what Collins calls an "asymmetry lottery."

It is of course tempting to suppose that the human situation is no different. The environmental bias includes the handedness of one's own parents, which explains why people are more likely to be left handed if one or other parent is left handed. Some observers have reported a maternal influence, so that a child is more likely to be left handed if the mother is left handed than if the father is. This might be attributed to closer contact between mother and child than between father and child. The difference is slight, however, and not all researchers have found it.[24]

Collins' strongest argument against genetic theories of human handedness was based on evidence from twins.[25] Monozygotic twins, popularly known as identical twins, are formed from the splitting of a single fertilized egg, and therefore carry identical genes. If the direction of handedness were under strict genetic control, then, monozygotic twins should always have the same handedness. In other words, there should be essentially perfect correlation in handedness between twin pairs. The facts are quite to the contrary. Collins combined the results of several surveys, yielding data on the handedness of 462 pairs of twins, and discovered a virtually complete lack of any correlation. That is, the handedness of one twin tells us virtually nothing about the handedness of the other.

We can illustrate this with reference to throwing dice. Suppose that throwing a six on a single die stands for left handedness, while throwing any other value stands for right handedness. We can predict quite well the distribution of handedness in monozygotic twins by considering what happens if we throw two dice independently. The predicted proportion of right-handed pairs in then $5/6$ multiplied by $5/6$, or $25/36$, that of mixed pairs is $2 \times 5/6 \times 1/6$, or $10/36$, while that of left-handed pairs is $1/6 \times 1/6$, or $1/36$. This is what is known as a *binomial* distribution, and it is what one expects if the handedness of one twin is quite independent of the handedness of the other.[26] The distribution of handedness is also approximately binomial among dizygotic (or fraternal) twins, who grow from separate fertilized eggs and bear the same genetic resemblance to one another as do ordinary nontwin siblings. Among nontwin siblings the distribution shows a slight positive relation, meaning that a child is slightly more likely to be left handed if a sibling is left handed than if the sibling is right handed, but it is still fairly close to the binomial.[27] The actual distributions, as tabulated by Collins, are shown in Table 7.3.

There has been some debate as to whether twins provide admissable evidence for genetic theories of handedness.[28] In particular, it has been suggested that twins are susceptible to "mirror imaging" tendencies, either because of their relative locations in the uterus or, in the case of monozygotic twins, because of special factors to do with the splitting of the egg. In folklore, some twins are said to be "mirror twins," one the left–right mirror image of the other, like Tweedledum and Tweedledee, that quarrelsome pair from Lewis Carroll's *Through the Looking Glass*. There is some evidence that mirrored features are more likely to occur in monozygotic twins the later the split occurs.[29] In the extreme case there is no split, and we have joined-together twins (sometimes known as Siamese twins); in this case, one twin exhibits reversal of the internal organs while the other has the internal organs the right way round. There is no evidence that such mirror imaging applies to handedness, and among twins who are separate at birth, reversals of the internal organs are in any case extremely rare.[30] The popular notion of mirror twins therefore seems to be largely a superstitious one. The very fact

TABLE 7.3

HANDEDNESS IN TWINS AND PAIRED SIBLINGS

The table shows the numbers and percentages of twins and paired siblings who are both right handed, of opposite handedness, and both left handed.

Pairings

	Both Right	Mixed	Both Left
Monozygotic			
Numbers	347	106	10
Percentages	74.9	22.9	2.2
Expected by Chance	74.6	23.5	1.9
Dizygotic			
Numbers	300	80	4
Percentages	78.1	20.8	1.0
Expected by Chance	78.4	20.3	1.3
Nontwin Siblings			
Numbers	3067	475	41
Percentages	85.6	13.3	1.1
Expected by Chance	83.1	15.8	1.1

The data are summarized by Collins (1970) from surveys of monozygotic and dizygotic twins by Wilson and Jones in 1928, Newman in 1937, and Rife in 1940 and 1950, and from Rife's 1940 survey of paired siblings. The percentages "expected by chance" were computed from the assumptions that the distribution is binomial (see text for explanation).

that handedness in twins so closely matches the binomial distribution implies that opposite handedness occurs in twins no more often than one would expect by chance, and no more often in monozygotic than in dizygotic twins. There does appear to be a slightly higher frequency of left handedness among twins than among the singly born, but this can be attributed to the effects of crowding in the uterus rather than to any special factors associated with the process of twinning itself.[31] The data summarized by Collins therefore stand as compelling evidence against the view that the direction of handedness is under genetic control.

More generally, there appears to be no precedent anywhere in biology for the idea that the direction of an asymmetry can be genetically coded. Michael J. Morgan of the University of London has examined the biological evidence and concluded that the genes are "left–right agnosic"—that is, they cannot encode the difference between left and right.[32] The only possible exception that he was able to discover concerned the direction of coiling in snail shells! Whether a shell coils clockwise or counterclockwise seems to be determined by a pair of alleles, with the clockwise allele dominant. But this is scarcely a convincing precedent for supposing that the direction of human handedness might be genetically controlled. For one thing, the influence of the genes controlling the coiling of the shell is expressed, not in the individual carrying the genes, but rather in the offspring of that individual.[33] If you are a snail it is your mother's genes that count, not your own. Moreover the inheritance of counterclockwise coiling does not always breed true; snails carrying two recessive alleles often produce offspring that coil clockwise rather than counterclockwise. In one strain the incidence of clockwise coiling was as high as 80 percent.[34] The bias toward clockwise coiling is therefore stronger than one would expect if the direction of coiling were completely under genetic control.

The reader may well be wondering what on earth the coiling of shells has to do with left–right asymmetries like handedness! The fact is that the distinction between clockwise and counterclockwise can be interpreted as a left–right difference. A clockwise snail becomes counterclockwise if viewed in a mirror, as the reader may verify by closely examining a corkscrew in a mirror. Genetic control over the direction of coiling therefore does imply genetic control over a left–right asymmetry, and seems to be a genuine exception to Morgan's dictum that the genes are left–right agnosic. But given the special features of this control, and the fact that snails and humans are very distant cousins indeed, we might well agree that this example has rather little bearing on handedness. Morgan did later modify his dictum slightly, concluding instead that "the inheritance of asymmetry is asymmetrical."[35] That is, even in the case of the snails, any genetic control over the direction of asymmetry seems to be dwarfed by the influence of left–right biases that are of nongenetic origin.

ANNETT'S THEORY

Despite these objections there have been persistent and often ingenious attempts to devise genetic theories of handedness.[36] We shall focus on one in particular, because in our view it stands out as conspicuously more successful than the others. This is the theory developed by Marian Annett,[37] whose measure of handskill was referred to earlier. We have here reinterpreted this theory slightly.

According to Annett, the majority of people inherit what she calls a "right shift." We may assume that these individuals carry a dominant allele like the one we previously labelled R. Among this majority the right hand is favored overall, but because of environmental influences the degree of right handedness varies, giving rise to a bell-shaped distribution. Because of this variation, some small proportion of this group will actually be classed as left handed. We may include pathological effects under the broad category of environmental influences. Annett suggests that the right shift is more marked for women than for men, perhaps because men are more susceptible to pathological influences at birth.

What is especially interesting about Annett's theory is that the alternative to the right shift is not a left shift, but is rather a *lack* of the right shift. That is, a minority of people inherit no genetic predisposition to be either left handed or right handed. Let us suppose that this is due to a recessive allele which we label N, for neutral.[38] The distribution of handedness for NN individuals will also be bellshaped, but will be symmetrical about the point of zero handedness. As is the case with rats and mice, half of these individuals will be left handed and half right handed, although a good many may be better classed as of mixed handedness (we do not mean to imply that these people are mouselike in other respects). The two hypothetical distributions are illustrated in Figure 7.3.

Barring those who are left handed because of extreme environmental or pathological influences, left handers can thus be seen as falling within the category of NN individuals. This neatly explains why only about half of the children of left-handed couples are left handed. Indeed, Annett herself carried out a study of the children of families in which both parents were left handed, carefully screening out those families in which

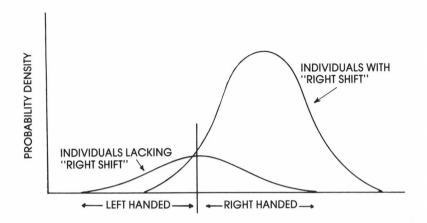

PROBABILITY DENSITY

INDIVIDUALS WITH "RIGHT SHIFT"

INDIVIDUALS LACKING "RIGHT SHIFT"

←— LEFT HANDED —→ | ←—RIGHT HANDED—→

FIGURE 7.3.

The larger bell-shaped curve represents the majority of individuals and is shifted to the right, so that nearly all of the individuals in this group are right handed. The smaller curve represents the minority who lack the right shift; half of these individuals are right handed and half left handed (after Annett, 1972, 1978).

one or other parent had had birth complications that might have accounted for their left handedness.[39] The children of the remaining families showed no overall difference between the left and right hand on the peg-moving task; of the forty-five children, twenty-three were faster with the left hand and twenty-two were faster with the right hand. These children had evidently inherited the lack of any predisposition to be either left or right handed, exactly as the theory would predict.

Another general argument in favor of a theory like Annett's is that it explains the rather diffuse and inconsistent laterality exhibited by left handers. We have already seen that left handers tend to be less left handed than right handers are right handed—although this could represent the "pull" of the right-handed world. However, left handers also show inconsistencies with respect to other measures of laterality, such as footedness,[40] and eye dominance,[41] while right handers are fairly consistently lateralized on these measures. We may suppose, in terms of Annett's theory, that *NN* individuals are essentially random with respect to different manifestations of laterality, while *RR* and *RN* individuals are subject to the same uniform lateralizing influence. The reader may recall from Chapter 6 that of the nine infants with a left tonic reflex studied by Gesell and Ames, four subsequently became left handed and five right handed—an essentially even split. As we shall see in the following chapter, right handers nearly always have language represented primarily in the left cerebral hemisphere, while left handers show a mixed pattern of cerebral dominance. The most bizarre finding of all, perhaps, is that right handers process the *word* "right" more quickly than the world "left," while there is no difference among left handers![42]

Fingerprints, which so often provide crucial evidence, have also furnished useful support for Annett's theory. The two hands usually differ with respect to the number and pattern of ridges on the skin of the fingers and palms. David C. Rife summarized five studies of fingerprints and handprints in a total of 3,095 right handers and 1,642 left handers, and in each study the asymmetry between the hands was less among the left handers than among the right handers.[43] Since the patterns of fingerprints and handprints are known to be inherited, presumably genetically, this evidence is sometimes cited in general support of genetic theories of handedness.[44] It favors Annett's theory particularly, since it is again consistent with the notion that most left handers belong to a subgroup of the population that lack consistent asymmetry, while the majority of right handers are genetically predisposed to be asymmetrical.

Annett's theory does not necessarily contradict Morgan's conclusion that the genes cannot encode the direction of an asymmetry. We can suppose that the right shift is not coded directly by the *R* allele, but rather that this allele permits the expression of some underlying asymmetry, possibly of molecular origin.[45] Consequently the two alleles, *R* and *N,* can be viewed as encoding whether or not a particular asymmetry will be expressed, rather than as encoding the direction of the asymmetry. There are in fact biological precedents for genetic control over the *degree* of asymmetry, if not over its direction. One example is of particular interest because it suggests a close parallel to Annett's theory. Among mice, as among humans and other vertebrates, the heart is asymmetrical and displaced somewhat to the left. There is a mutant strain of mice, however, in which this asymmetry is reversed in half the population.[46] Even after many years of inbreeding, the incidence of reversal has remained at 50 percent, suggesting that the direction of the asymmetry is randomly assigned, an outcome, one might say, of Collins's asymmetry lottery. We may liken these mice to the *NN* individuals of Annett's theory. They display no genetic predisposition toward either the normal or the reversed asymmetry of the heart.

It is a fine point whether Annett's theory can be reconciled with the evidence on the distribution of handedness among twins and siblings, particularly among monozygotic twins. The theory does allow for a random environmental component, so that we need not expect monozygotic twins always to show the same handedness. In fact, we might reasonably expect those twins inheriting the right shift to follow a binomial distribution, but one that is strongly biased toward right handedness. Those twins *not* inheriting the right shift should also follow a binomial

---

TABLE 7.4

HANDEDNESS IN TWINS

This table shows the numbers and percentages of monozygotic twins who are both right handed, of opposite handedness, and both left handed, as tabulated by Zazzo (see note 47) from his own and nine other surveys:

	Pairings		
	Both Right	Mixed	Both Left
Monozygotic twins			
Numbers	867	295	48
Percentages	71.7	24.4	4.0
Expected by Chance	70.3	27.1	2.6

Note that in this tabulation, the percentage of monozygotic twins of opposite handedness is less than one would expect according to a binomial distribution. The discrepancy is small, but sufficient to reconcile the data with Annett's theory.

---

distribution, but one that is unbiased; that is, a quarter should be left handed, half should be of opposite handedness, and a quarter should be right handed. The difficulty is that the sum of these two binomial distributions is not itself binomial, so the theory is therefore inconsistent with the data summarized by Collins, and shown in Table 7.3.

But the fault may lie with the data rather than with the theory. The surveys summarized by Collins were in some cases rather dated and were based on unreliable measures of handedness, possibly on unreliable techniques for assessing whether the twins were truly monozygotic. Annett herself has shown that her theory provides an excellent fit to another tabulation of handedness in 1,210 pairs of monozygotic twins.[47] Not surprisingly these data, shown in Table 7.4, reveal a systematic departure from the binomial distribution, as indeed the theory must predict. We still have some reservations about whether Annett's theory can explain all of the data, not only on monozygotic twins, but also on dizygotic twins and on nontwin siblings. The issue, however, is a complex one, hinging both on the adequacy of the surveys and on the mathematical assumptions one makes in fitting the theory.[48]

Whether or not Annett's theory is correct in detail, we think that it is surely the most convincing theory that has been proposed. It is broadly consistent with what is known about genetic influences over other biological asymmetries. It incorporates a component due to environmental and pathological influences. These influences, moreover, account for the fact that handedness varies in continuous fashion, despite the two basic genetic categories implied by the theory. The idea that left handers belong to a subgroup of the human population who lack a predisposition to be lateralized will in fact be a recurring theme in the remaining chapters of this book. For instance, the theory makes sense of a number of observations about the relations between handedness and the functional asymmetry of the brain, as we shall see in the next chapter. It also makes sense of certain observations about children who suffer difficulties with reading and speech, the topics of Chapters 11 and 12.

Chapter 8

Language and the
Left Cerebral Hemisphere

In 1836, at a meeting at Montpelier in France, one Marc Dax made a historic observation: among 40 patients suffering from disturbances of speech, all proved to have suffered injury to the left side of the brain.[1] This may have been the first explicit recognition that the left cerebral hemisphere is normally the dominant one for speech and language. However, Dax's report was not published until 1865 and initially made little impact. In the meantime, in 1861, a French scientist and physician, Paul Broca, had read an influential case study to the Anatomical Society of Paris in which he described the results of a postmortem examination of the brain of a patient known as ''Tan,'' so called because that was the only articulate sound he could make. Broca attributed Tan's inability to talk to a lesion in the frontal lobe of the left hemisphere of the brain, in a specific area now known as Broca's area (see Figure 8.1).[2]

Although Tan had lost the ability to talk, he could write normally and could understand both written and spoken language. He suffered no paralysis of the lips or tongue and indeed could move his tongue to the left or right when asked to do so. His disability seemed to be restricted to the specific movements involved in articulate speech. It is an example of *aphasia,* a general term for language disorders that cannot be attributed to disturbances of the muscles themselves, to loss of hearing, or to general mental deficiency. More specifically, Tan's aphasia is an example

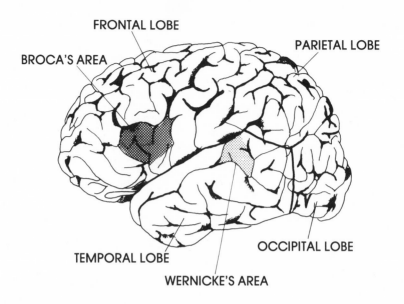

FRONTAL LOBE

PARIETAL LOBE

BROCA'S AREA

OCCIPITAL LOBE

TEMPORAL LOBE

WERNICKE'S AREA

FIGURE 8.1.

Diagram of the left side of the brain shows Broca's area and
Wernicke's area.

of *motor aphasia,* since the impairment is one of expression rather than
one of comprehension.

In 1874 Carl Wernicke described a kind of aphasia, sometimes called
sensory aphasia, that is essentially the converse of that described by
Broca.[3] The patient is virtually unable to understand the speech of others, but can talk fluently, even garrulously. However, his own speech is
meaningless, although it may be grammatically correct. One is reminded of the famous sentence produced by Noam Chomsky, the lin-
guist, to illustrate that a sentence can be syntactically correct but seman-
tically empty: "Colorless green ideas sleep furiously." (Chomsky went
on to say some quite interesting things.)[4] The impairment is also sometimes called *jargon aphasia,* since the victim's speech often contains
jargon and neologisms. One real-life example runs as follows: "I think
that there's an awful lot of mung, but I think I've a lot of net and tunged
it a little wheaten duhvayden."[5] This type of aphasia can usually be attributed to damage in the left temporal lobe of the brain in the area now
known as Wernicke's area (see Figure 8.1).

Wernicke also recognized another kind of aphasia, known as *conduction aphasia* or *central aphasia*, usually due to damage to the left hemisphere between Wernicke's and Broca's area. The patient can understand speech, and can usually even talk quite fluently, although with an excess of circumlocution and substitutions of sounds (e.g., "fots of fun" for "lots of fun").[5] The most striking symptom is the inability to repeat what someone else has said.[6] Curiously enough, there is another, somewhat complementary kind of aphasia called *transcortial aphasia*, in which the patient compulsively repeats what is said by another person, a symptom known as *echolalia*. Although some of these patients understand very little, their echolalic repetitions often correct the grammar of the original! It seems that the patients retain some knowledge of grammar (or syntax) even if they have no access to the meaning of an utterance.[7]

The striking feature of all these aphasias is that they are caused in the great majority of patients by damage to the *left* side of the brain, indicating that speech and language are represented primarily on that side. This asymmetry has been verified by a great many other observations and experiments, including the dramatic series of studies carried out on patients with so-called "split brains."

In the early 1960s, several patients suffering from severe epilepsy underwent an operation in which the nerve fibers connecting the two sides of the brain were cut. The purpose of this was to prevent the spread of epileptic activity from one side of the brain to the other. The operation proved more successful than expected, however, and the patients either had fewer epileptic seizures or ceased to have them altogether.[8] In their everyday activities, they were remarkably unaffected by the operation, and were seemingly as intelligent, efficient, and coordinated as before. Nevertheless, the patients offered a unique opportunity to assess the functions of each side of the brain without interference from the other side; indeed, subtle psychological testing revealed that the two sides acted as separate, autonomous entities, each with its own emotions and consciousness.[9]

It is possible to direct information to a single side, or hemisphere, of the brain of the split-brain patient, and so test only that hemisphere's capacities. One way to do this is to make sure the patient's eyes are fixated on a point, then briefly flash information to the left or right of that point. The flash must be sufficiently brief that the patient does not have time to move his eyes, yet long enough for the information to be visible and interpretable—a flash of about $1/10$ of a second is about right. Under these conditions, information projected to the right of the fixation point is projected wholly to the left hemisphere, while information to the left of fixation is projected wholly to the right hemisphere. This is illustrated schematically in Figure 8.2.

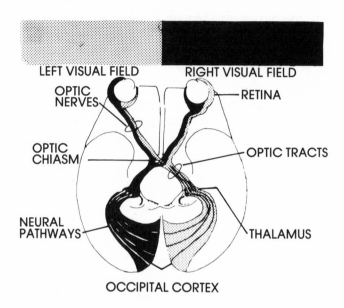

FIGURE **8.2.**

Schematic representation of the human visual system illustrates the fact that information in the left visual field is projected to the right side of the brain, and information in the right visual field to the left side.

Split-brain patients can easily name words or pictures of objects flashed to the right of fixation, but they cannot name words or pictures flashed to the left, indicating that the right cerebral hemisphere is essentially mute.[10] Similarly, they can name objects felt with the right hand, which is represented in the left cerebral hemisphere, but they cannot name objects felt with the left hand—provided that the hands are hidden from view. But although the right hemisphere cannot overtly name words, it can evidently understand them. For instance, split-brain patients can correctly point with the left hand to an object named by a word in the left visual field, even though they cannot name the object. One split-brain patient was asked to pick with his left hand from among fifteen objects that which "makes things bigger," and correctly chose a magnifying glass.[11] These and similar examples suggest that the right hemisphere is capable of understanding language at quite a sophisticated level.

Eran Zaidel at the California Institute of Technology has developed an ingenious technique for restricting visual input to a single hemisphere of a split-brain patient for minutes at a time, thereby overcoming one of the limitations of using brief flashes.[12] One eye is covered and the other is fitted with a contact lens with a small screen on it. Half of the screen is opaque, blocking out vision in half the visual field. The patient can look around freely, but can only see things that are to one or other side of the point of fixation. Zaidel asked the patients oral questions about pictures, with either the left or the right visual field blocked out. Although both cerebral hemispheres receive the oral question, only one hemisphere can act upon it, since the other hemisphere does not receive the relevant visual information. Zaidel was therefore able to test each hemisphere independently for its ability to understand words and sentences. He discovered that the right hemispheres of adult patients achieved a vocabulary about equivalent to that of a child between ten and sixteen years of age, and could understand both active and passive sentences. That is, the right hemisphere was only slightly less sophisticated in comprehension than the left, and the difference was apparently only a matter of degree.

These observations seem rather at odds with the evidence from aphasic patients. Damage to the left hemisphere often results in devastating loss of comprehension, as in the so-called sensory aphasia. Why does the intact right hemisphere not mediate comprehension in these patients? One possibility is that the left hemisphere may exert a negative or inhibitory influence on the right, whereas this influence is literally cut off in split-brain patients. An alternative possibility is that the two sides of the brain in split-brain patients are not typical of those in normal people. All of the patients had a long history of severe epilepsy prior to the surgery. This may have caused some rearrangement of language representation in the brain, including some compensatory representation in the right hemisphere. The extent of language representation in the right hemisphere is a somewhat controversial issue, although there seems to be fairly general agreement that the dominance of the left hemisphere is more pronounced with respect to the *production* of speech than with respect to its *comprehension*.

It is also possible to test for cerebral asymmetries in normal people by projecting information to just one hemisphere at a time. The measured differences are not absolute since each hemisphere is connected to the other through the commissures, but it appears that there is some loss of information in transmission from one side to the other, and some increase in time. Thus most people identify words and letters more accurately[13] and quickly[14] if they are flashed in the right than in the left visual field. Of course normal subjects, unlike split-brain patients, *can* name words and letters flashed in the left visual field because the right hemisphere does have access, via the interconnecting commissures, to the speech mechanisms of the left. The differences between left and right visual fields in normal subjects are therefore typically small, and cannot be demonstrated reliably on single presentations, or even in single individuals. One must usually test a group of people in order to demonstrate an effect convincingly.

Another way of testing for cerebral asymmetry both in split-brain and in normal people is to use a technique called *dichotic listening*. The subject wears earphones, and different information is played simultaneously to both ears. The information might be syllables, numbers, words, or even sentences, in which case the situation somewhat resembles that of a cocktail party where the listener might try to listen to two conversations at once (or to drop several eaves at once). Under these conditions, a split-brain patient can only report back the information presented to the right ear, implying that this information reaches only the left cerebral hemisphere.[15] Normal people can report verbal information presented to either ear, but there is usually a right-ear advantage, which is again taken as evidence for a dominance of the left hemisphere in the processing of language.[16]

Studies of cerebral lateralization in normal subjects have not proven very useful in determining the degree of lateralization or the absolute functional properties of each cerebral hemisphere, but they have provided a great deal of information about the range of functions that are lateralized. In visual studies, the right visual field advantage applies to words, letters, and even backward (mirror-reversed) letters.[17] In dichotic listening, the right-ear advantage has been demonstrated with spoken digits,[18] meaningful as well as meaningless words,[19] prose passages,[20] consonants,[21] vowels,[22] backwards speech,[23] and even, although perhaps less certainly, the grammatical and prosodic components of ordinary speech.[24] In other words, the dominance of the left hemisphere, whether relative or absolute, seems to apply to virtually every aspect of the perception, comprehension, and production of language.

The next question is whether the dominance of the left cerebral hemisphere extends beyond language. We have already seen that it is more pronounced with respect to the production of speech than with respect to comprehension, which suggests that the left hemisphere might exert a more general dominance in the control of movements. There is some evidence, for instance, that there is a left hemispheric dominance in the control of movements of the tongue and jaw, even when these movements have nothing to do with speech.[25] There is also a disturbance known as *apraxia,* that usually results from damage to the left cerebral hemisphere. Apraxia is characterized by an inability to do simple things on command (e.g., "Show me how you comb your hair"), even though the patient can evidently understand the command and does not suffer from paralysis of the muscles.[26] The disability seems to be confined to *sequences* of acts, since apraxic patients appear to have no difficulty when asked to copy static positions of the limbs.[27]

But it is the phenomenon of right handedness that most strongly suggests a more general dominance of the left hemisphere in the control of movements. Control over the extremities, including the hands and fingers, is very largely contralateral; that is to say, the left side of the brain controls the right hand, and the right side controls the left hand. Right handedness therefore implies a dominance of the left hemisphere in manual control. It is pertinent then to consider the relation between handedness and the lateralized representation of language in the brain.

HANDEDNESS AND CEREBRAL LATERALIZATION

It seems natural to suppose that there must be a link between right handedness and the fact that most people have language skills represented primarily in the left hemisphere of the brain, since both phenomena seem characteristically if not uniquely human, and both imply a dominance of the left hemisphere. It has long been observed that disturbances of language are associated often with paralysis of the right side.[28] Moreover Broca described the case of a left-handed woman with no impediments of speech or language following left-hemispheric damage, and inferred from this that left handers have speech represented in the right hemisphere.[29] Consequently, it seemed reasonable to many early investigators to speak of a ''dominant'' hemisphere, and to suppose that the left hemisphere was generally dominant among right handers, and the right hemisphere among left handers.

Yet as early as 1868 the English neurologist, John Hughlings Jackson, had remarked on the case of a right-handed person with aphasia and *left*-sided paralysis—evidently a right hander with speech represented in the right cerebral hemisphere.[30] Such cases of so-called *crossed aphasia* are by no means rare. In one review published in 1959, there were fifty-three cases of right handers with aphasia following damage to the right hemisphere, and sixty-six of left handers rendered aphasic by injury to the left hemisphere.[31] It is clear that the relation between handedness and cerebral lateralization for language is not so straightforward as the early investigators believed.

Data accumulated at the Montreal Neurological Institute on patients about to undergo brain surgery for chronic epilepsy have revealed how right-handed patients differ from left- and mixed-handed patients in terms of the relative proportions of left- and right-cerebral representation of language.[32] In many cases the epileptic focus is in the temporal lobe of the brain, in the vicinity of language-mediating areas; before attempting to remove the affected tissue, it is important for the surgeon to know whether language is represented on the afflicted side or on the other side. The method used to determine this is the sodium amytal test, developed at the Montreal Neurological Institute by Juhn Wada, who is now at the University of British Columbia.[33] Injection of sodium amytal into the carotid artery on one side causes a temporary inhibition of function on that same side of the brain. The procedure is to ask the patient questions following injection to each side in turn. The patient's ability to answer is suppressed when the injection is on the side that mediates language, but is relatively unaffected when it is on the other side. This permits an accurate assessment of the hemisphere that is dominant for language.

Out of 140 right-handed patients tested at the Montreal Neurological Institute, 96 percent had language represented in the left cerebral hemisphere, while only 4 percent had language represented in the right. Out of 122 left handers or patients with mixed handedness, 70 percent had language in the left hemisphere, 15 percent had language in the right, while the remaining 15 percent had language represented on *both* sides.[34] In another study based on the sodium amytal test administered to epileptic patients, 73 out of the 74 right-handed patients, or 98.5 percent, had language represented in the left cerebral hemisphere.[35] In other words, the vast majority of right handers do indeed have language represented in the left hemisphere, but so do the majority, albeit a smaller one, of *left* handers.

One might suspect that these figures are not representative of the normal population since they are based on epileptic patients, although the Montreal investigators did remove from their samples those patients with evidence of early brain injury that might have influenced cerebral lateralization. There are some other data, based on non-epileptic subjects, that seem to corroborate the Montreal findings. At the National Hospital in Queen Square, London, depressed patients are sometimes treated with electroconvulsive therapy (ECT), in which convulsions are induced by passing an electric current through the brain. ECT is delivered only to one side of the brain, and to different sides on separate days. The patient is asked simple questions as soon as he or she has recovered sufficiently to tell the examiner his or her own name. An ability to answer provides a good indication of whether language is represented on the side that received the current. Among fifty-two right handers, all but one were clearly left cerebrally dominant for language. Among thirty left handers apparently free of neurological disease, twenty-one (or exactly 70 percent) had language represented primarily in the left cerebral hemisphere, seven were right cerebrally dominant, while two were classified as "uncertain".[36] Of course, depressed patients may be no more representative of the normal population than are epileptics, although there seems no *a priori* reason to expect them to show unusual patterns of cerebral lateralization.

Nevertheless, some other studies do suggest a lower proportion of left handers as having language represented in the left cerebral hemisphere. In one study of 123 left-handed aphasics, for instance, only 53 percent were judged left cerebrally dominant for language, with 47 percent right cerebrally dominant.[37] Presumably, the nature of the evidence did not permit the investigators to detect bilateral representation of language. Even taking this into account, the data seem clearly at odds with the evidence based on sodium amytal and ECT tests. In terms of their early neurological history, aphasics may actually be more representative of the normal population than either epileptics or the chronically depressed. In any event, we take it that the proportion of left handers with left-cerebral representation of language lies somewhere in the range of 53 to 70 percent.

Of course, it is neither desirable nor ethical to administer the sodium amytal test or ECT to normal subjects, and tests of cerebral lateralization suitable for normal people have generally not proven sufficiently reliable to provide accurate data on the relation between handedness and cerebral lateralization. The dichotic-listening test is used routinely at the Montreal Neurological Institute as a rough screening test, but it fails to give perfect prediction of the results of the sodium amytal test. The proportion of normal right handers who display a right-ear advantage in dichotic listening is typically about 85 percent, which is significantly lower than the estimates of left-cerebral dominance based on the sodium amytal and ECT tests.[38] We attribute this to the unreliability and other vagaries of dichotic listening. Recently, however, Gina Geffen and her colleagues at Flinders University in Australia have developed an improved version of the usual dichotic listening test which, they claim, is in very close agreement with the results of tests following unilateral ECT.[39] We may therefore perhaps look forward to accurate estimates of the incidence of left and right cerebral dominance for language in normal Australian left and right handers.[40]

Similarly, tests based on comparison between visual fields have proven too unreliable for accurate estimates, although, like dichotic-listening tests, they tend to confirm the general observation that right handers show a higher incidence than left handers of left-cerebral dominance for language.[41] Again, however, there is a recent promise of better things to come. Jerre Levy, now at the University of Chicago, has developed an index based on two tasks: identification of syllables, which normally yields a right-field advantage, and localization of dots, which normally yields a left-field advantage. She claims that this index perfectly predicts cerebral lateralization,[42] but this claim has yet to be checked against more direct measures.

ANNETT'S THEORY REVISITED

It is instructive now to consider how Annett's theory about the inheritance of lateralization might be applied to the results of the sodium amytal tests carried out at the Montreal Neurological Institute. According to Annett's theory, which we introduced in the previous chapter, most people inherit a right-shift factor, so that their handedness and cerebral lateralization are subject to a strong lateralizing influence.[43] (Actually, it would make better sense now to call this influence a left shift, since it implies a dominance of the left cerebral hemisphere, but to minimize confusion we shall stick to Annett's terminology.) This explains why the great majority of right handers, 96 percent in the Montreal investigation, are left-cerebrally dominant for language.

Some individuals, however, are assumed to lack the right-shift factor. We assume that in these individuals handedness and cerebral dominance for language are established independently and at random. Among the left and mixed handers of the Montreal investigation, 15 percent were right cerebrally dominant and 15 percent had language represented in both cerebral hemispheres. We take it that these individuals belong to the group lacking the right shift. Since this group should display no overall bias in cerebral lateralization, we must add to it another 15 percent with left-cerebral dominance for language. Overall, then, 45 percent of the left and mixed handers belong to the special group lacking the right shift. We must also expect some right handers to belong to this group, which explains why there is a small proportion of right handers who are right cerebrally dominant for language.

However, we still have another 55 percent of left and mixed handers who do not belong to the recessive group lacking the right shift, and who are left cerebrally dominant for language. These may constitute the "pathological" left handers, those who are non-right handed because of birth stress or some other extreme environmental influence. This interpretation implies that such pathological influences typically cause a switch in handedness but not in cerebral dominance for language, which explains why many more people are left handed than are right cerebrally dominant for language. Must we therefore conclude that somewhat more than half of the left and mixed handers belong to this "pathological" category? This estimate may be too high since it is based on epileptic patients, although one would derive a very similar estimate from the post-ECT tests on the depressed patients studied at the National Hospital in London. Other investigations have yielded lower estimates of the proportions of left handers with left-cerebral dominance and one would therefore derive a lower estimate of the incidence of pathological left handedness. In the study of left-handed aphasics that we mentioned earlier, for instance, it was estimated that only 53 percent were left cerebrally dominant for language, suggesting that the proportion of pathological left handers among them may have been as low as 6 percent. We suggest that the true proportion in the normal population lies somewhere between these extremes of 6 and 55 percent!

Some writers have distinguished between *familial* left handers, those with at least one left-handed parent or sibling, and *nonfamilial* ones, those from right-handed families. This distinction should correspond roughly to that between left handers lacking the right shift, which is assumed to be an inherited condition, and those who are left handed for pathological reasons. As one might expect from Annett's theory, the evidence suggests that familial left handers show no overall bias in cerebral lateralization. Indeed, individuals in this category often have language skills represented on both sides of the brain. Nonfamilial left handers, on the contrary, seem to show the normal left-cerebral dominance for language.[44] To explain this, we must again assume that pathological influences such as birth stress may cause handedness to switch, but have little effect on cerebral lateralization. In the previous chapter, we cited evidence that left handers do show a higher incidence of minor pathologies.

The pattern of differences predicted by Annett's theory is evident in data on the very shape of the human brain. Marjorie LeMay of the Massachusetts General Hospital has pointed out that the brain, when viewed from the top, usually exhibits what she calls a torque (or twist), in which the frontal lobe on one side protrudes forward and the occipital lobe on the other side protrudes back. This asymmetry can be measured by a method known as computerized transaxial tomography (CTT), in which images are generated by computer from X-rays taken from around the circumference of the brain. It is also discernible in many cases in the external shape of the skull. Among most right handers, and also among the majority of children under one year old, LeMay found the torque to be counterclockwise; that is, the right frontal lobe protruded forward and the left occipital lobe protruded back (see Figure 8.3). Among left handers there were approximately equal numbers exhibiting a clockwise as a counterclockwise torque; nearly a third exhibited no torque at all. When LeMay separated familial from nonfamilial left handers, she found that the nonfamilial group more closely resembled right handers, suggesting again that this group included the higher proportion of pathological left handers.[45]

Finally, it has been observed that among right handers there is a positive correlation between cerebral lateralization, as assessed from differences between the visual fields and as assessed by differences between the ears in dichotic listening. That is, right handers who show large differences on one measure tend to show large differences on the other. Among left handers, however, there appears to be no correlation at all.[46]

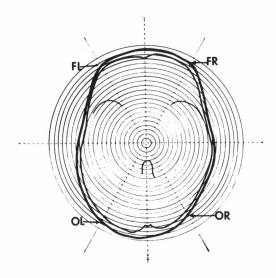

FIGURE 8.3.

Diagram of a brain viewed from the top shows the counterclockwise torque. The frontal lobe extends further forward on the right than on the left, while the occipital lobe extends further back on the left than on the right. (From M. Le May, "Asymmetries of the Skull and Handedness," **Journal of Neurological Sciences** 32 [1977]: 243–53. Reprinted with the permission of the author and the publisher.)

This again suggests a lack of consistent lateralization, as we might expect if a reasonable proportion of normal left handers belong to the recessive group lacking the right shift. Moreover, this result suggests that not only are handedness and cerebral lateralization randomly and independently established in this group, but different manifestations of cerebral lateralization are also independent of one another.

The evidence on cerebral lateralization therefore adds to the evidence reviewed in the previous chapter that some proportion of left handers (or more strictly, non-right handers) belong to a minority of the population that lack any consistent predisposing lateralization. Estimates of this proportion range from 45 percent to about 94 percent, depending at least partly on the population from which the sample is drawn. Of course, some small proportion of right handers would also belong to this minority. Estimates range correspondingly from about 5 percent to about 10 percent, assuming about nine times as many right handers as left handers. In genetic terms, we may perhaps say that those who belong to this unlateralized minority are less effectively *buffered* against environmental variations than are those who inherit the right shift. Handedness and other external asymmetries, and different manifestations of cerebral asymmetry, would all be established by random and perhaps independent environmental influences, some prenatal, some postnatal. The outcome may be considerable variation in the patterns of lateralization, and thus of cerebral organization. Perhaps this explains why left handers appear to be overrepresented in all extreme groups, including the highly gifted and the highly creative (Leonardo da Vinci scores on both counts), as well as among those with special problems, such as stuttering or reading disability. Those who inherit the right shift, by contrast, are provided with a strong and unifying lateralizing influence that tends to create a homogeneous product: right handed, left cerebrally dominant persons largely in favor of the established virtues.[47]

We shall continue to speculate on these matters from time to time, and we shall consider the role of cerebral lateralization (or the lack of it) in reading disability and in stuttering in Chapters 11 and 12.

THE DEVELOPMENT OF CEREBRAL LATERALIZATION

In Chapter 6 we argued that right handedness probably reflects a biological predisposition rather than the direct effects of learning or experience, even though handedness itself is not manifest until some time after birth. The argument that left-cerebral dominance is biologically preprogrammed is rather more direct. The strongest line of evidence has to do with an anatomical asymmetry of the human brain that appears to be related to the representation of language and that can be detected even before birth.

Although it has been known for over a hundred years that there are consistent structural asymmetries in the human brain, these were generally thought to be too small to account for the remarkable functional differences. More recently, objective measurements have revealed that some of these anatomical asymmetries are larger than hitherto suspected, and that they correspond at least roughly to areas known to mediate language. In 1968, Norman Geschwind and Walter Levitsky of the Harvard Medical School measured the asymmetry of the temporal planum, an area in the temporal lobe of the brain in the vicinity of Wernicke's area.[48] In 100 human brains, the planum was on average nearly one centimeter longer on the left than on the right, and one third larger in area. Sometimes the difference was very striking, with the left planum five or more times larger than the right; indeed, the right planum may even be absent altogether.[49] The left planum was the larger in 65 percent of cases, the two sides were equal in 24 percent, and the right planum was the larger in 11 percent. It should be noted that these figures do not correspond precisely to the proportions of individuals with language represented on the left, bilaterally, and on the right. This suggests some reservations about the significance of the asymmetry, but we suspect that the discrepancy probably has to do with the nature of the measurements. There is no good reason to suppose that relative size is the most appropriate measure, and some more subtle index of the anatomical asymmetry may correspond more closely to the functional asymmetry.

It was later shown that the asymmetry of the temporal planum is presented in fetuses and in newborns,[50] and indeed can be observed in the fetus as early as the 31st week of pregnancy.[51] It has also been observed that there are often additional ridges, or *gyri,* on one or other side of the temporal lobe, and that these occur more often on the right than on the left. This asymmetry is also observed in the brains of human fetuses, as well as in adult brains.[52] These observations suggest that the anatomical basis for the lateralized representation of language is established before birth.

It is not so clear precisely how or when these anatomical asymmetries are expressed as *functional* differences between the two sides of the brain. In one study, asymmetries in electrical potentials measured on the scalp were found to be present early in the first year of life.[53] The potentials evoked by speech sounds, including meaningless syllables, were generally larger when recorded from an area of scalp over the left temporal lobe than from an area over the right temporal lobe. The potentials evoked by a musical chord or a burst of noise were larger over the right temporal lobe. This was true of the majority of infants ranging in age from one week to ten months of age, as well as of older children and adults. This result suggests that the left-hemispheric specialization for processing speech sounds, as well as a complementary right-hemispheric specialization for perceiving nonspeech sounds, can be detected well before the infant learns to talk. Whether cerebral asymmetry is manifest psychologically at this early age is more controversial. One author has claimed that, on a dichotic-listening task, infants ranging from three weeks to three months of age showed a right-ear advantage for speech sounds and a left-ear advantage for musical sounds,[54] but her data are somewhat contentious.[55] Other evidence does suggest that the right-ear advantage for words is present in three-year-olds.[56]

Although the left hemisphere in most people seems predisposed to mediate language from before birth, the right hemisphere can nevertheless take over the representation of language if the left is incapacitated, provided that this occurs early in life.[57] In this respect the two hemispheres are sometimes said to exhibit *equipotentiality* for the representation of language—a slight misnomer, possibly, since the potential of the right hemisphere may never quite reach that of the left, at least among those disposed to be lateralized. Moreover, the right hemisphere's potential for language declines with age, so that by the age of puberty or thereabouts incapacitation of the left hemisphere results in more or less permanent aphasia. It is by then too late for the right hemisphere to mediate language, just as it may be too late for any person to learn language if he or she has been deprived of exposure to language during the so-called "critical period," the period from birth until about the age of thirteen years.[58]

In the first two years of life, however, equipotentiality may be very nearly complete. This is revealed by studies of people who have had one or other cerebral hemisphere surgically removed during infancy, a drastic operation that is sometimes necessary in cases of certain tumors that would otherwise prove fatal. Despite their severe loss, these people later appear remarkably normal in their ability to speak and to understand. Subtle tests reveal that those with removal of the left hemisphere are slightly worse at comprehension than are those with removal of the right hemisphere.[59] In one study, for instance, these groups differed in their ability to understand passive negative sentences, but not in their ability to understand passive affirmative or active negative sentences![60] But since the right hemisphere seems capable of some degree of comprehension even in normal subjects, the results of tests of comprehension are not nearly so striking as the fact that subjects with early removal of the left hemisphere can *talk*, with little or no impediment. By contrast, removal of the left hemisphere in adulthood nearly always results in more or less complete motor aphasia. At best, the patient may understandably retain the ability to swear, and in rare instances to sing, but ordinary propositional speech is almost always irredeemably lost.[61]

Since the right hemisphere's potential for mediating language, particularly speech, is not normally permitted expression, we must suppose that the left hemisphere somehow exerts an inhibitory influence. This influence is removed if the left hemisphere is incapacitated. Provided the critical period for the acquisition of language has not been surpassed, the right hemisphere can then take over the representation of language. There are other biological precedents for a mechanism of this sort. In female birds, for instance, the right ovary normally does not develop and in the adult is merely a vestige. But if the left ovary is removed, the right one then develops to a size that is larger than normal, suggesting the removal of an inhibitory influence.[62] Similarly, in certain species of crab, one claw is much larger than the other, but if the larger one is removed it regenerates as a smaller one and the smaller one is tranformed at the next moult into a larger form.[63]

The cerebral control of song in certain birds also provides a remarkable analogy to the phenomena of lateralization and equipotentiality in the human brain. Fernando Nottebohm of the Rockefeller University discovered that in chaffinches and canaries singing is controlled primarily from the left side of the brain through the hypoglossal nerve, which innervates the syrinx where the sound is produced. Once a bird has developed its song, cutting the right hypoglossal nerve has very little effect, while cutting the left nerve virtually destroys the song pattern. If the left nerve is cut before the bird begins its spring song, the right nerve takes over and the song develops normally—just as the right side of the human brain takes over speech and language skills if the left side is incapacitated before these functions have developed.[64]

In the normal development of song in these birds, the right hypoglossal nerve sometimes takes control over a few high-frequency elements which emerge relatively late in the repertoire. This suggested to Nottebohm that the pattern of lateralization might be established by a gradient in the rate of growth between the two sides. The left side may develop earlier and therefore gain control over the majority of song elements, while the later developing right side catches up only in time to secure control over the elements which appear late in the developmental sequence. Nottebohm suggests that such a gradient might underlie many phenomena of neural lateralization.[65] There is evidence, for instance, that such a gradient may also underlie the asymmetry of the heart in vertebrates, and that *situs inversus,* in which the heart and other internal organs are left–right reversed, is due to factors very early in embryonic development that tend to inhibit growth on the left, and so cause a reversal of the underlying gradient. Indeed, the phenomenon of situs inversus is itself somewhat analogous to that of equipotentiality, in which the representation of language is left–right reversed.

We acknowledge the danger of arguing from analogy, but it is tempting nevertheless to suppose that a similar gradient underlies left-cerebral dominance for language. Michael J. Morgan has taken the argument a step further to suggest that it is actually the *same* gradient that underlies cerebral asymmetry, the asymmetry of the heart, and perhaps other asymmetries as well, and that this gradient is ultimately of molecular origin.[66] All vertebrates would therefore possess this gradient, but the manner in which it is expressed would depend on environmental, pathological, and genetic factors. For instance, the genetic allele assumed to be responsible for the right shift postulated by Annett would allow the gradient to be expressed in handedness and in cerebral lateralization. People carrying the recessive allele would not display consistent handedness or cerebral asymmetries, but would still reveal the usual asymmetries of the heart and internal organs because these asymmetries are controlled by different genes. The reader may recall that in Chapter 6 we rejected the notion, prominent in history, that there might be a relation between handedness and the asymmetry of the internal organs. The lack of consistent handedness in animals other than humans, and the imperfect correlation in humans between handedness and situs inversus of the heart, suggest that there is no *direct* relation between these phenomena. We are now suggesting, however, that there might be an indirect relation, in that both may depend ultimately on a common underlying gradient. We pursue this theme in Chapter 13.

We know of no direct evidence that the development of cerebral lateralization is controlled by a gradient favoring earlier or more rapid development on the left, so the idea remains little more than a conjecture. However, there is a recent case history, interesting in its own right, that can be interpreted in terms of this gradient. A few years ago a girl named Genie was discovered living in a single room, isolated by her parents from virtually all human contact, and unable to speak even though nearly fourteen years old. She has since been rehabilitated and taught to speak and understand language reasonably well, to a point that has led some to question the idea that there is truly a ''critical period'' in the development of language.[67] The interesting point from our perspective is that language is evidently represented primarily in Genie's *right* cerebral hemisphere. We might interpret this to mean that the leading left hemisphere had already surpassed the critical period for language, but that the lagging right hemisphere remained within it, and was therefore able to accommodate some degree of language representation. Clearly, however, this is itself highly conjectural, and the authors who noted Genie's right-cerebral dominance place an entirely different interpretation upon it.

THE ORIGINS OF CEREBRAL ASYMMETRY

It is of course difficult to tell whether our ancient forbears were left cerebrally dominant for language. Some evidence may be gleaned from preserved or reconstructed skulls, but this cannot be considered decisive until more is known about the relations between asymmetries of the skull and functional cerebral lateralization in present-day humans. Indeed, the evidence may actually be misleading. For instance, studies of modern skulls generally reveal the left side to be longer than the right.[68] In one investigation reported in 1929 it was found that three-quarters of 729 male skulls from the 26th to 30th dynasties of ancient Egypt were longer on the right. This reversal has been taken as support for the theory, based initially on heiroglyphics and drawings (see Chapter 6), that the ancient Egyptians were predominantly left handed.[69] We suspect that differences in length between the sides of the skull have little to do with either handedness or with cerebral lateralization for language. In a study of East African skulls, it was again observed that the right side was generally longer than the left, but these skulls also typically exhibited the counterclockwise torque that is characteristic of right handers.[70]

Prehistoric evidence is especially difficult to interpret, since fossilized skulls are usually reconstructed from fragments; it may be impossible to tell whether external asymmetries were present in the original or whether they arose in the process of reconstruction. Sometimes, however, the surface of the brain leaves an imprint on the inside of the skull which may reveal asymmetries. On a cast of a skull of Neanderthal man found at La Chappelle-aux-Saints in France, the end point of the Sylvian fissure that runs along the upper boundary of the temporal lobe of the brain is higher on the right than on the left. A very similar asymmetry exists in the brains of most right-handed humans (see Figure 8.4) and is conceivably related more directly to the representation of language than to handedness itself. Neanderthal man lived over 40,000 years ago. There is some dispute as to whether this creature is a true human ancestor, although Marjorie LeMay has argued that it was probably capable of language. LeMay has also suggested that the same cranial asymmetry

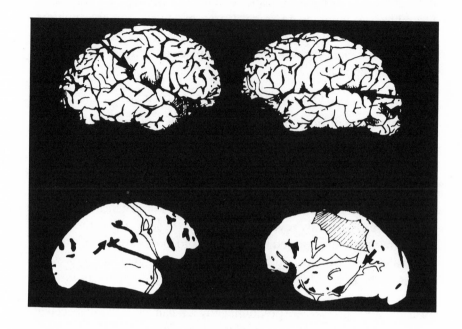

FIGURE 8.4.

Asymmetry of the sylvian fissure appears in the brains of modern humans **(top)** and Neanderthal humans **(bottom)**. The arrows indicate that the end point of the fissure is higher on the right side of the brain than on the left side.

can be discerned in two other fossil skulls, one from Peking Man and the other from *Australopithecus*.[71]

This asymmetry of the Sylvian fissure has also been observed in the brains of ten out of twelve orangutans and five out of nine chimpanzees. It was rare or nonexistent among samples of brains of other nonhuman primates, including gorillas, gibbons, Siamangs, and various species of monkey.[72] In another study, the Sylvian fissure was found to be longer on the left than on the right in the majority of humans and chimpanzees, but not in rhesus monkeys.[73] The presence of these asymmetries is especially interesting in the light of recent evidence that chimpanzees can be taught to communicate in a way that resembles human language, either by using sign language[74] or by arranging plastic shapes representing words on a board.[75] If the capacity for language is at all related to these anatomical asymmetries, we might expect the orangutan to prove an even more sophisticated conversationalist than the chimpanzee.

Be this as it may, there is evidence that the gorilla has a capacity for language at least equal to that of the chimpanzee despite the fact that only two out of a sample of seven gorillas' brains revealed the asymmetry of the Sylvian fissure (compared with five out of nine chimpanzees), and despite the fact that gorillas show poorer manipulative skill than chimpanzees. Francine Patterson at Stanford University taught Koko, a gorilla, to converse in American Sign Language using at least 375 different signs, more than double the number so far mastered by a chimpanzee. Patterson even estimated Koko's I.Q. on human intelligence tests to be between eighty-four and ninety-five, only slightly below the average for a human child of the same age. So far as we can judge from published accounts and photographs, Koko does not seem to exhibit marked handedness; she is described as left handed in pouring milk into a cup, but is predominantly right handed in typing.[76] We know of no evidence related to functional cerebral asymmetry, either in Koko or in any other gorilla.

Indeed, we know of only one study of functional asymmetry related to language in any nonhuman primates.[77] Five Japanese macaques and five other Old World monkeys were trained to discriminate ''coo'' sounds recorded from Japanese macaques in the wild. The sounds were played to the monkeys through earphones to one or other ear. Under one condition the monkeys had to discriminate two categories of coos, one typically emitted by estrous females soliciting males, the other emitted by males and nonestrous females in a variety of circumstances all apparently concerned with the seeking of contact. The Japanese macaques were all better at this discrimination when the sounds were played to the right ear than to the left ear. This was interpreted as a left-hemispheric dominance for the perception of meaningful sounds, analogous to the human left-hemispheric dominance for the perception of speech sounds. The other Old World monkeys, with one exception, did not display the right-ear advantage, presumably because the sounds conveyed no real-world meaning to them. Under another condition the monkeys discriminated the sounds on the basis of pitch, a dimension that has no communicative significance. One of two Japanese macaques showed a *left*-ear advantage, but the other, like the two other Old World monkeys that were tested, showed no evidence of lateralization. In short, functional left-cerebral dominance occurred only when the discrimination the monkeys had to make corresponded to a distinction that was meaningful to their own species.

Some authors have sought causal links between handedness and cerebral lateralization for language, but there is disagreement as to which was the cause and which the effect. The prehistoric evidence is not decisive. As we have seen there is some evidence that *Australopithecus* may have been predominantly right handed and may have exhibited the asymmetry of the Sylvian fissure that possibly indicates a capacity for language. In both cases the evidence is tenuous indeed. Raymond Dart, who discovered the fossil remains of *Australopithecus,* was equivocal over whether this prehistoric creature could talk, but seemed to conclude that it could not. "Articulate speech," he wrote, "came only about 25,000 years ago and was preceded by about 1,000,000 years of gesture and babble."[78] However, Dart echoed the common theme that language was intimately related to the development of tools, and that spoken language may have arisen from the sounds that naturally accompanied the gestures of our ancestors when they used tools.

The 18th century philospher Etienne Bonnot, Abbé de Condillac (1715–1789) argued that the earliest form of language was itself gestural. This theme has been pursued more recently by Gordon W. Hewes of the University of Colorado.[79] He notes, for instance, that chimpanzees can learn sign language but not vocal speech. As we have seen, the same is apparently true of the gorilla. Hewes also notes that right-handed people most commonly make expressive gestures with their right hands while they talk, while left handers (as the reader must surely expect by now) do not show a strong preference for either hand and commonly make bilateral gestures.[80] He argues that handedness evolved through toolmaking and the use of weapons and preceded the development of speech.

Yet one can easily reverse the argument and maintain that handedness is a consequence of the lateralized representation of language in the brain. The British neurologist, Lord Brain, argued that because nonhuman animals are equally divided in their preferences for one or other hand (or paw), it must have been the appearance of a "motor speech center" in the left hemisphere of humans that brought about the preference for the right hand.[81] W. W. Roberts, the Scottish neurologist, also argued for the priority of lateralization for speech, not only in evolution but also in the development of the child.

It is not improbable that the infant passes through an earlier, fleeting, simian phase [in which] rudimentary handedness can be detected. But true human handedness occurs only after the beginnings of speech, by which it is directed and to which it is limited. Its essential quality is its determination by speech.[82]

One argument for the priority of cerebral lateralization over handedness is that more people have language represented in the left hemisphere than are right handed. We interpreted this to mean that handedness is the more fragile phenomenon, more easily reversed by pathological influences early in life; this very fragility may mean that handedness is the more recent phenomenon in evolution, just as it appears later in the development of the child. We also reviewed evidence, admittedly still tenuous, suggesting that chimpanzees and Japanese macaques exhibit cerebral lateralization for language, although neither exhibits consistent handedness. Moreover, canaries and chaffinches display a striking asymmetry in the cerebral control of song. So far as we know these birds do not display any asymmetry resembling handedness. We do not mean to suggest that human cerebral lateralization derives from a common ancestry between ourselves and these delightful birds; the point is simply that the left-cerebral control of bird song provides a biological precedent for the emergence of cerebral lateralization in the absence of any overt manual asymmetry.

Yet these arguments can also be used as evidence that there is no causal relation one way or the other between handedness and cerebral lateralization for language. We have already argued that among left and mixed handers—or, more generally, among those lacking the right-shift factor postulated by Annett—these different manifestations of asymmetry seem to be independent of one another, suggesting that there is no intrinsic causal relation between them. Among those possessing the right shift, by contrast, both handedness and cerebral lateralization are apparently under the influence of the same underlying gradient. In these individuals, the left hemisphere may be generally dominant for the executive control of purposeful, sequential actions. We may suppose, then, that handedness and cerebral lateralization share a common cause and are not caused one by the other.

CONCLUSIONS

In this chapter we have pursued our theme that human laterality, including both right handedness and the left-cerebral dominance for language, is the genetically controlled expression of some underlying biological gradient. Cerebral lateralization for language appears to be innate, and may be detected in some nonhuman primates as well as in humans; in these respects, it is perhaps more obviously a part of our biological heritage than is handedness. Yet we cannot conclude that consistent cerebral asymmetry is a *necessary* prerequisite for language, since there appears to be a minority of people who inherit no consistent predisposition to be lateralized. Although some of these individuals may suffer some disabilities of language, including stuttering and difficulties with reading, the majority do not appear to do so.

In general, there are two sorts of biological asymmetries, those in which the majority of individuals display the same direction of asymmetry, and those in which the direction is determined randomly (i.e., by Collins' "asymmetry lottery").[83] For instance, in the species of crab we mentioned earlier, half of the individuals have the larger, crushing claw on the left and half have it on the right. Among nonhuman animals such as rats, mice, monkeys and chimpanzees, handedness seems to be determined on a random basis. Colwyn Trevarthen of the University of Edinburgh has documented the emergence of handedness in baboons as they learn a manipulative skill, but again there was no overall preference; among five baboons, two were left handed and three right handed.[84] Other asymmetries are under the influence of a consistent directional influence; these include the leftward displacement of the heart in vertebrates, the left-cerebral control of song in chaffinches and canaries, and of course handedness and cerebral lateralization in the majority of humans.

Yet nature seems to have been somewhat ambivalent in determining which principle should control human laterality, since there seems to be a minority for whom laterality is randomly assigned. What are the relative advantages of the two principles? As we have already suggested, consistent asymmetry may result in a more predictable product, one that is more completely buffered against environmental contingencies. There are also social and economic advantages in uniformity; for instance, tools and weapons only need to be manufactured for one of the two hands.

Nevertheless, the random principle may also have advantages. It results in a species in which individuals may be lateralized, but the species as a whole displays no overall bias. Such a species might be better adapted to the natural environment in which there are no consistent asymmetries one way or the other. In the case of human laterality, the fact that left handers are in a minority suggests that the advantage of inconsistent laterality may lie in the element of surprise. In early warfare, for instance, the left hander may have had an advantage because of his very unexpectedness and may have so still in modern substitutes like boxing and tennis. The left hander might also exhibit a capacity for what we might call cognitive surprise, the ability to see unexpected relations that might escape more conventional brains. We have already mentioned Leonardo da Vinci as an example; Charles Chaplin and Harpo Marx were also left handed.[85]

The late Sir Cyril Burt, the British educational psychologist justly renowned for his efforts to defraud the scientific community into believing that human intelligence is largely inherited, was not flattering in his description of left handers.

> . . .they squint, they stammer, they shuffle and shamble, they flounder about like seals out of water. Awkward in the house, and clumsy in their games, they are fumblers and bunglers at whatever they do.[86]

Yet a recent large-scale study of highschool students in California revealed essentially no overall difference in scholastic achievement between left and right handers.[87] In certain kinds of specific skills, left or mixed handers may actually be superior to right handers. For instance, left handers seem to be superior at associating verbal with nonverbal symbols, perhaps because the two sides of their brains are less differentiated.[88] This might account for the supposedly high proportion of left handers in the architectural profession.[89] It has also been reported that left handers, and especially those who are *weakly* left handed, are superior to right handers in acoustic memory for pitch,[90] but we do not know why this should be so.

In this chapter we have emphasized the dominant role of the left hemisphere of the brain. This has enabled us to treat both handedness and cerebral lateralization within a common framework, and to pursue our theme that, in most people, both depend on the genetically controlled expression of an underlying biological gradient. Historically, too, the emphasis has been on the left hemisphere as the leading or dominant one, to the point that, even as late as 1962, the British zoologist, J. Z. Young, could wonder whether the right hemisphere was merely a "vestige"—although he prudently allowed that he would rather keep his own than lose it.[91] Yet the tide was turning, and it is now clear that the right hemisphere is the more specialized for a number of cognitive and perceptual functions. Indeed, some authors have even hinted that the evolution of cerebral lateralization may have begun with the specialization of the right hemisphere; if true, this would of course create difficulties for the theme we have already developed.

We deal with the specialization of the right hemisphere, and its implications concerning the nature, development, and evolution of cerebral asymmetry in the following chapter.

Chapter 9

Complementary Specialization in the Two Cerebral Hemispheres

The river is an island [1]

You are river. This way and that
and all the way to sea two escorts
shove and pull you. Two escorts
in contention.
Left bank or right bank, how can
you be a river without either?
Thus are U bends made. Thus are
S bends made. Your direction
is assured and sometimes running
perfectly and quite straight.
A low bank on your left holds your
laughing stitches in. On your right
side skips another hushing your
loud protests.
You are river. Joy leaping down a greenstone stair-way: anger
cradled in a bed of stones.
You're a harbour; a lake; an island only when your banks lock
lathered
arms in battle to confine you: slow-
release you.

153

Go river, go. To ocean seek your
certain end. Rise again to cloud;
to a mountain—to a mountain
drinking from a tiny cup.
Ah, river
you are ocean: you are island.

[Hone Tuwhare]

Ever since the dramatic discoveries about cerebral lateralization were made in the 19th century, the emphasis has been on the dominance of one hemisphere, usually the left, over the other. The dominant hemisphere for language was also described as the major or leading hemisphere, while the nondominant hemisphere was the minor hemisphere, considered to be relatively unimportant. This unilateral view of cerebral lateralization still persists to some degree; it served us well in the previous chapter, where we tried to integrate handedness and cerebral lateralization for language within a common framework.

Even as early as 1864, John Hughlings Jackson had expressed a doubt about this one-sided view. If the "faculty of expression resides in one hemisphere," he suggested, "there is no absurdity in raising the question as to whether perception—its corresponding opposite—may be seated in the other.[2] It was nearly a hundred years before Jackson's suggestion was systematically explored and shown to contain a generous measure of truth. Another early forecaster of things to come, albeit an unwitting one, was the British imperialist novelist and poet, Rudyard Kipling, who included the following little poem in his novel *Kim,* published in 1901.

> Something I owe to the soil that grew—
> More to the life that fed—
> But most to Allah who gave me two
> Separate sides to my head.
>
> I would go without shirt or shoes
> Friends, tobacco or bread
> Sooner than for an instant lose
> Either side of my head.[3]

This anticipates in remarkable fashion the present-day obsession with the complementary modes of consciousness that are said to inhabit the two cerebral hemispheres.

The most striking demonstrations of right-hemispheric specialization have been provided by the split-brain patients. When asked to arrange blocks on a table to match a design on a card, patients proved much more proficient with the left hand than with the normally preferred right hand. Since the left hand is controlled primarily by the right cerebral hemisphere, this observation illustrates a right-hemispheric advantage. Similarly, split-brain patients proved much better at drawing a cube in perspective with the left hand than with the right (see Figure 9.1). The right hand was so inept in some cases that the eager left hand had to be physically restrained from taking over.[4]

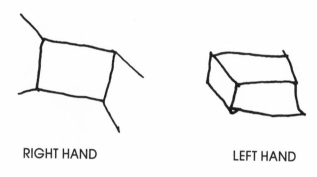

RIGHT HAND   LEFT HAND

FIGURE 9.1.

These drawings of a cube were made by the right and left hands of a split-brain patient. (From J. E. LeDoux, P. H. Wilson, and M. S. Gazzaniga. "Manipulo-spatial Aspects of Cerebral Lateralization: Clues to the Origin of Lateralization," **Neuropsychologia 15** [1977]:743–50. Reprinted with the permission of J. E. LeDoux.)

These observations might suggest a *motor* dominance of the right hemisphere, which runs counter to the theme developed in the previous chapter. We think however that the critical component that is represented in the right hemisphere rather than in the left is spatial rather than motor. Among intact right handers, it is the right hand that is the more proficient at drawing cubes in perspective, or at arranging blocks, or indeed at carrying out almost any manipulative task. We must suppose that the spatial information necessary for these tasks is supplied primarily by the right hemisphere, but is normally relayed via the interhemispheric commissures to the left hemisphere, which then directs the right hand in performance of the task. In the split-brain patient the commissures are cut, so the spatial information is denied passage to the left hemisphere, and the task must therefore be performed by the left hand. The left hemisphere and right hand may retain a measure of motor dominance, but this dominance is of little avail in spatial tasks involving a critical right-hemispheric component.

There is other evidence that the right cerebral hemisphere is normally the more specialized for spatial representation. Perception and memory of spatial patterns are often impaired by damage to the right hemisphere of the brain, but are seldom affected by damage to the left.[5] Studies of differences between the visual fields in identification of briefly flashed patterns have revealed a left-field advantage in normal people, implying a right-hemispheric superiority, for a range of nonverbal patterns, including pictures of faces,[6] nonsense shapes,[7] patterns of dots,[8] and lines in different orientations.[9] There even appears to be a right-hemispheric advantage for such simple visual tasks as judging depth,[10] color,[11] or fine shades of gray.[12] The right-hemispheric advantage for the perception of faces can be demonstrated informally by asking people to judge which side of a face, left or right, looks more like the *whole* face—Figure 9.2 provides illustrations and instructions. Most right handers choose the right side, which appears in the left visual field if one fixates the face centrally.[13]

The right-hemispheric advantage is not confined to spatial or even to visual tasks. Studies of dichotic listening in normal people have revealed a left-ear superiority, and therefore a right-hemispheric advantage, in perception of melodic patterns,[14] pitch,[15] timbre,[16] and harmony,[17] and also in perception of sonar sounds[18] and environmental sounds.[19] In touching pairs of nonsense shapes simultaneously, one with each hand, that touched by the left hand is usually identified more accurately than that touched by the right hand, indicating a slight right-hemispheric advantage.[20]

It is of interest that most blind people read braille more quickly and accurately with their left hands than with their right hands, again suggesting a dominance of the right cerebral hemisphere. In braille, the letters are represented by patterns of dots, which are touched by the fingers. The system was developed by Louis Braille in the early part of the 19th century, and was in general use from about the 1860s. Until quite recently it seems to have been taken for granted that the right hand would be the preferred one, perhaps because of the prevailing view that the left cerebral hemisphere was generally dominant over the right, es-

FIGURE 9.2.

The faces at the bottom were constructed from the separate halves of the face at the top. The one on the left is a symmetrical completion of the left half of the drawing (and thus of the right side of the face), while the one on the right is a symmetrical completion of the right half. Choose which one looks more like the original. (Most people choose the one on the left).

pecially for verbal tasks. Many blind readers use both hands, with the left hand actually running ahead of the right, but it was generally believed that the function of the left hand was simply to locate the ends and beginnings of lines. Yet the testimony of blind readers asserts a much more prominent role for the left hand. One early observer wrote: "when I have read much, the dots feel like wool to the right hand, but, on the contrary, like points to the left hand." As Shakespeare put it, "The hand of little employment hath the daintier sense." Recent experimental studies have confirmed that some three–quarters of blind readers prefer the left hand in reading braille and are more proficient with the left hand than the right.[21]

It may still come as a surprise that the right hemisphere should be favored in reading braille, since the task is a verbal one, seemingly no different in principle from reading ordinary script. Yet there is obviously a strong spatial component as well as the verbal one. Indeed, in identifying script of any sort, whether tactually or visually, there are presumably both spatial and verbal components, and one or other may predominate depending on the spatial complexity of the patterns and perhaps on the experience of the reader. One unpublished report suggests a right-hemispheric advantage in the recognition of briefly presented *handwritten* words, which is in contrast with the usual left-hemispheric advantage in recognizing words or letters in standard typescript.[22] Another study has revealed that the degree of left-hemispheric (i.e., right visual field) superiority in the identification of letters depends on the type face, and that more complex, scriptlike type faces may actually give rise to a right-hemispheric advantage.[23] Finally, Japanese readers show a left-hemispheric advantage in identifying *Hirakana* symbols, which resemble the letters of Western alphabets, but a right-hemispheric advantage in identifying *Kanji* symbols, which are ideographic in the traditional Chinese manner.[24] The more complex Kanji symbols evidently impose greater demands on spatial analysis, and thus call upon the more specialized resources of the right cerebral hemisphere.

The role of experience in determining the overall hemispheric advantage is illustrated by studies of the perception of Morse code. In interpreting dichotically presented sequences in Morse Code, untrained listeners display a right-hemispheric advantage, while skilled operators reveal a left-hemispheric advantage.[25] This again suggests a dissociation between identification of the pattern, which depends primarily on the right cerebral hemisphere, and translation into verbal symbols, which is a left-hemispheric specialty. With practice, the left hemisphere may be able to cope with the identification of the patterns, so that the specialized contribution of the right hemisphere is no longer necessary. It has also been observed that an initial right-hemispheric advantage in recognizing different musical instruments disappears as the listeners become more practised.

The perception of music also seems to depend on different specialized contributions from the two cerebral hemispheres. We have already noted the right-hemispheric advantage in the perception of melody, pitch, timbre and harmony, but we also noted in the previous chapter that there is a left-hemispheric advantage in the perception of rhythm. For example, Harold W. Gordon of the Hebrew University in Jerusalem found a left-hemispheric (right-ear) advantage in identification of dichotically presented melodies differing only in rhythm, no difference between hemispheres in identification of melodies differing only in pitch, and a right-hemispheric advantage in identification of chords.[26] In another experiment he found the right-hemispheric advantage for chords to be restricted to those with musical training, and to be more pronounced among men than among women.[27] To complicate matters further, there is evidence that while musically naive listeners display a right-hemispheric advantage in the recognition of melodies, musically experienced listeners display a *left*-hemispheric advantage; we discussed this phenomenon in the previous chapter. Yet there have been reports of musicians who retained their ability to appreciate and even compose music despite damage to the left hemisphere severe enough to cause aphasia. For instance, Maurice Ravel suffered sensory aphasia following an automobile accident at the age of fifty-seven, when at the height of his creative powers. Although his aphasia was moderately severe, he could still recognize tunes and identify errors with very high accuracy.[28] A more remarkable case is that of the Russian composer, V. G. Shebalin, who suffered a vascular lesion of the left hemisphere at age fifty-one that produced a severe sensory aphasia. Shebalin's musical abilities remained intact, and he is said to have even "executed a number of outstanding compositions" since the time of his misfortune.[29]

Sometimes, the relative advantage of one or the other hemisphere may depend on the task rather than on the nature of the objects or patterns to be processed. For instance, if pairs of letters must be judged the same or different depending on their physical shapes, the judgments are generally faster if the letters are presented in the left than in the right visual field, indicating a right-hemispheric advantage. If the judgment must be based on their names (so that *A* and *a*, which have different shapes, must now be judged as the same), then the judgments are generally faster if the letters are presented in the right visual field.[30] Letters may therefore elicit a right-hemispheric advantage if they are to be perceived simply as shapes, but a left-hemispheric advantage if they are to be perceived as verbal symbols. In an ingenious experiment with split-brain subjects, Jerre Levy and Colwyn Trevarthen have demonstrated right-hemispheric control when the subjects were required to match pictures on the basis of appearance, and left-hemispheric control when they were required to match them on the basis of function.[31] Figure 9.3 shows the pictures they used and the different ways in which they were to be

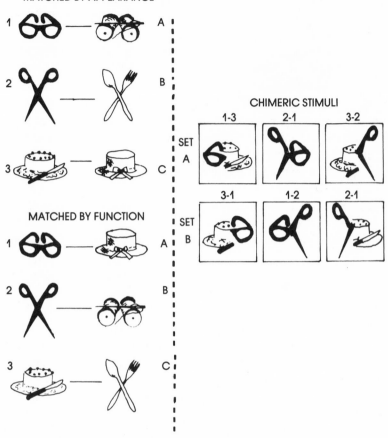

FIGURE 9.3.

These pictures were flashed to split-brain patients for matching by appearance (**e.g.**, the cake looks like the hat) or by function (**e.g.**, spectacles and hat are both things you wear). The pictures were presented as composites (**chimeric stimuli**) so that, for instance, the left hemisphere might "see" a hat and the right hemisphere a pair of spectacles. When asked to match by appearance, the patients tended to respond on the basis of the picture seen by the right hemisphere, but when asked to match by function they generally responded on the basis of the picture seen by the left hemisphere. (From J. Levy and C. Trevarthen, "Metacontrol of Hemispheric Function in Human Split-Brain Patients," **Journal of Experimental Psychology: Human Perception and Performance 2** [1976]:299–312. Reprinted with the permission of the American Psychological Association and J. Levy.)

matched. The results of this experiment showed that split-brain patients could activate the hemisphere appropriate to the type of processing required.

The direction of field differences can also depend on the prior mental set of the subject. Marcel Kinsbourne of the Hospital for Sick Children in Toronto has studied the ability of normal subjects to detect a gap on one or other side of a briefly exposed outline of a square. Normally, detection is as about as accurate if the gap is on the left as on the right—if anything, the left is slightly favored. But if the subject must remember a short list of words while performing this task, there is a bias in favor of the right of the square.[32] This left-hemispheric bias is evidently induced by the fact that verbal information is being held in memory, biasing attention toward the left hemisphere and thus toward the right side of space. There is some evidence that humming melodies or rehearsing melodies biases attention toward the right hemisphere and the left side of visual space.[33]

Kinsbourne has also suggested that mental activity in one or other hemisphere can bias eye movements or posture toward the corresponding side of space.[34] For instance, a person pondering a verbal question should be disposed to look to the right, while a spatial question should induce glances to the left. Several investigators have tried to verify these predictions by recording the directions in which people first look when asked a question. "Left-hemispheric" questions include verbal ones like "What is a word with three syllables?" or arithmetic problems like "What is the cube root of sixty-four?" "Right-hemispheric" questions include spatial ones, such as "How many edges are there on a cube?" or musical ones, such as "Is *Waltzing Matilda* in waltz time?"[35] The results of these experiments have not been unequivocal; about half of them have revealed the expected pattern of results, but the rest have been negative or inconsistent. A number of methodological difficulties cloud the issue, and clear-cut results may be impeded by some people's habitual tendencies to look left or right whatever the question, and by the fact that spatial questions often seem to cause people to stare straight ahead rather than to look sideways.[36] We recommend this line of research primarily as a party game, useful when all other attempts to entertain have failed.

To complicate matters even further, clinical observations have revealed a curious asymmetry in the contributions of the two cerebral hemispheres toward the awareness of the two sides of space. Damage to the right side of the brain often produces paralysis or anesthesia on the left side of the body, or an inability to see or react to objects in the left side of the visual space. The patient may neglect to clothe the left side of the body, and remain apparently unaware of the state of half-undress. When asked to draw a clock, the patient may omit the numbers 7 through 11, or attempt to squeeze all the numbers down the right hand side of the clockface. These symptoms almost always affect the left side of the body or of visual space. Damage to the left hemisphere only rarely produces a neglect of the right side.[37]

There seems to be at least an element of denial in these instances of left-sided neglect; the symptoms cannot be attributed wholly to a lack of sensation or motor control. Indeed, in one remarkable report, two patients apparently displayed a left-sided neglect of *imagined* space. In describing from memory the Piazza del Duomo in Milan, the patients tended to omit landmarks to the left of the imagined vantage point. When asked to take up an imagined vantage point on the opposite side of the square, the patients then proceeded to include landmarks they had previously omitted, and omit those they had previously included! On the few occasions when left-sided landmarks *were* reported, the patients mentioned them "in a kind of absent-minded, almost annoyed tone." This suggests that the neglect, or denial, may be as much emotional as perceptual or attentional.[38]

Evidence on the so-called hysterical neuroses, gained earlier in this century when this form of neurosis was more fashionable than it is today, presents a rather similar pattern of asymmetry. The symptoms included hysterical blindness, deafness, anesthesia, and paralysis. The French authority, Pierre Janet, observed that among those of his patients with asymmetrical symptoms, twice as many were afflicted on the left as on the right.[39] One might argue that right-handed patients might be unwilling to sacrifice their right hands to their neuroses, but the evidence is rather against this interpretation. Only a small proportion of patients suffered paralysis of the hands or arms, and the bias was in any case no more marked in the case of the hands than in the case of other parts of the body where the side of the affliction would be of little consequence.

These various findings have suggested that, in most people, the right hemisphere might be the more critically involved in emotion, or at least in the more negative emotions such as depression, anxiety and guilt. Disturbances of right-hemispheric functioning, whether of neurological or psychological origin, often result in neglect, denial, and a general loss of emotion—what Janet called "la belle indifférence." Conversely, damage to the left hemisphere may induce what has been termed the *catastrophic reaction,* including weeping, swearing, expressions of despair and guilt, and aggression.[40] Patients recovering from the sodium amytal test described in the previous chapter show opposite symptoms depending upon which side of the brain had been subjected to the injection. Injection to the left side provokes the catastrophic reaction, while injection to the right often induces denial that anything is the matter, sometimes amounting to euphoria or mania. The patient laughs, jokes, and expresses positive well-being.[41] Hone Tuwhare, author of the poem at the beginning of this chapter, correctly identifies the symptoms but has reversed the left-right polarity; it is the *right* side that "holds your laughing stitches in," the left side "hushing your loud protests."

Interpretation of these emotional effects is not entirely straightforward, since they might be secondary consequences of the lateralization of language representation. The catastrophic reaction to disruption of the left side of the brain might be simply an understandable response to the impairment of speech, while the euphoria that sometimes accompanies insult to the right hemisphere might be an expression of relief that language is not affected. Recent studies of interhemispheric differences in the perception of emotion suggest however that there may be a more fundamental explanation. In studies of dichotic listening, for instance, there is evidence for a right-hemispheric advantage in the identification of emotional sounds such as laughing and crying,[42] and in the identification of the emotional intonations of sentences.[43] Similarly, there is a left visual-field advantage in identification of the emotional expressions of faces.[44] In all of these studies of perceptual asymmetries in normal people, it is difficult to separate the emotional component from the purely perceptual one; nevertheless, there is some evidence that the interhemispheric differences are greatest for the most extreme emotions depicted, and especially for the most extreme *negative* emotions.[45] This suggests that there may be a genuinely emotional component to the differences.

THE DUALITY OF THE BRAIN

Given this rather bewildering array of interhemispheric differences, can we find any simple underlying principles? Many authors have tried to embrace all of the differences within a single duality, but there seem to be exceptions to every rule. As we have seen, John Hughlings Jackson suggested that the "major" hemisphere might be specialized for expression, the "minor" hemisphere for perception. Although this dichotomy does capture a good deal of the evidence, there are exceptions: the left hemisphere, for instance, seems to be the more specialized for the perception of words and letters, and for the perception of rhythm.

The idea that the left hemisphere may be predominantly verbal, the right hemisphere nonverbal, also captures a good many of the findings,[46] but again not all. The left hemispheric involvement in perception of rhythm, and in the production and coordination of nonverbal motor sequences, constitute exceptions. These same examples constitute exceptions to the related idea that the left hemisphere is specialized for symbolic representation, the right hemisphere for visual and analog representation.[47] It has also been suggested that the right hemisphere is specialized for spatial representation,[48] but this does not explain its superiority in the perception of melody or environmental sounds. Again, however, we must stress that there is a good deal of truth in each of these suggested dichotomies, but none seems entirely sufficient by itself.

In recent years there has been a comprehensive and sustained attempt to characterize the functions of the two cerebral hemispheres in terms of complementary modes of consciousness. This movement was led by Joseph E. Bogen, one of the neurosurgeons involved in the split-brain operations in Los Angeles in the early 1960s,[49] and was later popularized by Robert E. Ornstein in his book *The Psychology of Consciousness.*[50] Bogen identified the left hemisphere with what he termed the "propositional mind" and the right hemisphere with the "appositional mind," although he made it clear that these terms were not entirely sufficient. Indeed, the dichotomy between the two modes of consciousness may be so deep and fundamental, according to Bogen, as to transcend any simple verbal labels. Roughly, then, the left hemisphere represents analysis, reason, logic, order, and Western philosophical thought, while the right hemisphere stands for synthesis, intuition, imagination, creativity, and Eastern philosophical thought.

This theme was anticipated in a remarkable way by Count Maurice Maeterlinck (1862–1949), the Belgian man of letters, who distinguished between what he called the Western and Eastern lobes of the human brain. He wrote as follows:

> The one produces here reason, science, and consciousness; the other secretes yonder intuition, religion and subconsciousness. The one reflects

only the infinite and the unknowable; the other is interested only in what it can limit, what it can hope to understand. They represent in an image that may be illusory, the struggle between the material and moral ideals of humanity. They have more than once tried to penetrate each other, to mingle, to work in harmony; but the Western lobe, at least over the most active part of our globe, has up to the present paralysed and almost destroyed the efforts of the other. We owe to it not only our extraordinary progress in all the material sciences, but also catastrophes such as we are experiencing today, which, unless we take care, will not be the last nor the worst. It is time to rouse the paralysed Oriental lobe.[51]

Except that it lacks specific reference to the left and right cerebral hemispheres this passage, published in 1914, might have been written in the 1970s.

It is not difficult to find other precedents for the distinction drawn by Bogen. Bogen himself mentions the pre-Confucian Chinese concepts of yin and yang, the Hindu distinction between Buddhi and manas, the Levi–Strauss dichotomy between the positive and the mythic. But there is a danger of overinclusiveness. Just as it is difficult to find objects in the real world that are neither male nor female sex symbols (in the Freudian sense), so it is difficult to discover distinctions that cannot be grafted onto the two cerebral hemispheres. It is ironical, for instance, that the Marxist dichotomy is round the wrong way, for is not capitalism represented in the *left* hemisphere, the proletariat in the *right*? We think also of C. P. Snow's "two cultures" of the sciences and the arts,[52] popularized at around the time the surgeon's knives were poised to divide the brains of their epileptic patients. The sciences seem clearly to belong to the rational left hemisphere, the arts to the intuitive right.

Much of the spin-off from this characterization of hemispheric duality concerns the idea that the right hemisphere is the more creative. In a recent issue of the *Los Angeles Times*, a teacher of art is quoted as saying that the essence of her method is to teach people to "gain access to the right hemisphere and to be able to use it for education in general."[53] The reader need only pick up almost any issue of *The Journal of Creative Behavior,* nestling uncomfortably in the university library alongside its more dour and respectable sisters, to discover references to the suppressed creativity of the right hemisphere. Witness, for instance, the plaintive reference of one recent author to "the tragic lack of effort to develop our children's right brain strengths. That potential—a source of equally essential creative, artistic, and intellectual capacity—is at present largely unawakened in our schools."[54] There is more than an echo in these lines of Maeterlinck's earlier plea: "It is time to rouse the paralysed Oriental lobe."

It was Bogen who suggested that the right hemisphere might be the more creative, yet even he admitted that there was virtually no evidence for this.[55] More recently, Oliver Zangwill of Cambridge University has observed that patients with damage to the left frontal lobes of the brain often do particularly badly on verbal tests of divergent thinking, supposedly a measure of verbal creativity. He infers that the left hemisphere is the more critical for literary creativity, suggesting that hemispheric differences in creativity have more to do with the verbal or nonverbal nature of the creative enterprise than with creativity itself. Zangwill also cites evidence that the effects of lesions of the right hemisphere on the work of professional painters is not nearly so crippling as one would expect if the right hemisphere were crucial to artistic creativity. He goes so far as to conclude that "the right hemisphere is by no means as vital to artistic expression as is the left to literary creation."[56]

The notion of *hemisphericity,* as it is now termed, has also been used to characterize the difference between individuals. Some individuals are said to be predominantly left-hemispheric in their style of thinking, others predominantly right-hemispheric. At one time it was thought that individuals could be placed in these two categories according to whether they tended to look right or left when asked questions. We have already seen that this may depend partly on the question—although even that is in doubt—but the evidence for *any* kind of consistency in the direction of lateral eye movements (LEMs) is at best weak. In a recent review of this evidence, it was concluded "that variables that ought to correlate with LEMs if the latter are indicators of hemisphericity tend not to, and variables that do correlate with LEM patterns are only tangentially related to hemispheric asymmetry."[57] Another approach has been to compare different occupational groups, representing presumed left- and right-hemisphere ways of thinking, on measures of cerebral lateralization. Even the perpetrators of the notion of hemisphericity have found little support for their views in this line of research. For instance, Robert E. Ornstein and David Galin found no overall difference in the direction of lateralization according to electroencephalographic (EEG) measures between lawyers, supposedly left-hemispheric, and sculptors and ceramicists, presumed to be right-hemispheric.[58] In another study, there appeared to be no systematic differences between students of sculpture, psychology, and law.[59]

We believe that assignment of different styles of consciousness to opposite sides of the brain reflects at least in part the age-old symbolic potency of left and right. We have already seen how different values have
been assigned to the left and right *hands*. Thus the Pythagoreans linked
the odd numbers, the one, the male, the light, the straight, and the good
to the right, while the left was associated with the even, the many, the
female, the dark, the crooked, and the evil. Few dichotomies seem to
have escaped linkage to the left–right polarity at some time or place in
history. Left and right attract mythical ideas because they are at once
alike yet opposites; this is as true of the hands as of the cerebral hemispheres. Indeed, it remains something of a mystery that the human cerebral hemispheres should prove so different in function, yet so similar in
structure. To be sure, there may be an element of hyperbole in the contrast. We have seen, for instance, that there *are* structural differences,
and the functional differences may well have been exaggerated in the
swell of interest in cerebral lateralization. Nevertheless we suspect that
the contrast remains sufficiently mysterious to attract mythical conceptions of its significance.

To a limited extent, the modern assignment of values to the left and
right cerebral hemispheres bears the traces of the ancient linkage of values to the left and right sides of the body. However the polarity is naturally reversed, since each hemisphere is associated with the opposite
side of the body. For instance, the notion that the right hemisphere is
intuitive and the left hemisphere logical can be related implicitly to the
assignment of female values to the left side of the body and male values
to the right, given the common folklore that women are more intuitive
than men. Yet there is no evidence that women are more right-
hemispheric than men. Rather, the evidence suggests that women show
a lesser degree of cerebral lateralization of verbal skills in the left hemisphere and of lateralization of nonverbal or spatial skills in the right.[60] If
there is any neurological basis for differences in cognitive style, we suspect that it is more likely to be found in differences in *degree* of cerebral
lateralization than in differences in reliance on one or other hemisphere.

To understand present conceptions of cerebral lateralization, it is important to examine the dichotomies existing in contemporary thought. It
may be no coincidence that the more transcendental notions about hemispheric duality emerged at a time when there were sharp political divi-
sions within Western society, particularly in the United States. The left
cerebral hemisphere seems to have assumed something of the character
of the military and industral establishment, dominant, linear, coldly ra-

tional, while the right hemisphere stands for the creative disorder of the flower children. The war in Vietnam may be responsible, at least in part, for the explicit linking of Western values to the left hemispheres and Eastern values to the right. Quite apart from the political and military affiliations, there has also been something of a trend in education against the emphasis on verbal and symbolic skills, and in favor of more artistic skills, lateral thinking, and freer forms of expression. This may reflect in part the influence of television. We suspect that this movement was initially independent of neurological theories, but later found natural expression in the distinction between the hemispheres.

Among the more abiding myths is the belief in so-called psychic phenomena, such as clairvoyance, telepathy, psychokinesis, precognition, astral projection, and so on. This belief has been reinforced in recent years by the dubious exploits of Mr. Uri Geller[61] and by the equally dubious experiments of Dr. Harold E. Puthoff and Mr. Russell Targ of the Stanford Research Institute.[62] We shall let the reader guess which cerebral hemisphere is thought to be responsible for these phenomena. Right![63]

We do not mean to suggest that the prevailing views of hemispheric duality can be explained entirely in terms of contemporary social and political folklore. They do derive some support from the empirical evidence. Some of the evidence we reviewed does reveal that perceptual asymmetries have to do with the way the perceived patterns are interpreted, rather than with the patterns themselves. We suspect that the more analytic style of the left cerebral hemisphere derives from that hemisphere's involvement with language and symbolic representation, and is not a distinct, superordinate property. Moreover, the evidence suggests that cerebral lateralization is relative rather than absolute; as Zangwill puts it, "cerebral dominance is in all probability itself a graded characteristic, varying in scope and completeness from individual to individual."[64] Proponents of hemispheric duality, we think, have overgeneralized and excessively dichotomized the true nature of cerebral lateralization.

Consciousness and the Left Hemisphere

There is another aspect of the mythology of cerebral lateralization that is somewhat in conflict with the notion of hemisphericity, although it was explicit in the extract we quoted from Maeterlinck. This is the idea that only the left hemisphere is conscious, while the right hemisphere is a mere automaton. This idea has been repeatedly stated by Sir John C. Eccles, the neurophysiologist, largely on the grounds that split-brain patients cannot verbally express the thoughts or perceptions of their right hemispheres. He wrote that "the goings-on in the minor (right) hemisphere, which we may refer to as the computer, never come into the conscious experience of the subject."[65]

Eccles appears to have simply confused consciousness with speech. As we have seen, evidence from split-brain patients indicates that their right hemispheres are capable of comprehending verbal symbols or utterances, even though they cannot produce articulate speech. The right hemisphere of the split-brain patient can mediate nonverbal expression, through pointing or responding bodily to verbal commands. Patients undergoing the sodium amytal test do not appear to lose consciousness when the dominant hemisphere is suppressed, even though their speech or verbal comprehension may be inhibited. In one study, for instance, patients were able to manipulate a switch with the left hand when the left hemisphere was suppressed, indicating that the right hemisphere was still able to monitor the signals and organize the appropriate responses.[66] These and many other observations imply strongly that the right hemisphere is capable of awareness and responsiveness and is at least in these respects conscious.

In his provocative book *The Origin of Consciousness in the Breakdown of the Bicameral Mind,* Julian Jaynes of Princeton University presents a more subtle argument for associating consciousness with the left cerebral hemisphere. He suggests that the mind of the *Iliad* or of the Old Testament was bicameral (without cerebral lateralization) and lacked responsibility for action. Instead, people of that era were guided in their behavior by hallucinations, interpreted as the voices of the gods. Hallucinations eventually proved inadequate as a means of social control, especially during the physical and social upheavals of the second millennium before Christ. Through the evolution of left-hemisphere specialization, people acquired a concept of self and of responsibility for their own actions. The left hemisphere came to represent man (or, we hope, woman, as the case may be), leaving the right hemisphere to the gods. Jaynes finds vestiges for the bicameral mind even in modern times, citing evidence that hallucinations are more common than is generally supposed in normal, healthy individuals, and that they are more readily induced by electrical stimulation of the right than of the left hemisphere.[67]

Jaynes' argument implies that cerebral lateralization evolved *after* the development of language. It seems extremely unlikely that so dramatic a functional change could have occurred in so short a time by the normal, selective processes of evolution. Jaynes was aware of this difficulty and argued that the brain is especially adapted to rapid evolutionary change because of the tightness of coupling between different centers, implying that a minor anatomical alteration could bring about a major functional shift. However, we know of no other biological precedent for this argument. Moreover, the neurological evidence suggests that the brain is functionally rather insensitive to anatomical disturbances. We are left with the impression that the coupling between brain centers is characterized more by redundancy and plasticity than by tightness.

We suggest that arguments like those presented by Eccles and Jaynes are prompted more by myth, or perhaps by wish fulfillment, than by facts. In this case the myth may reflect the Cartesian belief that humans are fundamentally different from other animals, specifically in that only humans possess consciousness. Again, the elusive nature of the difference between the cerebral hemispheres seems to provide a peg on which to hang the myth. The apparent discrepancy between functional asymmetry and (relative) structural symmetry is suggestive of a uniquely mental component, identifiable perhaps with consciousness, and transcending the physical properties of the brain. To those with this dualistic notion of consciousness as inhabiting the realm of the nonphysical, it may have been disturbing to learn from the studies of split-brain patients that cutting the commissures could apparently create a split in consciousness itself. According to Zangwill, therefore, Eccles' attempt to install consciousness solely in the left hemisphere was "little more than a desperate rearguard action to safeguard the existence and indivisibility of the soul."[68]

In any event, it seems more and more likely that neither cerebral lateralization nor consciousness is unique to humans. We have seen that the anatomical basis for cerebral lateralization may have been present in prehistoric humans, and may be present in some nonhuman primates. A functional left-cerebral dominance for processing communicative vocalizations may be present in Japanese macaques. These observations, although admittedly rather tenuous, are in opposition to Jaynes' view that left-cerebral dominance is of very recent origin in human evolution. It is appropriate to recall here the fact that birdsong is controlled primarily by the left cerebral hemisphere in chaffinches, canaries, and spar-rows. By this token, both cerebral lateralization and consciousness should be for the birds. It is ironic that Jaynes' book should have ap-peared in the same year (1976) as an equally provocative book by D. R. Griffin, called *The Question of Animal Awareness.* Largely on the basis of recent discoveries about the versatility and sophistication of com-munication among animals, Griffin suggests that some nonhuman ani-mals possess a consciousness and self-awareness not unlike our own.[69] In Francine Patterson's account of Koko, the gorilla who learned sign language, we read of Koko's capacity to lie her way out of trouble.[70] This seems to leave little doubt that Koko's consciousness includes self-awareness and a sense of personal responsibility. We doubt that any go-rilla god spake unto Koko and said "Lie, or there'll be trouble."

A BIOLOGICAL PERSPECTIVE

We have suggested that current conceptions of cerebral lateralization suffer two main defects. One is that the differences between the cerebral hemispheres are seen as absolute rather than relative. In particular, they are portrayed as representing the opposite poles of some fundamental dichotomy in human thought. Yet Brenda Milner of the Montreal Neu-rological Institute, one of the most exacting of investigators in this field, has reminded us that the two hemispheres also have much in common;[71] we suspect, in fact, that they are more alike than different. The second defect is that cerebral lateralization is often portrayed as unique to hu-mans and thus conveying some property of thought or consciousness that sets us apart from the other animals. We suspect that there is at least a trace of the book of Genesis in such a conception. In this final section we shall try to present a biological perspective on cerebral lateraliza-tion, stressing the continuity rather than the discontinuity between hu-mans and other species.

In Chapter 4, we discussed the evolution of bilateral symmetry. We pointed out that the molecules of living matter are fundamentally asym-metrical, and that bilateral symmetry is an adaptation to the fact that the environment impinges on organisms without any consistent left–right bias. Since symmetry is an adaptation rather than a fundamental prop-erty, it is readily abandoned when it is no longer adaptive or when an asymmetrical system proves more expedient. In discussions of cerebral lateralization, it is all too easily forgotten that lateral asymmetries abound in nature. There seems no good reason to suppose that there is anything very unique or special about the asymmetry of the human brain.

An excellent and succinct account of biological asymmetries is provided by A. C. Neville in his book *Animal Asymmetry*.[72] Many asymmetries, like human handedness and cerebral lateralization, have been superimposed on a structure that was evidently symmetrical at an earlier stage of evolution. For instance, flatfish have both eyes on the same side of the body, and the fiddler crab has one large and one small claw. One of our favorite asymmetries is that of our compatriot, the New Zealand wrybill plover, which has its beak bent to the right. This oddity has been something of a mystery to some naturalists, who have tended to regard it with the condescension all too familiar to those of us who were raised in the colonies. The following extract illustrates the point.

> For all we know it may be a silent grief to respectable wrybill to see their little ones grow up with this horrid distortion of the proboscis, to reflect that in the councils of the great plover family their breed has been sent to Coventry—relegated for all time to South Canterbury.[73]

On closer study, however, it is clear that the curve of the beak is a useful adaptation, making it easier for the bird to get its beak under stones to turn them over in the search for food. It also enables the bird to use its beak as a kind of sieve to extract tiny crustaceans from surface water in the mudflats of northern New Zealand.[74]

Many of the functional asymmetries to be observed in nature concern actions that are manipulations *on* the environment rather than reactions *to* it. Internally generated, purposeful actions are not so tied to the spatial constraints of the environment as are more reflexive, "stimulus-bound" actions. The advantages of symmetry are correspondingly less telling, and there may even be advantages in an asymmetrical system. For instance the curved beak of the wrybilled plover is clearly an advantage in turning over stones. Given that this is a purposeful act, there is no serious disadvantage in the fact that the bird can only turn over stones from the left. The bird can nearly always maneuver so that a stone is to its right, or else choose another stone—it need leave no stone unturned. Sometimes the advantages of asymmetry in manipulative actions have to do with different specialization in paired organs. For instance, the lobster has one heavy claw adapted for crushing and one lighter nipping claw adapted for picking up food; again, crushing and nipping may be considered purposeful actions. In the gribble, a small marine isopod that annoyingly destroys submerged timber by boring into it, one of the mandibles is like a rasp and the other like a file—useful tools, no doubt, for its destructive trade.[75] Human handedness might be considered somewhat analogous to these examples in that the right hand might be considered specialized for ''operating,'' the left hand for ''holding,'' in Bruner's terminology. The analogy breaks down somewhat in that the specialization of the human hands is not apparent in the structure of the hands themselves, but seems to reside rather in the brain structures that control them.

In other cases, too, the advantage of asymmetry may have to do with the control of action rather than with the action itself. The lateralized control of song in certain birds may have evolved because of the conflict that would have arisen had both hemispheres been equally dominant. Birdsong is internally generated and is sequential, not spatial, and so is not constrained by the spatial features of the environment (except in the indirect sense that it has to do with territoriality). Similarly, the lateralized control of human speech may have been an adaptation to minimize interhemispheric conflict. The same reasoning applies to the control of manipulative skills. In the previous chapter we cited the evidence of Trevarthen that baboons spontaneously develop cerebral dominance as they acquire a complex manipulative skill. This serves as a prototype for the evolution of human handedness, which is more apparent in manipulative operations on the environment than in reactions to the environment. For instance, in the bizarre game of cricket, still practiced in the farthest flung outposts of the old British Empire, a fielder in the slips (*sic*) may react equally quickly to catch a ball that flies to his left or right, but in throwing the ball he relies on a single throwing arm.

Besides the advantage of unilateral control, one may argue that there are surely extra advantages to be gained by having the two cerebral hemispheres differentially specialized, if only because it avoids duplication of representation. The folded, wrinkled human brain is itself testimony to the limitations imposed by the volume of the human skull, as the brain doubles back on itself to discover extra capacity. However it is not altogether clear that the storage of knowledge is a matter of specific spatial location. Damage to specific locations in the brain does not disrupt specific memories, for instance. Rather, representation of specific memories seems to be distributed over wide regions of the brain, implying a good deal of duplication. Indeed, the two hemispheres of the split-brain patient evidently share a good deal in common, since the patients appear normal and well integrated in their everyday behavior. As we noted in the previous chapter, it requires subtle psychological tests to reveal interhemispheric differences. We are not denying that the cerebral hemispheres *are* differentially specialized, but the human brain also exhibits a good deal of the bilateral organization that is characteristic of all species.

We suggest, then, that the decisive influence in the evolution of cerebral lateralization in humans was the advantage conferred by unilateral control, especially in the case of internally generated, purposeful sequences of action. Both speech and manipulative actions fall into this category, and both are controlled predominantly by the left cerebral hemisphere. This does not mean, however, that left-hemispheric specialization is concerned exclusively with actions. Given that the left hemisphere in most people controls the production of speech, it is understandable that the perception and comprehension of speech should be biased in favor of the same hemisphere, since the integration of input and output is presumably accomplished more efficiently within a hemisphere than across hemispheres. Note, however, that the evidence reviewed in the previous chapter suggests that lateralization is more pronounced for production than for comprehension, suggesting that its origin is motor rather than perceptual.

There seems to be a motor component underlying other left-hemispheric perceptual advantages as well. For instance, we noted earlier that there is a left-hemispheric superiority in the perception of rhythm, but this may be a secondary consequence of the demonstrated left-hemispheric superiority in the production of rhythmic sequences.[76] Similarly, the left hemisphere appears to be superior to the right in judgments of simultaneity, temporal order, and duration,[77] but these in turn may reflect a left-hemispheric advantage in fine motor control. Again, we have seen that trained musicians show a left-hemispheric advantage in recognizing melodies, while musically inexperienced listeners show a right-hemispheric advantage. We might, however, attribute this to the fact that trained musicians are primarily involved in the production of music, so that the motor component is more prominent.

The simplest explanation of right-hemispheric specialization is simply that it is gained by default. The left hemisphere, having assumed the dominant role in language and in purposeful actions, may have forfeited some of its capacity for functions that would otherwise be represented bilaterally.[78] This interpretation is consistent with the evidence that right-hemispheric advantages are typically rather small, and cover a wide range of nonverbal functions, including very elementary ones as judgments of depth or hue. These functions scarcely suggest a superordinate mode of consciousness. Rather, many of them are functions that one would expect to find represented bilaterally in nonhuman primates. This is not to say that the fruits of human evolution have been deposited entirely in the left cerebral hemisphere. No doubt the human brain has evolved sophisticated perceptual or spatial skills that are uniquely human, and that are also more strongly represented in the right than in the left hemisphere because of the left-hemispheric preoccupation with language and executive motor control.

We have maintained the emphasis on left-hemispheric specialization as the primary influence in human cerebral lateralization. This emphasis is an historical one, and ties in with the theme developed in the previous chapter concerning the role of a common left–right gradient underlying the development of handedness and cerebral lateralization. Despite romantic appeals for a reawakening of the oriental lobe, we note that neurosurgeons continue to hold the left hemisphere more precious than the right in planning operations on epileptic foci. Nevertheless, it is worth considering briefly the possibility that we have wrongheadedly reversed the polarity of the evolutionary gradient, and that *right*-hemispheric specialization is primary.

William C. Webster of Carleton University in Ottawa has suggested that right-hemispheric specialization for the representation of space may have evolved because bilateral representation would tend to create a confusion of left and right, resulting in spatial disorientation.[79] We are naturally somewhat sympathetic to this theory, since Webster cites our own argument that a symmetrical system could not tell left from right (see Chapter 2). There is evidence that women are inferior to men in spatial ability, and are more confused about left and right than men are.[80] Consistent with Webster's theory, women also show the lesser degree of cerebral lateralization.[81] We might also note that women appear to be superior to men in verbal ability,[82] despite their more bilateral representation of language, which again suggests that the primary pressure toward asymmetrical representation had to do with spatial rather than verbal skills. However, the interpretation of differences between men and women is notoriously difficult, and the implications for theories about the evolution of lateralization are in any case oblique.

In our view, the bulk of evidence suggests that Webster's theory puts the cart before the horse. We argued in Chapter 4 that symmetry evolved precisely because the natural environment exhibits no consistent left–right bias. In coding spatial events, the advantages of mirror-image equivalence seems to outweigh any advantage of mirror-image *discrimination,* which favors bilateral symmetry rather than asymmetry. Of course, mirror-image discriminations are more important in the artificial human environment than in the natural environment, and we do make frequent use of the labels "left" and "right" in describing spatial scenes or in giving directional instructions. However, the asymmetries of the artificial human environment seem largely the products of human handedness, and the use of the labels "left" and "right" surely depends on the prior specialization of the *left* hemisphere for verbal representation. These considerations suggest again that the asymmetrical representation of space in the human brain is a secondary consequence of the left-hemispheric dominance for handedness and language.

We suggested in Chapter 2 that animals in the natural world are hardly ever called upon to tell left from right. Indeed it is much more likely that they will be required to treat left–right mirror images as equivalent. Nevertheless, it is sometimes suggested that left–right discrimination is necessary for successful navigation.[83] It is true that humans often make use of the labels "left" and "right" in navigating, or in giving directional instructions, but this may be because the labels are available and convenient rather than because they are necessary. In navigating over familiar terrain, it is generally possible to navigate with reference to landmarks, independently of the concepts of left and right. For instance, if you try to give instructions on how to go to a certain location in your own neighborhood without using the labels "left," "right," or their equivalents, you will find it difficult and inconvenient, but *possible.*

Some sense of left and right does seem to be necessary in migration over unfamiliar territory, where specific landmarks may be unknown. For instance, certain warblers migrate every year from central Canada to the southeast coast of the United States, where they pause to accumulate subcutaneous fat before proceeding on the long overwater flight to the lesser Antilles or the northern coast of South America. These birds evidently calculate the direction of flight relative to the north-south line, and thus fly to the *left* of this line in a southeasterly direction. Presumably, this calculation requires an internal sense of which is left and which is right, implying some structural (perhaps cerebral) asymmetry.

Interestingly enough, however, some birds evidently make a left–right confusion and fly south*west* instead of southeast. These "vagrant warblers" can be observed in the area around San Francisco before they set out on a futile overwater flight, only to perish in the Pacific.

For his doctoral dissertation at Stanford University, David F. De-Sante has experimentally studied the preferred directional orientations of the vagrant warblers.[84] Since the warblers migrate at night, he held them in cages under clear, moonless night skies. The birds showed clear but equal preferences for two axes, one running from northwest to southeast, representing the correct line of migration, the other running northeast to southwest, the vagrant direction. DeSante concluded that the birds were unable to tell left from right. He argued that the vagrant birds choose the direction of migration according to the direction of the prevailing wind, but having chosen a direction they maintain it. The prevailing wind is from the west, but an occasional easterly across the Canadian prairies brings a fresh crop of vagrants to California. The majority of birds, however, are not influenced by the wind and choose the correct direction.

DeSante's suggestion that the vagrant warblers belong to a subclass of warblers lacking a directional sense is strikingly reminiscent of Annett's theory that left-handed humans belong to a subclass lacking consistent lateralization. DeSante did not present any evidence on how those warblers that migrate successfully to the East Coast would orient if held in cages, so his theory remains conjectural. The fact that warblers belong to the order of passerine birds suggests an even more fascinating conjecture. Chaffinches, canaries, and sparrows are also passerine birds, and the reader will no doubt recall that singing in these birds is controlled primarily by the left side of the brain. Could it be that the warbling of warblers is also under left-hemispheric control? If so, this asymmetry might well provide the birds with the left–right sense that enables them to migrate successfully. We might then expect to find no such asymmetry among the vagrant warblers, who might also w-w-warble with a stutter (see Chapter 12). There is another dissertation here for somebody.

Note that this admittedly fanciful account has led us back to the suggestion that the asymmetry required for directional migration is secondary to an asymmetry of executive motor control. DeSante also observes that the migration of warblers is probably a relatively recent phenomenon, occurring within the last 20,000 years. If these birds do indeed display an asymmetry of vocal control, it seems very likely that this would have preceded the evolution of migration. This lends further credence to the idea that the motor asymmetry is prior, but permits a complementary asymmetry governing migration. We might argue analogously that the human ability to tell left from right was a useful spin-off from the lateralization of executive motor control, but was not in itself a decisive factor in the evolution of lateralization.

Part of our reason for supposing that left-hemispheric specialization is primary is that right-hemispheric advantages seem relatively slight compared with left-hemispheric advantages. If there is an exception to this rule, however, it is to be found in the very striking right-hemispheric dominance for spatial manipulations to be observed in split-brain patients. As we noted at the beginning of this chapter, the right hand of the split-brain patient is peculiarly inept at arranging blocks to match a pattern, or at drawing a cube in perspective, and the eager and efficient left hand must sometimes be prevented from helping out. This asymmetry rivals in degree the left-hemispheric superiority for verbal skills. It is important to note, however, that the areas of the right hemisphere that mediate these manipulospatial skills are directly opposite language-mediating areas in the left cerebral hemisphere.[85] Moreover, the corresponding areas mediating manipulospatial skills are bilaterally represented in nonhuman primates.[86] These considerations prompted the authors of a recent discussion of this problem to reach precisely the conclusion we are advocating here.

> . . .we feel that the superior performance of the right hemisphere of split-brain patients on a variety of manipulospatial tasks may not reflect the overall cognitive style and evolutionary specialization of the right hemisphere, but instead may represent localized processing inefficiencies in the left parieto-temporal junction due to the presence of language.[87]

So far, we have stressed the evolutionary aspect of the proposition that left-cerebral specialization is prior to right-cerebral specialization. In the previous chapter, we also proposed that the development of cerebral lateralization in the growing child might be guided by a left–right gradient favoring earlier development on the left. As a corollary to this, we might suppose that the right hemisphere gains certain specialized advantages only because of the left hemisphere's prior commitment to language and executive motor control. In other words, our idea that right-hemispheric specialization is achieved by default might apply in development as in evolution. Some authors have objected to this interpretation on the grounds that the infant is concerned with spatial concepts *before* she or he is concerned with language. Earlier development on the left should give rise to left-hemispheric specialization for spatial rather than for verbal skills. It might be argued on these grounds that there is a left–right gradient favoring earlier development on the *right*.

One counter to this argument is that left-hemispheric specialization is not restricted to verbal skills, but includes manipulative and executive motor functions as well. In any event, there is no good evidence to suggest that the child is not concerned with verbal skills even in early infancy. The infant can discriminate speech sounds very early in the first year of life,[88] and this is a skill normally associated with left-cerebral specialization. But perhaps the most critical evidence for the priority of left-hemispheric specialization has to do with the phenomenon of equipotentiality.

As we pointed out in the previous chapter, the notion of a left–right gradient, with the left hemisphere leading in development, provides a simple explanation for equipotentiality with respect to the representation of language. If the left hemisphere is damaged or even removed the gradient is effectively reversed, and the right hemisphere can then assume the functions of the left, provided of course that the damage occurs before some "critical period." This argument is essentially unidirectional and allows no provision for the left hemisphere to take over the specialized skills of the right hemisphere if the latter should be incapacitated. Bruno Kohn and Maureen Dennis of the Hospital for Sick Children in Toronto have studied patients who have had one or other hemisphere removed in early infancy. Their data seem to confirm the unidirectionality of interhemispheric compensation. Although early removal of the left hemisphere results in reallocation of verbal process in the right hemisphere, incapacitation of the right hemisphere does not bring about reallocation of right-hemispheric skills in the left hemisphere. Rather, "the subjects' spatial abilities depend on a *left*-hemispheric mediation of processes which are characteristic of right hemisphere functions in the human brain."[89] That is, the subjects apparently use inappropriate verbal strategies to solve spatial problems.

This suggests that it is the specialized left-hemispheric functions that have the higher priority, and can switch to the right hemisphere if the left is damaged, while the more subordinate right-hemispheric specialities remain inevitably confined to the right.

CONCLUSIONS

The phenomenon of cerebral lateralization illustrates again the age-old paradox of left and right. The two sides of the brain, like the two hands, are at once alike yet different. This paradox no doubt accounts for the symbolic potency of the distinction, which has served as a vehicle for most of the dichotomies—philosophical, political, religious—that have occupied the human intellect. As a result, the functional differences between the hemispheres have been overemphasized and overdramatized at the expense of the considerable overlap between them as well as at the expense of the continuity between humans and other animals. We have tried to restore a proper perspective by emphasizing the relativity of interhemispheric specialization and by seeking general biological principles that might govern the evolution of asymmetries, not only in humans but in other species as well.

We should add, however, that we have no objection to the various dichotomies themselves. It is perfectly acceptable to contrast the rational with the intuitive, the propositional with the appositional. We welcome moves to foster creativity in our schools or to develop the visual in addition to the verbal imagination. What we do object to is the facile association of these dichotomies with the two halves of the brain. It is, on the face of it, rather unlikely that the various ways in which the human intellect can be dichotomized should coincide precisely with the midsagittal split through the brain.

We have ourselves tried to adopt a more cautious biologically oriented approach, seeking other biological asymmetries that might provide insights into the nature of cerebral lateralization. There is perhaps a danger that we have neglected the uniquely human element, but given the powerful motives for believing ourselves different from and superior to other animals, we think it healthier to seek evidence of continuity rather than of special status for humans. According to Sir William Osler, the Canadian physician, the only criterion that clearly distinguished humans from other species was the insatiable desire of humans to take medicine.[90]

In rejecting the more radical theories about cerebral lateralization, we may seem to lean conservatively to the right. On the other hand, we have maintained the historical bias in favor of the left as the leading hemisphere. We suspect that the primary influence in the evolution of lateralization was the specialization of the left hemisphere for the executive control of sequential actions, a specialization now manifest in the left-hemispheric control over speech and manipulative skills involving the hands. This specialization was no doubt facilitated by the evolution of an upright stance which freed the hands, and to a lesser extent, the vocal organs, from environmental constraints, allowing them to be used for more manipulative purposes. We have suggested that this evolutionary development may provide a sufficient explanation for the ensuing pattern of lateralization, although there will no doubt be those who will insist on a more active component underlying right-hemispheric skills. The area is likely to be a focus of research and debate for some years to come. We shall have achieved our purpose simply if we have fueled that debate and prompted a more biological perspective.

Chapter 10

Development of the
Left-Right Sense

*And should I not spare Ninevah, that great city, wherein are more than
sixscore thousand persons that cannot discern between their right hand
and their left hand; and also much cattle?* [Jonah 4:11]

The "persons" referred to in this circumlocutory passage were children (although we suspect that the cattle may also have had difficulty telling left from right). It is of course a commonplace observation that young children have a special difficulty in learning the difference between left and right, and the problem has evidently been with us at least since the days of the Old Testament. Most parents will have experienced the difficulty of teaching their two- or three-year-old to identify the right hand, even though the child may already exhibit a fairly consistent preference in eating or drawing. Later on, at the age of five or six, the child may confuse mirror-image letters when learning to read, and in the first fumbling attempts to write may produce letters, words, or even whole sentences in mirrored script. We show an example from one of our own children (who shall be nameless) in Figure 10.1.

These errors and confusions are quite normal, and should not cause alarm. We have already argued, in Chapter 4, that there is an inborn tendency to treat left and right as equivalent, and that this is an evolutionary adaptation to the fact that left and right are equivalent in the nat-

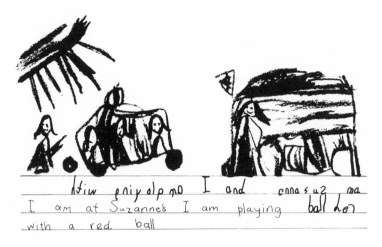

FIGURE 10.1.

This example of spontaneous mirror writing was done by a five-year-old child. The lighter script shows the teacher's correction.

ural environment—as well as in the environment of the preschool child. For instance, a chair is equally likely to be facing either way, and Mom, Dad, and the cat are equally familiar in left and right profile. There may be slight biases, in early exposure to books, for instance, or in a parent's nagging insistence that a child use the right hand to hold a spoon or crayon, but the overriding impression is one of indifference with respect to left–right orientation, especially during the very early years.

Research shows that left–right skills develop in a progressive manner. By the age of six years, most children can reliably indicate the left and right sides of their own bodies, but they still have difficulty labeling the left and right sides of other objects or other people, and do not really master these more complex operations until the age of about ten years.[1] The task of applying the labels ''left'' and ''right'' to objects other than one's own body requires more than just the ability to tell left from right, as we pointed out in Chapter 2. It also requires the ability to map one's own body coordinates onto the object in question. An eight-year-old might therefore fail to identify the left and right hands of another person because he cannot make the mental transformation necessary to understand which hand corresponds to his *own* left or right hand, and not because he cannot tell left from right.

This may not be the only factor, however. Confusions about the directionality of script persist beyond the age at which children can identify the sides of their own bodies even though no mental transformations are required, presumably because there is no explicit relation between the left–right orientation of letters or words and the sides of the body. In a study carried out in the 1930s, Helen Davidson found that between five and ten years of age, children remained more confused by the left–right mirror-image pairs *p* and *q, b* and *d*, than between the up–down pairs *p* and *b, q* and *d*.[2] Unfortunately her test was not a pure measure of mirror-image discrimination. Each child was given a sheet of paper with a sample letter on the left side and a box containing four rows of ten letters. She was told to look at the sample letter, then mark each letter in the box that was exactly like the sample. This task does not strictly require the ability to tell left from right because the letters need not be labeled; the child can simply compare each letter to the sample and note whether it is the same or different. Nevertheless we suspect that this would have proven a cumbersome strategy and the children probably did try to label the letters in some way. It is therefore likely that they were victims of genuine left–right confusion.

Davidson also suggested that the difficulty may have lain partly in the child's interpretation of the instructions. Some children evidently noticed that the letters faced different ways but "did not consider that this fact made them different." Of course this in itself is testimony to the salience of left–right equivalence in the recognition of patterns. As Davidson points out, recognition of *b*'s and *d*'s as the "same" is "similar to that in which a child recognizes a chair no matter which way the seat is facing. A chair turned upside down might possibly be another matter, however."

We do not think this can fully explain Davidson's results, though. For one thing, most children realize that orientation *is* important in the identification of letters, and in this respect identifying a letter is not like identifying a chair. Davidson noted that there were only "one or two isolated cases" in which the children appeared to consider left–right orientation unimportant. Moreover, Michael French at the University of Auckland carried out a similar study in which he gave children special instructions on the importance of orientation. He found that the instructions reduced left–right and up–down confusions by approximately equal amounts. But left–right confusions remained the more frequent, suggesting that the difficulty was not simply a matter of how the children interpreted the task.[3]

Juliet Vogel of Rutgers University has recently described similar results in a test that provides a more unequivocal measure of mirror-image discrimination.[4] She showed pictures of objects to children and college students, and then tested for recognition by showing pairs of pictures and asking her subjects to pick out which of each pair had been in the original series. Five-year-olds could not discriminate the originals from their left–right mirror images; relying on sheer guesswork, they were correct on about half of the trials. Nine-year-olds were correct on about three-quarters of the trials, while the college students, no doubt fighting for the academic reputation of their university, managed about 85 percent correct. These differences between the different age groups could not be attributed simply to differences in memory for the objects, since even the youngest children could easily pick out an original picture from a completely new one. An example of the discriminations is shown in Figure 10.2.

FIGURE 10.2.

Discriminations like this one were used by Vogel. The left panel shows one of the original pictures. Later, the subject must pick which of the right-hand pictures was the original one. (From J. M. Vogel, "The Development of Recognition Memory for the Left–Right Orientation of Pictures," **Child Development 48** [1977]:1532–43. Reprinted with the permission of the Society for Research in Child Development, Chicago, Illinois.)

Vogel, like Davidson, also wondered if the younger children may have simply failed to appreciate the relevance of left–right orientation, so she chose three further groups, aged six, eight, and ten years, and gave them special training in reporting of the left–right orientations of pictures. As a result of this training, only the two older groups showed any significant benefit in the recognition test. The six-year-olds could understand the training task well enough and perform it accurately, but this did not help them solve the mirror-image discriminations.

These studies suggest that children have great difficulty making left–right mirror-image discriminations up until the age of about six years, and show gradual improvement thereafter. However, it is not clear whether the age of six is critical, as it is the age at which children normally enter school and encounter left–right discriminations in learning to read and write, or whether there is some more fundamental neurological explanation, perhaps related to the growth of lateralization in the nervous system. We can gain some insight into this issue by considering further studies in which the emphasis is on *teaching* left–right discriminations, rather than on just testing them.

Now there seems little doubt that even very young infants can be taught the simplest kind of left–right differentiation, in which all that is required is a consistent response in one or other direction. Four-months-old infants can be taught to turn their hands to either the left or right of the midline, where the reward for a correct turn is brief access to a nursing bottle.[5] Of course, infants may learn this task by detecting some consistent asymmetry in the environment, but we suspect that they actually learn it in relation to some asymmetry within themselves. For instance, one study suggests that most infants learn more readily to roll their heads to the right than to the left,[6] and we noted in Chapter 6 that the tonic neck reflex in infants normally involves turning the head to the right. Besides, we saw in Chapter 3 that simple, unidirectional left–right response differentiations seem to cause other animals no difficulty, and we can think of no reason why human children should be an exception.

By contrast, mirror-image discriminations are very difficult for young children to learn. Rita G. Rudel and the late Hans–Lukas Teuber of the Massachusetts Institute of Technology tried to teach children to discriminate vertical from horizontal lines, oblique lines that were mirror images of one another, upright from inverted U-shapes, and left–right mirror-image U-shapes.[7] On each of these four discrimination tasks, the children were shown the pair of shapes fifty times and simply told to choose which one was correct. The correct one was sometimes on the left, sometimes on the right, according to a random schedule. At first the children could only guess, but since they were told each time whether their choice was correct they had ample opportunity to learn. Most of the children in the youngest age groups, aged three to four years, and all of the older children learned to discriminate between the vertical and horizontal lines and between the upright and inverted U-shapes. The two left–right discriminations proved considerably more difficult, especially for the younger children. None of the twelve three-year-olds and only one of the twelve four-year-olds learned to discriminate the mirror-image obliques, and only one three-year-old and two four-year-olds mastered the left–right U-shapes. As Figure 10.3 shows, discrimination of the left–right pairs improved with age, but even among the eight-year-olds, the oldest group studied, it remained poorer than discrimination of the other two pairs.

Figure 10.3 also reveals a marked improvement on the left–right discriminations between the ages of five and six. This may well have coincided with the period in which the children received their first intensive instruction in reading and writing, which could perhaps explain the sudden improvement in left–right discrimination. This explanation is also consistent with data gathered by Robert Serpell, who repeated Rudel and Teuber's experiment with Zambian children.[8] These data, which are also plotted in Figure 10.3, show that the improvement in left–right discrimination occurred about three years later among Zambian children than among American ones. Since Zambian children are introduced to reading and writing some years later than American children, the data are again consistent with the idea that left–right discrimination is markedly facilitated by experience with script.

In these last two studies, the tasks included the discrimination of mirror-image obliques, and there have been many other studies showing that children find this discrimination extremely difficult.[9] As we noted in Chapter 3, however, this task is ambiguous. For one thing, mirror-image obliques are at once left–right and up–down mirror images; for another, the difficulty may have to do with the fact that the lines are oblique, and not with the fact that they are mirror images. There is evidence that young children do experience difficulty with oblique lines in tasks other than those requiring discrimination of mirror images. Indeed, David R. Olson of the Ontario Institute for Studies in

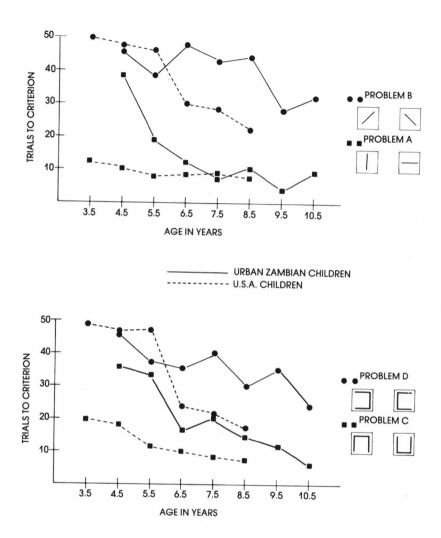

FIGURE 10.3.

Lines on the two graphs show the number of trials it took American and Zambian children of different ages to learn various discriminations. Notice that there is an abrupt improvement in mirror-image discriminations between 5 and 6 years of age for American children, and between 8 and 9 years for Zambian children (after Serpell, 1971).

Education has devoted an entire monograph to the child's concept of the diagonal, based largely on the observation that children under the age of about seven years find it almost impossible to fill in a diagonal on a checkerboard.[10]

Peter E. Bryant of Oxford University has argued that the child's difficulty in discriminating mirror-image obliques is indeed a consequence of the obliqueness of the lines and has little to do with the mirror-image relation. The difficulty arises, he suggests, because there are typically no other oblique lines in the environment against which to match the lines to be discriminated. By contrast, discrimination of horizontal from vertical is easy because there are usually many examples of horizontal and vertical lines that match the stimulus lines; for instance, the lines are usually displayed on cards with rectangular borders. Bryant has shown that children can readily master the discrimination of obliques if oblique matching lines are provided.[11]

Although we accept that children have difficulty coding oblique lines, we do not think that this is their only source of difficulty in discriminating mirror-image obliques. Bryant's experiments are equivocal, because in his experiments supplying matching obliques he also supplied a left–right cue. In one study, for instance, he showed that children could easily discriminate mirror-image obliques if diamond-shaped borders were drawn around the stimulus lines. However the top two edges of the diamond were in different colors, one red, one blue, and this of course provided a consistent cue as to which was left and which was right. Moreover, the improvement is apparently effective only if the children are given prior training to draw their attention to the borders around the lines. In another study in which no such training was provided, children continued to have great difficulty discriminating mirror-image obliques regardless of the shape of the borders and regardless of whether they were colored or not.[12]

In a study conducted by one of us (M.C.C.), children had greater difficulty with obliques that were exact mirror images than with obliques that were oriented on opposite sides of the vertical but at different angles to it (although Bryant failed to observe this effect in his studies).[13] This suggests that there is a component attributable to the difficulty of true mirror-image discrimination. But it is again Figure 10.3 that clinches our conviction that the difficulty with mirror-image obliques is truly an index of children's inability to tell left from right. Notice that the results for mirror-image obliques are rather closely parallel to those for left–

right mirror-image U-shapes, which contain no obliques at all. This suggests that the two discriminations share a common component. That component, we think, must be the necessity to tell left from right.

Let us return now to the question of what explains the development of the ability to discriminate mirror-image patterns. Figure 10.3 certainly suggests that there is a rapid improvement associated with experience with directional script. To a degree, then, learning to read and write might bring about the improvement, although this can scarcely be the whole explanation since left–right discriminations remain more diffi-cult than other kinds of discriminations at least until the age of ten years. The difference can even be detected in adulthood, as we saw in Chapter 3. We suspect that a child's "readiness" to learn left–right discrimina-tions, and thus to learn to read and write, probably does increase with age, probably as a consequence of the child's own laterality. Indeed, there may well be a "spurt" in the growth of laterality at around five or six years of age. It may be for this reason that formal schooling is intro-duced in most societies at this time. We shall pursue this later in the chapter. We suspect that left–right skills are not rigidly determined by the growth of laterality, however, and indeed that it is possible to teach some degree of left–right discrimination at almost any age, although the ease and extent to which one can do so is limited by the level of matura-tional development.

We now consider some of the principles that govern the effective teaching of left–right skills. Since some children have more difficulty than others, these principles may be of practical concern to parents and teachers, especially in cases where a child is having special difficulty learning to read or write.

EFFECTIVE TEACHING OF LEFT–RIGHT DISCRIMINATIONS

In Chapter 4, while discussing left–right discriminations in animals, we suggested that mirror-image discriminations are often acquired through the mediation of response asymmetries. There is evidence that this principle applies equally to the case of human children learning mirror-image discriminations. For instance, Wendell Jeffrey of the University of California at Los Angeles tried to teach four-year-olds to attach different names, "Jack" and "Jill," to two stick figures, one pointing left and the other pointing right.[14] The figures were shown one at a time, and the children were simply told whether the name they gave was right or wrong. Most of the children failed to learn the correct names. Half of them were then told to push a button located in the direction in which the figure pointed—the arrangement of figures and buttons is illustrated in Figure 10.4. After mastering this they were returned to the naming task, and now did much better than before, and much better than the remaining children who had continued with the original task.

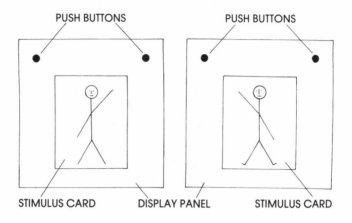

FIGURE 10.4.

The stick figures and arrangement of buttons represent those used in the experiment by Jeffrey. In one phase of the experiment, the children had to press the button the figure pointed at. This helped the children discriminate the names of the figures.

There seems little doubt that the asymmetrical actions, which did not require the ability to tell left from right, served to mediate the naming task, which did. Jeffrey observed that even after the children were told to stop pushing the buttons, they made asymmetrical movements. One child, for instance, lifted a shoulder on the side of the appropriate button before supplying the correct name. Others would look at the button before naming the figure. Clearly, it was easier for the children to discriminate their own movements to left or right than to discriminate the left–right asymmetries that these movements copied. One reason for this could be that asymmetrical actions are more closely linked to the child's internal sense of her own asymmetry than are asymmetrical visual patterns.

Some years later, in 1966, Jeffrey showed how a similar procedure could help four-year-olds learn to discriminate mirror-image obliques. Our group of children had to press a near button for one of the oblique lines and a far button for the other. This task, which is a genuine mirror-image discrimination, proved very difficult. For another group of children, Jeffrey added arrowheads to the bottoms of the oblique lines, and placed the buttons to the left and right of the lines. The children were required to press the button on the side indicated by the arrowhead. This task proved relatively easy, presumably because it does not require any ability to tell left from right. However, training on this task greatly facilitated the children's subsequent ability to apply different verbal labels to mirror-image obliques, as in the task that Rudel and Teuber used in their study. Once again, the training seems to have taught the children to map the left–right distinction between the stimuli onto that between the sides of their own bodies.[15]

Yet another variation on this theme is provided by J. Christopher Clarke and Grover Whitehurst of the State University of New York at Stony Brook.[16] They trained kindergarten children to discriminate the left–right and up–down mirror-image patterns illustrated in Figure 10.5. As one might expect, the left–right patterns proved the more difficult to discriminate. This task proved easier when the children were instructed to touch the patterns on a particular side before labeling them than when they touched the patterns in the center, on both sides, or not at all. Notice that touching the patterns on one side effectively converts the discrimination from a mirror-image discrimination into a simple discrimination between colors. We encountered a similar example in Chapter 3, where the subjects were pigeons, not children.

The same general principle is implicit in a technique advocated by Grace Fernald, a pioneer in the development of remedial techniques for poor readers.[17] Using his preferred hand, the child is taught to trace over letters or words that he finds difficult to discriminate, saying the letter or word as he does so. Suppose that the child is being trained with mirror-image letters such as *b* and *d*. So long as the same hand is always used and tracing begins on the same side of the letters (say, the side opposite the hand used), the tracing would produce different, non-mirror-image sensations of movement (known as kinesthetic sensations) from the mirror-image letters. If some sort of "internalization" of this tracing activity were possible, the child might eventually be able to generate these kinesthetic cues without having to carry out the actual tracing, and so discriminate the letters. The tracing movements would also be ac-

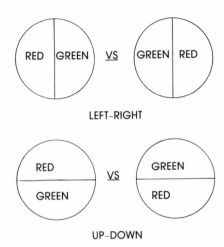

FIGURE 10.5.

These colored patterns were used by Clarke and Whitehurst[20] in their experiment on mirror-image discrimination in children. Notice that if a child touches the left–right mirror-image patterns on the right, say, and looks only at that side, the discrimination is then effectively only a discrimination between red and green.

companied by corresponding eye movements, and these too might eventually be internalized to provide the consistent asymmetry necessary for the child to discriminate the letters.

Even rather general training in asymmetrical body skills may have a specific influence on left–right discriminations. In one study, mentally retarded children were given practice on such skills as catching and throwing a ball with the left hand, or imitating asymmetrical poses such as a boy holding a ball up in his right hand.[18] This proved to have a beneficial effect in the children's ability to make left–right response differentiations to verbal commands. Again, the training may have drawn the children's attention to the relation between their own laterality and that of objects in the environment. It may also have heightened the children's "feeling" for the difference between their own left and right actions. These kinds of activities have often been advocated for children with reading problems,[19] although we know of no experimental tests of its effectiveness with such children.

So far, we have focused on techniques designed to overcome the specific problem of left–right discrimination. Needless to say, there are also many general considerations to keep in mind when teaching any discrimination—the subject should be well motivated, the feedback unambiguous, the rewards for correct discrimination effective, and so on. We need not dwell on these matters here. There is, however, one general technique that has proven particularly effective with difficult discriminations, and that has been used, with mixed success, in teaching mirror-image discriminations. This technique is known as *fading*.

The basic idea is to first teach an easy discrimination, and then alter the stimuli in gradual steps toward the desired end. If the changes are sufficiently smooth, discrimination will be maintained throughout, and pupils will often master a difficult discrimination with virtually no errors. For instance, suppose we wished to teach a child to discriminate between two slightly different tilts of a line, perhaps only two degrees apart. We might begin by making the angle large, and then gradually reducing it, making sure that discrimination is accurate before introducing any change. If discrimination breaks down at any stage, it is possible to back up to an earlier stage and ease the subject more gently toward the desired goal.

Fading procedures can prove treacherous, however, as is illustrated by the unsuccessful attempt of an American psychologist, Sidney Bijou, to teach retarded children to pick out from a set of five patterns the one that matched a sample pattern.[20] The alternatives included the mirror image of the sample as well as the sample itself, and the children showed a high degree of mirror-image confusion. In an attempt to overcome this, Bijou changed the shape of the mirror-image pattern slightly so that it was no longer the exact mirror image of the sample. He then gradually altered its shape back again until the mirror-image relation was exact. Once this final step was achieved, the discrimination always broke down, no matter how finely graded the steps. The same problem occurred in another experiment, attributed to L. T. Stoddard,[21] in which fading was used in an attempt to teach children to pick out a particular oblique line from seven other lines with the mirror-image orientation. The stimuli and the fading sequence are shown in Figure 10.6. Again the discrimination broke down at the final step, when the choice was between pure mirror images.

The problem with these procedures was that, at the beginning of the fading sequence, the children learned to match the stimuli on the basis of differences unrelated to left–right orientation. In Bijou's procedure, the

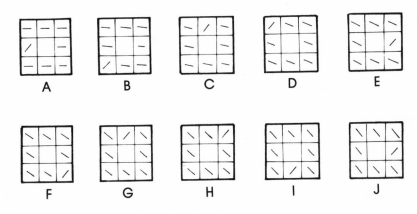

FIGURE 10.6.

A fading sequence like this was used in experiment attributed to Stoddard. The task is to pick out the line that is different from the other seven. The discrimination always broke down at J, when the critical line was the mirror image of the others.

sample was distinguished from the other alternatives by its shape, while in Stoddard's it was distinguished by the *degree* of tilt. These differences disappeared once the final step was reached! Fading procedures will work only if the same *rule* for discriminating the shapes applies at all stages of the fading sequence.

Cheryl Harper of the University of Waikato in New Zealand has successfully incorporated fading procedures into a program to teach retarded children to discriminate left–right mirror images.[22] One such procedure, known as *fading of a prompt,* was used to teach the children to discriminate mirror-image flag-shaped forms. First, the children were taught to point in the direction that each flag pointed in, thus establishing a link between the left–right orientation of the flags and the children's own laterality. The trainer then designated one flag as "right" and the other as "wrong." Over the next series of trials the trainer touched one or the other card and asked, "Which way is the right card pointing?" or "Which way is the wrong card pointing?" depending on which card was touched. Fading was then introduced as the experimenter no longer actually touched the card, but merely pointed to it. Over successive stages the experimenter's finger was gradually withdrawn, until finally she no longer pointed at all. At this stage most children were able to indicate the right or wrong card on request.

Harper also used other fading procedures, with mixed success. One successful procedure, which she called *fading by construction,* involved progressive alteration of the shape of one stimulus towards its final form, while keeping the other form constant. Importantly, the altered feature of the form was that which distinguished it from its mirror image; an example of the series of stimuli in the fading sequence is shown in Figure 10.7. As in the earlier procedure, the children were required to point to the correct card on each trial. Two unsuccessful procedures involved fading out a colored edge added to the asymmetrical feature of one of the pair of forms, and fading out a colored background behind one of the pair. These procedures were probably unsuccessful because they required attention to an irrelevant source of difference between the stimuli, namely color, and the children therefore failed to learn the skills necessary for left–right discrimination.

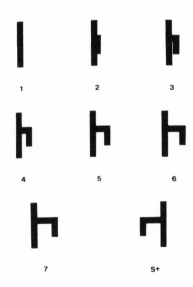

FIGURE 10.7.

Example of a successful fading sequence used by Harper. One stimulus, labeled S+, remained constant, and the other changed from a vertical bar (Step 1) to the mirror image of S+ (Step 7).

Properly constructed fading sequences can be remarkably effective in training difficult discriminations, including those between left–right mirror images. The evidence we have reviewed also suggests that mirror-image discrimination requires attention to the relation between the orientations of the stimuli and the sides of the subject's own body. The skill of discriminating between mirror-image forms therefore involves at least two components: discriminating between one's own left and right sides, and projecting this distinction onto the external forms. Effective remedial procedures should address themselves to both components. Cheryl Harper's fading of a prompt seems to come closest to incorporating all the ingredients for successful training of mirror-image discrimination, and might therefore serve as a useful model for teaching children who are experiencing special difficulty in learning to read.

STRUCTURAL ASYMMETRIES AND GROWTH
OF THE LEFT–RIGHT SENSE

As we have seen, one can usually achieve at least some limited success in teaching young children to tell left from right, but it is generally easier to wait until they are six or seven years of age before attempting to teach the sorts of complex mirror-image discriminations required in, say, learning to read. Up to a point, one can attribute this to the fact that older children are better at learning complex skills in general, although it is by no means universally true that skill in learning increases with advancing age. Witness, for instance, the ease with which young children pick up a foreign language that is often the despair of their parents, or even of their older siblings. There seems little doubt that the ability to learn mirror-image discriminations and the more complex left–right differentiations depends at least in part on the development of structural asymmetries in the nervous system.

We argued earlier that asymmetries are more obvious in those parts of the nervous system concerned with action than in those parts concerned with perception. In evolutionary terms, the advantages of asymmetry over symmetry are to be found in manipulations of the environment rather than in reactions to it. As in evolution, so in development—or, to appeal to the biological adage, ontogeny recapitulates phylogeny. We should therefore not be surprised to see that simple left–right response differentiations emerge first in the repertoire of left–right skills, and that response asymmetries play a general role in the learning of mirror-image discriminations.

The most obvious response asymmetry is handedness. In Chapter 6 we cited the evidence of Gesell and Ames that handedness develops gradually over the first years of life and may not be stable until the child is about eight years of age. The development of left–right discriminations is roughly parallel to the development of handedness. The child learns the sides of his or her own body at about six years and gradually learns more complex discriminations over the next four years or so. We suggested earlier that the introduction of reading and writing in schools might have a decisive influence in the development of left–right skills, but that influence might also be at least partially reversed; that is, the practice of introducing reading and writing at around six years of age might be in part a response to the child's developing laterality. We cited the conviction of Gesell and Ames that handedness is a matter of growth, not of training. Since handedness plays an obvious role in development of the ability to tell left from right, we are forced to the conclusion that this ability is also at least partly dependent upon maturation.

The role of handedness has already been apparent in the training procedures we have reviewed—in Fernald's tracing technique, in Harper's fading of a prompt. Indeed, handedness seems the *only* cue by which a child could distinguish left from right. It is quite common for children to go through the motions of writing in order to determine which is the right hand. English-speaking children are no doubt aided in this by the happy coincidence that *write* and *right* are homophones. In Roman Catholic cultures, children often briefly make the sign of the cross before deciding which hand is which, as we have already noted. Arthur Benton of the University of Iowa has shown that accuracy in left–right discrimination is higher the more extreme the preference for one or other hand. He has also observed that children with one-sided disabilities are relatively good at telling left from right, while otherwise normal adults who profess to experience frequent left–right confusions tend to be ambidextrous.[23]

Some authorities have suggested that eye dominance might be critical in the development of left–right discriminations involved in reading, but we do not think this likely. The dominance of one or other eye is by no means as obvious or consistent as is the preference for one or other hand. Even adults are often not sure, until tested, which is their dominant eye. We therefore think it unlikely that eye dominance is sufficiently salient to serve as a cue for telling left from right. However, eye dominance might conceivably play an indirect role in the development of directional eye movements, which *are* critical in learning to read, and which might well facilitate the discrimination of mirror-image letters or words, at least in the case of scripts that are written laterally in a consistent direction.

We have stressed the role of handedness and of motor asymmetries in the development of the ability to tell left from right. Eventually, however, asymmetries related to movement would give rise to sensory asymmetries; that is, the two hands or sides of the body *feel* different, and we may become aware of a perceptual gradient between the left and right sides of the visual field. Stage entrances, for instance, are more dramatic from the left than from the right, and paintings often lose their impact if viewed in a mirror. Arthur Benton suggests that the sensory component, or what he calls the ''left–right sense,'' emerges during the fifth and sixth years of life.[24]

We doubt that the asymmetries of the internal organs contribute significantly to the left–right sense. Nevertheless, we may draw attention here to a mnemonic used by actors on the French stage. One side of the stage traditionally leads off to the *cour,* or courtyard, while the other leads to the *jardin,* or garden. From the viewpoint of the actor the *cour* is on the left, and his mnemonic for this is that the word ''cour'' resembles *coeur* which is French for ''heart.'' Should he become confused as to which is which, then, he may perhaps be reminded by the anxious beating of his heart.

Finally it is possible, even likely, that the left–right sense depends to some extent on the development of cerebral lateralization. As we saw in Chapter 8, lateralization can be detected in electrophysiological measurements in early infancy and in anatomical measurements even before birth. Evidence on the development of psychological manifestations of lateralization is conflicting. Several studies carried out in the late 1960s and early 1970s suggested that the right-ear advantage in reporting dichotically presented words emerges somewhere between four and seven years,[25] and this again corresponds reasonably well with the age at which children begin to learn to read and write and to become proficient in left–right skills. In another study, it was found that the right-field advantage in recognition of printed words was present in fourth-graders, but not in second graders.[26] However, we also cited evidence in Chapter 8 that the right-ear advantage in dichotic listening can be detected in three-year-olds,[27] and, according to one controversial study, in infants aged three weeks to three months.[28] Gina Geffen of the Flinders University in Australia has carried out several studies suggesting that the right-ear advantage in dichotic listening remains constant at least from the age of five years, although the ability to focus attention on one or other ear may improve with age.[29]

We suspect that cerebral lateralization does show progressive changes with age, perhaps up to the age of puberty, and the different cognitive skills become lateralized at different ages. For instance, M. Philip Bryden and Frances Allard of the University of Waterloo have argued that the perception of elementary speech sounds, or phonemes, is the last of the auditory verbal skills to lateralize, and that this lateralization is not complete until the age of about eleven years.[30] Carol Tomlinson–Keasey and her colleagues at the University of Nebraska, Lincoln, have also suggested that lateralization of the left cerebral hemisphere is not complete until adolescence and that the processing of written materials lateralizes later than the processing of spoken materials.[31] The idea that lateralization develops up until the age of puberty has also been advanced to explain why men show a higher degree of cerebral lateralization than do women, since girls reach puberty earlier on average than boys do.[32]

In Chapter 8, we reviewed evidence that the two sides of the brain are equipotential with respect to the representation of language early in life; that is, language is normally represented primarily in the left cerebral hemisphere, but the right hemisphere can take over if the left is incapacitated. Equipotentiality gradually decreases until the age of puberty. To explain these facts, and to reconcile them with the fact that left-cerebral dominance can be detected at or before birth, we suggested that the left hemisphere normally develops ahead of the right, and so gains prior access to language functions. This theory implies a gradual build up of the lateralized representation of verbal skills in the left hemisphere until puberty. Again this conforms remarkably well to the evidence that left–right skills also develop progressively over the first ten or so years of life.

We shall have more to say about the relation between left–right skills and cerebral lateralization in the following chapter. Our concern there is not with the developmental aspect, but rather with the proposition that people who lack consistent lateralization may be more than usually prone to reading disability, perhaps because they suffer left–right confusions.

CONCLUSIONS

If one fact emerges strongly from this chapter, it is that the child of five or six years is at a critical stage in the development of left–right skills. That is also the stage at which handedness begins to stabilize, and cerebral lateralization becomes sufficiently pronounced to be measurable by routine tests of dichotic listening. At that age, too, the child starts school, and begins in earnest to learn to read and write. Both verbal and left–right skills continue to develop progressively until the child reaches early adolescence.

It is notoriously difficult in the study of child development to disentangle the causes from the effects. One could argue that the spurt in left–right skills and in manifestations of laterality is a direct result of the child's exposure to school. Certainly, a child will not learn to tell left from right unless taught to do so, and learning to read and write includes the learning of left–right skills, implicitly if not explicitly. We suspect though that children are not really ready to learn left–right skills until they are about five or six years of age, and that this is one of the reasons why formal schooling is normally begun at that age. The growth of physical asymmetries sets limits on the development of a left–right sense, but does not rigidly determine it.

Educational influences, we think, are of two basic kinds. First, there are influences that help develop the child's own laterality. These include the teaching of unimanual skills, like throwing or writing, instruction in reading, and perhaps generalized exposure to verbal culture which facilitates the development of left-hemispheric specialization for language. To be effective, these influences depend on some degree of asymmetry in physical maturation. Secondly, and perhaps more importantly, the child must be taught to exploit her own left–right sense, and to map it onto the objects and symbols of the world about her.

One reason that we have stressed the importance of physical maturation is that certain individuals do not appear to be consistently lateralized, and there is some evidence that these individuals do not develop a strong left–right sense and may consequently experience some difficulty in reading and writing. We have already suggested that this lack of lateralization may be inherited. In the following chapters we consider some of the pathological implications of incomplete lateralization, including its possible role in reading disability and stuttering.

PART THREE

The Psychopathology of Left and Right

When thou doest alms, let not thy left hand know what thy right hand doeth.

[Matt. 6:3–4]

Chapter 11

Dyslexia

It's with blood that letters enter.
[Cervantes, *Don Quixote*]

One theme that has already emerged from our discussions of handedness and cerebral asymmetry is that some people lack consistent lateralization. They may be ambidextrous, or show mixed patterns of handedness, footedness, and eye dominance, or have speech represented in both hemispheres of the brain. Left handedness does not appear to be an entity in its own right (as it were) but is part of this more general pattern of inconsistent lateralization. Left handers show mixed patterns of asymmetry on all other manifestations of laterality, such as the representation of speech, eye dominance, footedness, anatomical asymmetries of the brain, and so forth. Following Marian Annett, we argued that the lack of a consistent lateralizing influence may be inherited, perhaps according to simple Mendelian principles. In some cases, however, departures from the usual pattern of right handedness and left-cerebral representation of speech may be caused by injury or pathology, including lack of oxygen at birth.

Whether inherited or pathological, departures from the usual pattern of lateralization may cause problems. Some of these problems are purely mechanical, as when the left hander fumbles with right-handed scissors, or when the budding marksman with opposite handedness and eye dominance tries to aim a rifle. Some are social, as when societies vilify the left handers as awkward, unclean, or possessed by evil spirits. Yet, as we have seen, left handers have persisted in approximately the same proportion throughout recorded history, sustained partly perhaps by the value of surprise that is conferred upon them in such activities as primitive warfare and its modern equivalents in sport. Moreover, if ambidexterity rather than left handedness is the true expression of the inherited lack of lateralization, we do not have to look far to find activities in which it is an advantage to be ambidextrous rather than strongly single handed.

With the surge of interest in cerebral asymmetry, it has become fashionable to attribute oddities of deportment or personality to anomalies of cerebral lateralization rather than of handedness. Again, lack of lateralization appears to be a mixed blessing. On the positive side, the individual with speech represented on both sides of the brain is unlikely to suffer long-term impairment of speech following one-sided damage to the brain, while the person with speech represented unilaterally may well suffer permanent disruption of speech if the damage is on the critical side. We have already noted that left handers, who are more likely to have bilateral representation of speech than are right handers, may have slightly superior ability in mental rotation, memory for pitch, and in the association of verbal with nonverbal symbols—a useful aptitude, perhaps, in fields like architecture. It may also be the case that individuals without consistent lateralization are genetically less well buffered against environmental variations than are those with strong lateralization and thus show a more varied range and style of cognitive abilities. Here we think of such varied geniuses as Leonardo da Vinci, Harpo Marx, and Charlie Chaplin—all left handers.

On the debit side, those lacking cerebral lateralization may be especially susceptible to psychological problems. In trying to identify these problems we must tread warily, however. The very fashionability of ideas about cerebral lateralization has led to exaggerated and uncritical claims about its role in psychological phenomena of all kinds. As we have already seen, where psychological ills were once attributed to witches or spells or phases of the moon, they may now be blamed on atypical lateralization. In addition, it is often difficult to tell whether a problem arises directly from anomalies of lateralization or whether it is an indirect consequence of social or interpersonal pressures. For instance, throughout the ages left handers have been victims of ridicule and abuse, and this, rather than their left handedness, may partially at least explain why they are overrepresented in almost every pathological group, including schizophrenics, epileptics, hyperactive children, and disabled learners, not to mention the male sex generally. Of course, atypical lateralization may itself result from injury or pathology, so it is not always clear which is the cause and which the effect.

In this and the following chapter we shall concentrate mainly on two pathological conditions that may be linked in different ways to weak or inconsistent lateralization: specific reading disability (or dyslexia) and stuttering. In neither case is the argument immune to the difficulties of interpretation that we have just raised. On the other hand, both relate to themes that have already been featured in this book, so there is a reasonable *a priori* case for supposing that lateralization, or the lack of it, may be implicated. In particular, we shall suggest that left–right confusion arising from the lack of cerebral lateralization may sometimes be at the root of dyslexia, and that stuttering may often occur because of a failure of one or other side of the brain to assert dominance clearly in the control of vocalization. These particular themes are by no means merely recent speculation, flotsam on the tide of the latest fashion to attribute nearly everything to anomalies of cerebral lateralization, but go back some fifty or sixty years. In particular, both themes were energetically pursued by an American pioneer of research into children's problems with reading, writing, and speech, Samuel Torrey Orton (1879–1948).[1] Orton's ideas were widely accepted in the 1920s and 1930s, challenged and to some extent forgotten after the Second World War, and revived to some degree, although in modified form, in recent years.

We shall not claim that the lack of cerebral lateralization invariably causes dyslexia or stuttering, neither shall we contend that these disabilities are always due to lack of lateralization. Our claim is simply that these conditions may occur more frequently among those lacking consistent lateralization than among those with the usual left–cerebral dominance for language. Those inheriting the lack of any predisposition toward lateralization might in fact show quite varied and even marked patterns of laterality. In such an instance, only a small proportion would therefore be susceptible to disability. Because of the element of chance, therefore, we do not expect high correlations between these disabilities and indices of lateralization, neither do we expect strong evidence for inheritance of dyslexia or of stuttering. A theory that begins with the expectation of only weak correlations might itself be justly accused of weakness and yet both disabilities have evaded any other simple explanation. Any theory that purports to shed at least some light on them is surely better than no theory at all.

SPECIFIC READING DISABILITY: AN OVERVIEW

I struggled through the alphabet as if it had been a bramble-bush, getting considerably worried and scratched by every letter. After that, I fell among those thieves, the nine figures, who seemed every evening to do something new to disguise themselves and baffle recognition. But at last I began, in a purblind groping way, to read, write, and cipher, on the very smallest scale.

Thus were the reminiscences of Pip, the hero of Charles Dickens's *Great Expectations.* Although Pip does not seem to have been dyslexic, his vivid description of his early encounter with script may give some insight into the predicament of the disabled reader.

Reading is an extremely complex skill, involving spatial perception, oral comprehension of spoken language, memory, and fine motor control. There may be many different reasons, then, why a child may fail to learn to read properly. One authority, Alex Bannatyne, suggests that these may range from slight defects in the central nervous system to equally slight impediments in hearing, from deficiencies in decoding visual patterns to difficulties in remembering the associations between spoken sounds and written symbols.[2] Some children, he observes, simply lack the motivation to learn to read. Although our concern in this chapter is with the role of left–right confusions and the lack of cerebral lateralization, we emphasize again that these are not the only influences underlying reading difficulties.

The specific term *dyslexia* is now quite widely used to refer to reading and spelling disabilities relatively free from association with other disturbances such as mental retardation, sensory deficits, impairment of speech, or emotional problems. Sometimes a further distinction is drawn between developmental dyslexia (implying a developmental and maturational anomaly) and acquired dyslexia (implying brain damage). Despite their different origins, however, these two forms of dyslexia may not be easy to distinguish on the basis of symptoms.[3] Estimates of the incidence of dyslexia vary widely, owing largely to the lack of agreed criteria as to the degree of impairment that distinguishes the dyslexic from the child who is merely a slow reader. For example, a study of Edinburgh children showed that 9.1 percent of children between seven and a half and ten and a half years of age had reading quotients of less than 85 percent of their intelligence quotients. The majority of these were one and a half to two years behind their expected reading age.[4] Of over 2,000 children studied in the Isle of Wight, almost 4 percent were two or more years retarded in reading skills.[5] In Dunbartonshire, 15 percent were still without independent reading skills after two years of instruction.[6] In the United States, one study reported variation in the percentage retarded by more than two years between 3 percent in suburban schools and 28 percent in metropolitan schools.[7]

These figures notwithstanding, effective remedial measures have been hampered by arguments about the existence of specific dyslexia as a clinical entity and the status of evidence as to cause. Educators in particular have been reluctant to accept the usefulness of the term dyslexia on the grounds that it may lead to indiscriminate prejudgment of the cause of reading retardation and hence may serve as a mere label for parents and teachers to latch onto as an excuse for poor attainment. The pros and cons of this controversy have been nicely discussed elsewhere.[8]

Some definitions of dyslexia suggest that it applies only to children of at least normal intelligence, although there seems no reason for supposing that other children might not suffer from it. In fact, the literature often depicts the dyslexic as one who in all other respects may be highly talented. Perhaps this is because the affliction is more noticeable among otherwise gifted people. The English neurologist MacDonald Critchley[9] remarked that the reading faults exhibited by the dyslexic "are unlike those met in the case of a dullard, or a poorly educated person." Another investigator has chronicled the case histories of several exceptional men who may have been dyslexic, among them the inventor Thomas A. Edison, the surgeon Harvey Cushing, the sculptor Auguste Rodin, and President Woodrow Wilson.[10] On somewhat surer grounds, it has been said that Hans Christian Andersen was dyslexic.[11] Although dyslexic women are relatively rare, they are currently represented by at least one well known member of their sex, the actress Susan Hampshire.

It is doubtful whether dyslexia is ever quite so circumscribed as this idealized characterization would suggest. On the contrary, the diversity of symptoms has led a number of investigators to try to distinguish subgroups of dyslexics on the basis of clusters of symptoms. Sandhya Naidoo, formerly of the Word Blind Centre for Dyslexic Children in

London, has described three types, each with a characteristic grouping of signs.[12] One is characterized by delays and disorders in the development of speech and language, another by disorders of the visual perception of space and by clumsiness, and the third involves both sets of symptoms.

It has been suggested that dyslexia might be specific, not to reading generally, but to the reading of specific languages, notably those of Western culture. There is evidence for instance that reading problems are comparatively rare among Japanese children.[13] In Japan, children are usually taught two different scripts—first, the *Kana*, in which the symbols correspond more or less to syllables and are combined to form words, and later the *Kanji* script, in which the symbols are based on Chinese ideographs and stand for whole words. In neither case is there any confusion created by reversing a symbol, since no two symbols are mirror images of one another. There can be no mirror-image confusion in *reading* the symbols. Although children may often reverse a symbol in *writing*, the error is regarded as relatively unimportant and is usually short-lived. It is also relevant to note that Japanese is traditionally written in vertical columns and read from top to bottom, although the left-to-right arrangement is also used, borrowed from Western culture. It is therefore reasonable to conclude that any child suffering acute left–right confusion would have less difficulty learning to read Japanese than learning to read English.

Yet this is surely not the only possible reason why reading disability is less common among Japanese than among Western children. One study has shown that slum children in Philadelphia who were unable to learn to read English script could nonetheless be readily taught to read English represented by Chinese characters, and even write their own stories in Chinese script.[14] The characters were presented left to right as in English, so it is unlikely that the original difficulty with English had much to do with poor left-to-right scanning. The investigators admitted that the very novelty of the approach may have overcome a poor motivation to read among these children, but they suggested that the main reason for their success lay in the level at which the language was represented by the symbols. English script is difficult to learn to read because the elements represented by the letters are phonemes, the smallest meaningful units of speech, and are in many cases unpronounceable by themselves. For instance, one cannot pronounce a consonant like *d* or *k* in the absence of a vowel either following or preceding it. By contrast, scripts in which the symbols correspond to syllables, as in Kana, or to words, as in Kanji or Chinese script, are easier to learn because each symbol can be pronounced. It is therefore easier for a child to grasp the nature of Japanese symbols than of Western symbols.

Finally, there is evidence that dyslexia runs in families, suggesting that it may be genetically inherited. For instance, Richard Masland of Columbia University recently reported to the Orton Society, established in 1949 to further the work pioneered by Orton, on a study of the families of twenty dyslexic children. He claimed that 45 percent of the first-degree relatives of these children were also dyslexic.[15] We shall encounter further evidence for the inheritance of at least some kinds of dyslexia in the studies discussed below.

ORTON'S THEORY

Before we turn to experimental studies, we shall examine Orton's theories about the role of left–right confusions and cerebral lateralization in reading disability. In his extensive clinical experience with children suffering from problems of reading and writing, Orton was struck by the frequency with which these children wrote backwards, in mirror writing, or confused letters or words (like *was* and *saw*) that were mirror images or near mirror images. Orton also observed that children with these difficulties often appeared to lack a consistent cerebral dominance or that they came from families in which there was some incidence or history of mixed laterality. He concluded that mirror-image confusion was a result both of the symmetry of the two hemispheres of the brain and the failure of one side of the brain to dominate the other.

Orton supposed that the symmetrical arrangement of the hemispheres would necessarily result in the two halves recording events with opposite left–right orientations. As he put it:

> The exact symmetrical relationship of the two hemispheres would lead us to believe that the group of cells irradiated by any visual stimulus in the right hemisphere are the exact mirrored counterpart of those in the left.[16]

He argued from this that the dominant hemisphere normally recorded events in the correct orientation while the nondominant hemisphere recorded them in the reverse orientation. The physical arrangement of the word CAT, for example, would be correctly recorded in the dominant hemisphere, but would be recorded as though it were TAO in the nondominant hemisphere, as illustrated in Figure 11.1. If a child failed to

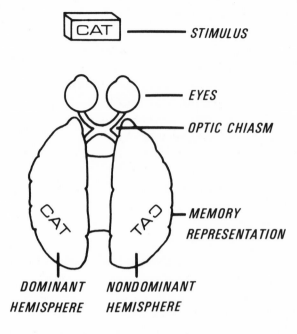

FIGURE 11.1.

This schematic drawing illustrates Orton's theory that a particular pattern, such as the word CAT, would be represented in correct orientation in one side of the brain, but as though left–right reversed in the other (after Orton, 1925).

learn to suppress the activity of the nondominant hemisphere, the reversed record would intrude to create left–right confusion. Orton coined the term *strephosymbolia,* meaning "twisted symbols," to describe this condition.

Although this theory bears a resemblance to the one we developed in Chapter 4, it is muddled and wrong. There is actually no reason at all to infer from the symmetry of the brain that one half would record patterns correctly while the other half would record them as though they were left–right reversed. One might as well argue that a camera that was left–right reversed would produce mirror-imaged photographs, or that a person's writing would be normally oriented on a left-hand page but magically reversed on a right-hand page. In fact there is every reason to believe that each half of the brain records information correctly. In Chapter 4, we suggested that memory traces might be left–right reversed in *transfer* from one side of the brain to the other, but this is a different proposition altogether.

It may have been partly because of this irrational quality that Orton's theory gradually lost favor. Although we know of no authors (besides ourselves!) who have stated explicitly what was wrong with the theory, several seem to have sensed that something was the matter. In 1960, for instance, Oliver Zangwill wrote of Orton that:

> . . . he linked his observations with a decidedly speculative theory of brain function which few have had the temerity to accept. For these and other reasons, Orton's work has fallen into disrepute, especially among educational psychologists. None the less, Orton deserves great credit for being the first to study these problems in a systematic way and to envisage them within the framework of genetic neurology.[17]

Moreover Orton was not wrong in all of his ideas. Even if the detail of the theory is irrational, it is still reasonable to attribute left–right confusions to the bilateral symmetry of the brain, a point we have been at pains to make in the early chapters of this book. Conversely, one might plausibly link the ability to tell left from right, and therefore to discriminate left–right mirror images, to the emergence of cerebral asymmetry, as we suggested in the previous chapter. Finally, Orton was clear that the problem was one of memory, not of perception,[18] even though his neurological theory makes no provision for the distinction. That is, Orton recognized that a child who is prone to left–right confusions does not actually *see* letters or words as though left–right reversed, but simply has difficulty remembering which way round they are supposed to be.

EVIDENCE OF LEFT–RIGHT CONFUSIONS

Although much of the evidence Orton cited was anecdotal, based simply on observations of individual patients, he also referred to evidence of a more experimental nature.

> That the mirror-image reversals play a significant role in strephosymbolia is adequately supported by our earlier studies in Iowa. The errors made by a group of reading disability cases were tabulated and compared with those made by a carefully selected control group of normal readers of the same grade and intelligence, and the errors of reversal were found to be significant statistically for the reading disability cases at each of the four reading grades that were studied. Not only was this so, but the frequency with which errors by reversal appeared in the work of a given case proved to correlate with the amount of his retardation in reading, that is, with the severity of his disorder.[19]

Several other studies have similarly shown that poor readers make more left–right reversals of letters and words than do normal readers, although poor readers also make more errors of other kinds.[20]

Not all investigators have found left–right confusion to be a conspicuous characteristic of poor readers. In one study of 429 second graders in Reno, only ten children showed left–right confusions along with severe reading problems, but these were among the forty-three considered by their teachers to be the poorest readers.[21] Other evidence reinforces the idea that left–right reversals occur most frequently among the most severe cases and are more likely to be observed in children referred to clinics for remedial reading than in poor readers picked from the classroom.[22] Two recent studies have shown that poor discrimination of mirror images is specific to left–right mirror images, and does not apply to up–down mirror images.[23]

Poor readers also seem to be especially prone to spontaneous reversals. For example, they are more likely than normal readers to make left–right errors in reproducing pictures from memory[24] or reconstructing matchstick figures.[25] Boys who read normal printing poorly do *better* than normal readers when the printing is mirror-reversed,[26] and may also be better at mirror writing.[27]

Left–right confusion may also be inferred from the tendency of some dyslexics to make regressive eye movements during reading. Alex Bannatyne has suggested that dyslexics are less able than average readers to inhibit a natural tendency to scan the environment in either direction. He mentions evidence that in normal readers the ability to scan to the right increases with age after the commencement of reading instructions, accompanied by a decrease in regular movements and fixations during a scan. Most dyslexics showed poorly lateralized scanning in either direction with more short pauses and general oculomotor instability, although there are some exceptions.[28]

In his monograph of 1960, Oliver Zangwill examined a group of twenty dyslexic patients and noted that thirteen of them showed some manifestation of left–right confusion, either in the form of letter reversals, right-to-left scanning, or confusion over the left and right sides of the body.[29] If left–right confusion is characteristic of at least one subgroup of dyslexics, then a subject later described by Zangwill and his colleague C. Blakemore may be as close to a typical case as one is likely to find. Indeed this person fits rather well into the idealized picture of the dyslexic as in other respects rather gifted.

The subject, D.A., was a 23 year old postgraduate student who had always regarded himself as an exceptionally slow reader and writer as well as a poor speller. He had achieved a bachelor's degree in biology largely on the basis of good intelligence combined with an excellent memory for lectures and demonstrations, and confessed that he had done very little reading in the course of his undergraduate career. He was right-handed for writing, tennis and throwing, but a left-handed batsman [in cricket]. He was left-footed and left-eye dominant, and had always found exceptional difficulty in distinguishing left from right. His mother and maternal first cousin were likewise partly left handed.[30]

What a splendid example, conforming in every respect to our own (and Orton's) theoretical conceptions! He exhibits left–right confusion and reading disability, and appears to belong to that subgroup of people who inherit no disposition to be lateralized. We cannot but wish him success in his academic career.

Closer analysis of D.A.'s reading disability revealed that it was due primarily to an inability to scan from left to right. Recordings of his eye movements showed an excessive number of regressive movements when he would look back at words he had already read. Oddly enough, he seemed to be able to scan from right to left more rapidly than from left to right, although his ability to read mirror writing was not tested. His problem was evidently a failure to learn an asymmetric habit rather than a simple motor disability, since his saccadic eye movements to flashing lights were normal. He seemed to have no difficulty identifying individual letters, digits, or even words exposed very briefly, for 40 milliseconds or less, although his ability to spell was appalling.

The role of eye movements in left–right confusion is often misunderstood. In his 1946 monograph, *The Master Hand,* Abram Blau recognized the importance of left-to-right eye movements in the discrimination of mirror-image words and letters, but maintained that if a letter is scanned from right to left it is actually *seen* as though mirror reversed.[31] This is surely wrong. The orientations of patterns or objects in the world appear stable no matter how we move our eyes over them. Besides, as we have already pointed out, left–right confusion is a confusion of labeling, not a confusion of perception itself. Eye movements are important in determining the *order* in which we extract information from the printed page, or from the world about us, and a consistent left-to-right scan may serve as a *mnemonic* for helping a child distinguish a *b* from a *d,* but it does not alter the way in which a person perceives orientation.

We have often heard it said that a dyslexic child "sees things backwards." That is wrong. Many dyslexic children have extremely accurate perception and excel in skills or sports that require good hand–eye coordination. What is unique about reading as a visual skill is the directional component, and this component is merely a matter of convention, critical in the interpretation but not the perception of the orientation of letters and words. For most if not all other visual skills, it may be something of an advantage to be able to scan with equal facility in either direction. The reluctance or inability of the dyslexic child to learn a particular directional habit may be an expression of the evolutionary advantage that is conferred by symmetry for the perception of the everyday natural environment.

In summary, there is considerable evidence that children with reading disability have special difficulty forming the asymmetrical habits required by reading. Of course nearly all children make left–right confusions when learning to read, and perhaps experience some difficulty in learning to scan the printed page from left to right. As MacDonald Critchley observed, "the dyslexic individual is not unique in making reversals and translocations, but he is conspicuous in making so many of them and for so long at a time."[32]

LATERALITY IN DYSLEXICS

Early studies on laterality in dyslexics were concerned with handedness or eyedness rather than with cerebral lateralization. This was inevitably so because no simple ways of directly measuring cerebral dominance had been developed. Even so, Orton claimed that 69 of his 102 cases were of opposite handedness and eye dominance and that many were also ambidextrous or came from families with some history of mixed or left handedness.[33] Among the 20 cases studied by Zangwill, only 8 were described as "fully right handed," the rest showing at least some degree of left handedness. Ten of the cases came from families with one or more members who were not right handed.[34] Many other studies have reported similar associations between dyslexia and either mixed handedness[35] or left handedness.[36] The incidence of left handedness may be taken as evidence for the role of incomplete cerebral lateralization on the grounds that left handers exhibit less pronounced lateralization than do right handers (see Chapter 8).

On the other hand there are also a number of studies showing no relation between dyslexia and left handedness or ambilaterality.[37] The apparent conflict between these studies is no doubt due in part to variation and inadequacy in the measurement of handedness, but another contributing factor is surely the failure of some studies, large-scale surveys in particular, to differentiate between degrees of severity among the dyslexic subjects. As seems to be the case with left–right confusion, weak laterality seems characteristic of only a subgroup of poor readers, often those with the most marked disability.[38]

The high proportion of familial left handedness among dyslexics has received special attention in yet another recent article by Oliver Zangwill[39] in which he records the family pedigrees of two dyslexic patients. One child was predominantly left handed, the other somewhat ambidextrous though predominantly right handed. Both family trees included many relatives with reading or spelling problems and either left handedness or ambidexterity extending back three generations. This association between dyslexia and familial left handedness or ambidexterity has also been reported in a few other case histories, but has been overlooked in most studies of larger populations, save in one study of ninety-eight dyslexic boys reported by Sandhya Naidoo.[40] Not only were there significantly more left handed and ambidextrous children among the worst fifty-six readers than among the remaining forty-two, but an analysis based on clusters of symptoms revealed two subgroups in which there were familial reading and spelling difficulties associated with left handedness.

In a recent review, Martha Bridge Denckla of the Harvard Medical School has argued that what she terms "visual-perceptual factors," which we take to include left–right confusions and reversals, are relatively unimportant in dyslexia.[41] Even among the minority who display these symptoms, she claims, the perceptual problems are usually transient and tend to be dominated by more general difficulties with language, including problems with articulation, naming, and the sequencing of words or syllables. Yet Denckla also reports data on the laterality of children referred to her clinic that are rather strikingly similar to those described by Orton in the 1930s, data which she has "tried in vain to escape." Nearly two-thirds of the children are right handed, right footed, and *left* eye-dominant, while many of the others also show departures from the usual right-sided preferences. Denckla lays stress on the high frequency of left eyedness, and suggests that this may favor right-to-left scanning, thus interfering with the reading of English and other left-to-right scripts. She also asserts that left eyedness is strongly associated with familial left handedness—that is, the majority of left-eyed children have at least one first-degree relative who is left handed. These observations lend further support to the association between dyslexia and the inherited lack of consistent lateralization.

Denckla's argument that left eyedness may favour right-to-left eye movements does not seem entirely rational, since it would imply that reading disability in Israel, say, should be associated with right eyedness, and indeed that there should be an unusually high incidence of reading disability among those who read Hebrew or other right-to-left scripts. We know of no evidence to support these predictions. Yet reports of left eyedness and a preference for reversed scanning among dyslexics are remarkably common. We suspect that left eyedness may only cause problems when it is associated with right handedness. This particular combination implies that the left cerebral hemisphere is dominant in control of the hands, while the right cerebral hemisphere is dominant in control of the eyes. Consequently, if a child learns a directional habit with the right hand, say in learning to write or to track the words in reading, there might be a tendency, through interhemispheric left–right reversal, for this habit to be reversed when it is transferred to eye movements. In fact, a group of Australian psychologists found a remarkably high incidence of what they called *crossed control* in children with reading disability. In crossed control, the side of the controlling eye in central binocular vision is opposite the preferred hand.[42] Our account of the role of eye dominance is admittedly speculative, however, and the more cautious conclusion to be drawn from Denckla's data is that problems in learning to scan in a particular direction are due simply to weak or inconsistent laterality, and that opposite handedness and eyedness is just one manifestation of this.

In recent years, influenced by technological advances, investigators have focused on direct measures of cerebral lateralization rather than on handedness or eyedness. Several studies have shown that poor readers, unlike their more literate peers, do not exhibit the usual right–field advantage in identifying briefly flashed words, implying a deficit in cerebral asymmetry for verbal processing—although not all investigators have observed this effect.[43] Similarly, Paul Satz of the University of Florida has reviewed 13 studies of differences between the ears in dichotic listening, and found at least some evidence for reduced lateralization among poor as compared to normal readers.[44] He also observed that this was more generally true of younger than of older children with reading problems, suggesting that some children may be victims of a lag in the development of cerebral asymmetry. In one study of boys aged five and a half, seven, and twelve years, for instance, the right-ear advantage for processing words increased with age, but the increase for disabled readers lagged behind that for normal readers, and was still not fully developed in the twelve-year-old disabled readers.[45] If cerebral asymmetry does not develop beyond puberty, as some have suggested, some children may never become fully lateralized and reading problems may persist.

Many of these studies were carried out on groups of children drawn from normal classrooms, and there may therefore have been few genuine dyslexics among them. Moreover, many investigators were not especially concerned to separate those with specific reading problems from those with more generalized linguistic deficiencies. The role of weak or inconsistent lateralization may therefore be ambiguous—it may well predispose a child to left–right confusions or regressive eye movements, or it may reflect a deficit in the specialized functions of the left cerebral hemisphere. Indeed, in one recent study, poor readers were shown to be deficient in the processing of verbal *acoustic* information.[46] Clearly, these children were not dyslexic in the strict sense of the word, but it may well be the case that the majority of children suffering from reading problems are actually victims of a more general retardation in language. In fact, reading may be a particularly sensitive indicator of linguistic problems generally.

Some authors have stressed particular patterns of anomalous cerebral lateralization rather than a global lack of asymmetry. For example, Tony Marcel, now at the Medical Research Council's Applied Psychology Unit in Cambridge, England, together with Paul Rajan, compared good and poor readers aged from seven to nine years on two tests of lateralization.[47] The poor readers showed a lesser degree of right visual-field superiority than the good readers in identifying briefly flashed words, but the two groups showed equal *left* visual-field superiority in the perception of faces. Marcel and Rajan concluded that reading disability was related to deficiencies in left-hemispheric specialization, but that right-hemispheric specialization was normal in retarded readers. Ironically, Sandra Witelson of McMaster University reported essentially the converse pattern of results in a group of reading-impaired boys aged from six to fourteen years, but paradoxically she drew more or less the same conclusions![48] The poor readers showed the same right-ear advantage in dichotic listening as the good readers, but unlike the good readers, they failed to show evidence for right-hemispheric specialization in the recognition of nonsense shapes presented simultaneously to each hand (*dichaptic* presentation) or in the identification of human figures flashed to one or other visual field. Witelson noted that the poor readers performed badly on the dichotic-listening test despite the right-ear advantage and concluded that they were deficient in left-hemispheric skills. To compensate, she suggested, poor readers try to adopt inappropriate, holistic, "right-hemispheric" strategies in reading. Such children, she quaintly proposed, have "two right hemispheres and none left."

The idea that the disabled reader is fundamentally a right-hemispheric, holistic perceiver has a certain popular currency.[49] This is no doubt derived in part from the fashionable notion that the left hemisphere is an analytic, sequential processor, while the right hemisphere is holistic, spatial, and intuitive. We have already argued in Chapter 8 that this characterization is too simplistic, and that there is little evidence to support the view that individuals can be classified into left-hemispheric and right-hemispheric "types." Yet, up to a point we can accept the view that dyslexics may lack the ability to scan visual displays in a systematic, sequential manner, perhaps because they have difficulty forming consistent directional scanning habits. Again, in a restricted sense, the reader who is prone to left–right confusions (or left–right equivalence) might be regarded as a more holistic perceiver than one who is not. However we do not think that these difficulties reflect a right-hemispheric mode of processing so much as a *lack* of hemispheric asymmetry.

The evidence we have reviewed so far is reasonably consistent in showing that disabled readers very often show atypical patterns of laterality, although there seems relatively little consistency in the precise nature of these patterns. No doubt some of the discrepancies between studies are due to different definitions or criteria of reading disability, different ages at which children are examined, different ways of testing laterality, and so forth. But there is perhaps another source of variability. Our main premise was that those inheriting the lack of consistent lateralization might be more than usually prone to reading disability. However, a characteristic of those lacking a biological predisposition to asymmetry is that actual manifestations of asymmetry are likely to be extremely variable, giving rise to a wide variety of possible effects, some positive, some negative. One of the characteristics of left handers, for instance, is simply the large variety of different patterns of asymmetry they manifest—even visual and auditory measures of cerebral lateralization fail to show any correlation, whereas they are clearly correlated in right handers.[50] In the person lacking the predisposition to asymmetry, different manifestations of laterality are at the mercy of random influences and occur in chance combinations. Only a small proportion might reveal that particular anomaly or cluster of anomalies that lead to left–right confusions and problems with the spatial component of reading. A somewhat higher proportion might fail to develop properly lateralized representation of language and suffer reading problems as part of a more generalized impairment of language.

The capricious nature of reading disability is illustrated by a study carried out by Harold W. Gordon in Haifa, Israel, on twelve dyslexic children and their families.[51] These children were markedly better at what Gordon called "right-hemisphere" tasks, involving mental rotation, perceptual completion, and block design, than at "left-hemisphere" tasks involving serial processing, word production, and immediate recall of series of digits. A control group of normal readers showed no overall difference in skill between the two kinds of tasks. Gordon concluded that the dyslexic children were "locked" into a right-hemispheric mode of processing. A slightly different interpretation, but one that is more consistent with our own line of reasoning, is that the dyslexic children were essentially unlateralized, and thus lacked the serial skills typical of left-hemispheric specialization, although they evidently compensated in terms of spatial, non-serial skills. But the interesting point is that 90 percent of the first-degree relatives of the dyslexics showed the same profile of skills as did the dyslexics themselves, even though most of them claimed never to have had any difficulty with reading. This study therefore provides support for our contention that dyslexia results from an inherited lack of lateralization, but it also suggests that not all those who inherit this condition become dyslexic. We do not know precisely what it is that causes some of these individuals to become dyslexic, while others apparently learn to read without difficulty.

Albert M. Galaburda and Thomas Kemper of the Boston University School of Medicine have examined the brain of a man, killed in an accident, who had been dyslexic.[52] They discovered that the usual asymmetry of the temporal lobes, in which the temporal planum is larger on the left than on the right (see Chapter 7), was absent in this man's brain. Again, we have evidence of lack of asymmetry in a dyslexic. The brain also revealed other anomalies, such as cell bodies in the most superficial layer of the cortex where they are normally absent, and islands of cortical tissue in the white matter of the brain where they do not belong. It is conceivable that dyslexia is the combined result of lack of structural asymmetry and other anomalies that are not yet fully understood.

In conclusion, then, what can be said of the bewildering and often conflicting array of evidence on reading disability? First, there seems little doubt that weak or inconsistent laterality is an important factor, perhaps even in the majority of dyslexic children. This may in turn cause a child to be unusually prone to left–right confusions and reversals. We suspect however that simple confusions between letters like *p* and *q* or words like *was* and *saw* are fairly transient, and may emerge as a serious problem only in the most severely dyslexic. The difficulty of learning directional scanning habits may be more central to the problem. In the skilled reader, movements of the eye across the printed page involves mechanisms that are intricate and subtle.[53] The eye moves in a series of discrete, ballistic jumps, known as *saccades*. The distance one is to move the eye must be calculated before the movement begins, much as one must calibrate the swing of a golf shot to hit the ball the required distance. In reading, this calculation is made with astonishing speed, and takes into account aspects of the meaning and physical layout of the script in ways that we are usually unaware of. Any uncertainty or hesitancy over the direction in which the eye must move could seriously disrupt the intricate sequence of operations.

In the early stages of learning to read, eye movements may be essential in establishing the sequences of letters in words, but with extended practice the words are seen as wholes. In the skilled reader, the eye may make only one or two fixations per line. The disabled reader, with deficient scanning habits, may simply never learn these intricate skills, may never learn the sequences of letters in words and so remain unable to spell properly, or may never learn to read the order of words fluently from the printed page. Such a person might well be characterized as a *holistic perceiver,* although more from his inability to analyze the sequential properties of script than from a superordinate perceptual style. The consistent lateralization may also result in more general deficits in sequential processing that go beyond difficulties with eye movement. We suggested in the previous chapter that the basis of cerebral lateralization may be in the evolution of purposeful, sequential actions. This could explain why many children with reading disability also have difficulty with sequential aspects of spoken language. Such children would not be classed as "dyslexic" in the strict sense of the term, although the distinction between the child with a specific reading disability and the child with more general problems with language may often be a fine one.

IMPLICATIONS FOR TREATMENT

Finally, we turn to the question of whether our somewhat tentative conclusions regarding the role of left–right confusion, cerebral lateralization, and dyslexia have useful implications for treatment of the disorder.

Possibly the most important point to be made is that left–right factors are applicable only to a minor, though significant, proportion of dyslexics. Remedial procedures arising from considerations about laterality, or directed at left–right confusion, will not be appropriate in all cases. We must emphasize again that reading disability, even in its purest form, may have many different causes. This realization has led to an understandable impatience with those writers who have advocated a single cause, or more particularly a single treatment, for all cases of dyslexia. The idea of poor cerebral dominance as a single or major cause of dyslexia has been promoted by more than a few over enthusiastic proponents since Orton first suggested it. We noted earlier that the idea fell into disrepute and remains suspect in the field of education, where the emphasis is on empirical rather than theoretical approaches to learning difficulties. In relation to some of the more speculative neurological fancies, this type of scepticism is no doubt justified and beneficial, but we can see no reason why neurological theories should not occasionally suggest a successful strategy for treatment that no amount of empirical observation would reveal.

Of course one hardly needs a neurological theory to appreciate that an older child who persists in left–right reversal errors during reading, would benefit from a training program directed to teach the specific left–right discriminations and differentiations that are lacking. In the previous chapter we reviewed a number of alternative procedures that have so far been used and showed the value of a theoretical understanding of the developmental basis of left–right discrimination in the design of effective training strategies. This amply illustrates the value of an effective neurological theory even at the most superficial level of application.

Another approach to the treatment of dyslexia emphasizes the complementary strategy of altering the task to one in which the deficit in discrimination is irrelevant. For example, it has been suggested that the teaching alphabet should be modified for dyslexics to a multi-fontal form in which the shapes of some letters are changed to prevent confusion of mirror images[54] (see Figure 11.2). Through fading procedures, the multi-fontal alphabet would eventually be replaced by the standard one. As we saw in the previous chapter, however, fading procedures can prove treacherous when applied to mirror-image discriminations, and an effective remedial program requires awareness of the theoretical issues involved.

FIGURE 11.2.

The multifontal alphabet, designed to minimize mirror-image confusions and make the letters more distinctive (From B. Sklar and J. Hanley, "A Multifontal Alphabet for Dyslexic Children," **Journal of Learning Disabilities** 5 [1972]:48. Reprinted with the permission of B. Sklar.

A third approach to remedial work is to try to influence cerebral lateralization itself. Perhaps the best known proponent of this approach is the educationalist Carl Delacato, formerly of the Institutes for the Achievement of Human Potental in Philadelphia. He has advocated a variety of physical exercises which supposedly produce a neurological reorganization, including increased cerebral lateralization.[55] The enthusiasm of Delacato and his followers for this approach has not been matched by those who have reviewed its effectiveness.[56] Controlled studies have not only failed to show any effect of these exercises on cerebral dominance, but their influence on reading skills is also in doubt. On the other hand, even Delacato's approach seems preferable to the view, sometimes expressed, that because dyslexia is caused by weak cerebral dominance it is a neurological rather than an educational problem which no amount or type of reading therapy is likely to help (although at least one proponent of a neurological theory has suggested measures for preventing the development of inappropriate reading strategies in young children.)[57] In our view, attempts to modify lateralization itself are at this stage premature, and it seems more prudent to direct remedial programs at deficiencies in the reading skills themselves.

Finally, what if there are no clear-cut solutions to the problem of reading disability? In spite of large-scale attempts to study reading failures and to develop more effective strategies to teach children to read, the problem seems as much with us as ever it was, at least if we are to judge from the complaints of the higher-education authorities as featured in the popular press. Some blame permissive teachers, others blame television, but the simpler interpretation is that a certain proportion of children will find it very difficult to learn to read properly no matter how reading is taught. Those who find this an unacceptably bleak prospect should take some heart from the resourcefulness of many dyslexics themselves. MacDonald Critchley[58] notes that many of them do learn to read, but develop their own special strategies for doing so. We think, for instance, of those highly verbal, literate, often creative people who remain appallingly bad at spelling—one such person was the English novelist Evelyn Waugh,[59] considered by some to have been the finest prose stylist of recent times. Other dyslexics may develop compensatory skills, such as design, sculpture, or acting—we have already mentioned Auguste Rodin and Susan Hampshire. If at least some dyslexics belong to that subgroup of unlateralized individuals, then the relatively low incidence of reading disability may be a small price to pay for the diversity of talent and offbeat genius that these individuals so often bestow on our culture. One is reminded of a remark by Charles Lamb in his *Last Essays of Elia* (1883): ''He has left off reading altogether, to the great improvement of his originality.''

How better to conclude this chapter, then, than by noting yet another talented dyslexic who fits our idealized characterization? Tommy

Smothers, one of the two famous Smothers Brothers prominent in American television comedy, was the worst speller in his class and a very slow reader. He claims he was put in the "dumb square" at square dancing because he could not tell left from right. When two psychologists interviewed him, they discovered that he was right handed and left eyed! He may even have exhibited some of the more general difficulty in sequencing that many disabled readers show, since he claims that he was particularly prone to spoonerisms or malapropisms.[60] We all, but ourselves especially, have cause to be grateful to people like Tommy Smothers.

Chapter 12

Stuttering

"In that case," said the Dodo solemnly, rising to its feet, "I move that the meeting adjourn, for the immediate adoption of more urgent remedies—"[Lewis Carroll, *Alice in Wonderland*]

The Dodo, in Lewis Carroll's *Alice in Wonderland*, represents Carroll himself. Its name is derived from the way Carroll pronounced his real name when he stuttered: "Do-Do-Dodgson." It seems likely that stuttering[1] was an inherited condition in the Dodgson family, since according to one biographer eight of the eleven Dodgson children were afflicted by it.[2] We may also recall Carroll's fondness for mirror-writing and his obsession with mirrors generally. Although we earlier discussed the idea that he might have been a changed left hander, these various symptoms suggested that he may at least have been rather weakly lateralized.

As many of our more mature readers will remember, the late King George VI of England was also afflicted with a stutter. He had particular difficulty with the letter *k,* and in his speeches or broadcasts on radio the phrase "His Majesty" was always substituted for "King." It is not unreasonable to suppose that his condition was due in part to an anomaly of lateralization. Although a right-handed golfer, he was a talented left hander at tennis, and played with modest success at Wimbledon. One

227

photograph also shows him holding a telephone to his left ear with his left hand.[3]

In Chapter 9, we argued that lateralization in the nervous system evolved primarily in relation to the control of internally generated, purposeful actions. If control is delegated to one side, potential conflicts are overcome. The need for unilateral control may have been especially acute with respect to the organs of speech, including tongue, lips, palate, and vocal chords. These organs are connected bilaterally to motor centers of the brain, so that any conflict between the two sides of the brain would create special difficulties. Moreover speech is a highly skilled act, requiring intricate, high-speed, precisely timed sequences of movements, and any source of disruption could have severe consequences. We believe that these are good reasons for supposing that the lateralized control of speech was primary in the evolution of lateralization.

These considerations provide reasonable *a priori* grounds for supposing that lack of cerebral dominance may disrupt the fine control of articulation and so cause stuttering. This idea seems to have been proposed first by Samuel Torrey Orton, who suggested it to his colleague Lee Edward Travis at the University of Iowa in the mid-1920s. Travis elaborated the "dominance theory" in his book *Speech Pathology,* published in 1931.[4] The theory was the springboard for most of the studies of stuttering carried out at the University of Iowa by Orton, Travis and their associates in the 1920s and 1930s, but, like the dominance theory of reading disability, it gradually lost favor. Indeed, in a volume published in 1955 to mark thirty years of research at Iowa it is scarcely mentioned, except in a historical context.[5]

According to Wendell Johnson, who followed Travis as director of the Speech Clinic at Iowa, the dominance theory lapsed for want of evidence. The investigators failed to discover any neurological differences between stutterers and other people. Even the early evidence that stutterers were more likely to be left handed, or to come from families with histories of left handedness, did not seem to be corroborated in later studies at Iowa, although the issue was somewhat shrouded by problems associated with the measurement of handedness. Johnson concluded that "the more skilled and meticulous the investigators became, the more they found stutterers to be, from a neurophysiological point of view, like other people."[6]

We suspect there are other reasons for the change of emphasis. In the

1940s and 1950s, it became fashionable to seek emotional or psychological causes for pathological conditions like stuttering and reading disability. We may recall that Abram Blau, in his 1946 monograph *The Master Hand,* even attributed left handedness to "emotional negativism." The emphasis also shifted somewhat away from discussion of causes and toward the rehabilitation of stutterers. Understandably, investigators may have preferred the more optimistic view that stuttering was of psychological rather than neurological origin and therefore more amenable to treatment. Johnson himself argued that most instances of stuttering were as much the fault of the victim's parents as of the victim himself. If a child did not speak fluently, some parents found this unacceptable and communicated their dissatisfaction to the child. The child came to perceive his own speech as faulty, which only served to increase the impediment. Stuttering was therefore a result of a "vicious circle" in the interaction between some parents and their children. Johnson proposed that therapy should be directed as much to the parents or listeners as to the stutterer himself.[7]

The idea that stuttering might be due to a faulty perception by the stutterer of his own speech was given some support by studies of the effects of delayed auditory feedback, first carried out in the early 1950s.[8] In this procedure the subject's speech is recorded and played back, in echo-like fashion, after a brief delay. If the delay is of the order of a fifth of a second, even the normal speaker loses her normal fluency and begins to sound like a stutterer. This led to the suggestion that stutterers suffer some defect in perceiving their own voices, producing an effect comparable to that of delayed auditory feedback. Of course this does not prove that the defect has anything to do with the interactions between the stuttering child and his parents, and in any event it has been argued that the resemblance between stuttering and the effects of delayed auditory feedback is no more than superficial.[9] For instance, listeners can readily distinguish between the two from tape recordings.

We think that the time is ripe for a revival of the "dominance theory." With the growth of techniques to measure cerebral dominance, the theory can now be tested more effectively than was the case in the 1920s and 1930s. As we shall see, much of the recent evidence supports it. Moreover, with the remarkable development of the discipline of neuropsychology over the past two decades, it is no longer quite so unfashionable to attribute minor pathologies to neurological anomalies. At the same time, however, we share the concern of the educationalist or speech therapist that the label "neurological" can often serve merely as an excuse not to attempt treatment. In any event, we do not wish to claim that lack of cerebral dominance is the sole cause of stuttering, or even that it is a sufficient cause in individual cases. The child who inherits the lack of any disposition to be lateralized may be placed at greater risk, but the actual onset of stuttering may have some emotional or traumatic origin.

STUTTERING AND HANDEDNESS

It is still widely believed that stuttering is somehow related to left handedness, and in particular that it is caused by forcing a natural left hander to write with the right hand. Perhaps surprisingly, the true incidence of left handedness among stutterers is still in doubt. While there are a number of surveys showing a much higher incidence of left handedness and ambilaterality in stutterers than in the general population, there are almost as many studies showing no such differences between the two groups.[10] None of the studies compared stutterers and non-stutterers with respect to how many of their immediate relatives were left handed.

Theories relating shifted handedness to stuttering imply either that changing the writing hand causes a change from unilateral to bilateral control of speech, or that it causes emotional conflicts, either of which may cause stuttering. As with the studies of left handedness, there is a marked lack of uniformity in surveys of the incidence of changed handedness among stutterers.[11] On present evidence, all that can be said is that there are some cases in which stuttering began after a child was induced to change from the left to the right hand for writing. Estimates of the percentage of cases in which this occurred vary from 0 to 70 percent! In any event, it is dubious whether this bears on the issue of laterality, since it has yet to be shown that changed handedness has any influence on the cerebral representation of speech control.

It is of course difficult to separate left handedness or switches in handedness from the more general condition of inconsistent lateralization. As we have noted many times in this book, left handers show mixed patterns of lateralization quite apart from whether they have been forced to write with the right hand. Moreover, there is no doubt an element of self fulfillment in the theory that a switch in handedness causes stuttering. As we have seen, it has been suggested that Lewis Carroll was a changed left hander, but the evidence for this seems to have been that he stuttered! We know of no independent evidence that he exhibited any tendency to left handedness.

We now examine the evidence relating to cerebral lateralization in stutterers.

CEREBRAL LATERALIZATION IN STUTTERERS

The association between familial left handedness, weak cerebral dominance for speech, and stuttering, was confirmed in a remarkable way by a series of clinical cases described in 1966 by a Philadelphia neurologist, R. K. Jones.[12] Jones described four patients, referred for neurosurgical treatment of brain injury in the region of the presumed speech areas. These patients had suffered severe stuttering since childhood. Three were left handed and one right handed, but all came from families with a high incidence of left handedness, suggesting that they belonged to that subgroup of the population inheriting no consistent predisposition to lateralization (see Chapter 8). Their neurological problems were of recent origin and quite unrelated to their stuttering. The cerebral hemisphere in which speech was represented was determined both pre- and post-operatively by means of Wada's sodium amytal test. Before the operation, the test showed a most unusual state of affairs; in each patient, speech control was bilaterally represented. Following surgery to the damaged cerebral hemisphere each patient was able to speak without stuttering. The post-operative Wada test now revealed unilateral control of speech by the unoperated hemisphere; in three cases this was the right, in one the left.

What is remarkable about Jones's report is that all four patients had familial associations with left handedness, bilateral representation of speech, and remission of stuttering following surgical instatement of unilateral speech control. This must be regarded as strong evidence not only of an association between stuttering, bilateral control of speech, and familial left handedness, but also of a causal relation between bilateral control and stuttering. Since these observations are based on only four cases it would seem unwise to generalize to all or even the majority of stutterers, but it may reasonably be taken to indicate the existence of a subgroup of stutterers in whom anomalous cerebral dominance is a significant causal factor.

Two subsequent reports[13] concerning testing by sodium amytal of stutterers have not confirmed Jones's findings, the usual left dominance for speech being found in six out of seven cases. These patients, however, were unlike those of Jones in at least one other respect—all but one were right handed, and the pattern of handedness in their families was not reported.

Another relevant series of cases has been reported by a neurosurgical group at St. Anne Hospital in Paris.[14] Several epileptic stutterers were described as regaining fluent speech following surgery to either the right or left cerebral hemisphere to relieve epilepsy. In two of these cases the patients, who were under local anaesthesia, began to speak fluently in the course of the surgery itself. One account reads as follows:

> During this operation, when we were starting the resection of the fusi-form gyrus, we were astonished to hear the subject articulate with ex-traordinary ease and to express his surprise at no longer stuttering. Fol-lowing this intervention, the patient was entirely cured of his epileptic attacks and his stammer.

With respect to their relevance to a possible link between bilateral speech control and stuttering, these observations seem consistent with those of Jones. Most of the subjects were described as right handed, but again the handedness pattern in their families was not reported.

By far the majority of studies of cerebral lateralization in stutterers have used the dichotic-listening test described in Chapter 9. The usual procedure has been to administer the test to a group of stutterers and a matched group of nonstutterers, then compare the percentages of each group showing a right- or left-ear advantage in the recall of words or other speech sounds. Some experiments have also compared groups on the mean *absolute* difference (that is, on the size of the difference without regard to its direction) between left-ear and right-ear scores, although this can in some cases be difficult to interpret. Of ten studies reviewed, most reported a significantly greater number of stutterers than nonstutterers showing a left-ear advantage.[15] Of these, some also noted significantly smaller ear differences in the stuttering group, compared to the normal group. However, two studies[16] showed similar, high proportions of subjects showing a right-ear advantage among both stutterers and normals.

The usual dichotic-listening test is sensitive to cerebral lateralization for the *perception* of spoken sounds, however, whereas the theory we are considering has to do with dominance in the *production* of speech. Indeed, Harvey M. Sussman and Peter F. MacNeilage of the University of Texas found that stutterers did show the usual right-ear advantage in the perception of dichotically presented syllables, but, unlike nonstutterers, they did not show a right-ear advantage in a dichotic task that may be sensitive to lateralization in speech production.[17] The subjects heard a tone that varied continuously but randomly in frequency played in one ear. Another tone was played in the other ear, and the subjects could alter its frequency by moving their jaws to one or other side. Their task was to match the frequency of this tone to the other tone by making appropriate movements of the jaw. Nonstutterers were better at this when the tone under their control was delivered to the right ear; Sussman and his colleagues had earlier reported similar results when the frequency was controlled by movements of the tongue rather than the jaw. A group of twenty-eight stutterers, however, showed no overall difference between ears. Sussman and MacNeilage suggest that this task provides a measure of cerebral dominance in control of articulators, including tongue and jaw. Their result therefore seems to provide good support for the theory relating stuttering to lack of dominance in motor control, although Sussman and MacNeilage point out that some individual stutterers did show quite marked asymmetry.

Sussman and MacNeilage's result also reminds us that different indices of cerebral lateralization may not be correlated, especially among left and mixed handers and among those assumed to lack consistent lateralization. Indeed, even the dichotic tracking task may not yield an exact measure of lateralization for the production of *speech,* since the tracking movements of the jaw were nonvocal in nature, although this test is probably more germane to the cerebral-dominance theory of stuttering than is the usual dichotic-listening test. It remains a curiosity, however, why so many of the other studies of dichotic listening in stutterers revealed an overall *left*-ear advantage. It is also worth noting that in all of these studies only right-handed stutterers were included. Considering the evidence for the increased incidence of left handedness among stutterers, a purely right-handed sample cannot be regarded as truly representative. Nevertheless, the fact that handedness and ear advantage were so frequently opposite to one another among the stutterers in these samples is further evidence that stutterers often show inconsistent lateralization.

Although the lateralization of visual perception is not directly germane to questions about stuttering, there is one study comparing the two visual half-fields in perception of briefly flashed words by stutterers and normals.[18] Surprisingly, the stutterers (all right handed) demonstrated a left visual half-field advantage, again reversing the result shown by the normal subjects. Many of the stutterers, but none of the normals, showed no difference between the half-fields.

In two other studies, electrical potentials were recorded over the scalps of stutterers and matched normals while they performed both verbal and nonverbal tasks. In one, slow potential shifts were measured over the speech-motor area on both sides of the brain. There were larger changes on the left in 80 percent of normals and 28 percent of stutterers in the moments preceding speech.[19] In the other study, the measure was the incidence of alpha waves, whose frequencies range from 8 to 12 cycles per second, while the subjects read out loud.[20] Alpha waves were diminished in incidence, implying brain activation, over the left hemispheres of the normals but over the *right* hemispheres of the stutterers. Again, this reversal of asymmetry is rather surprising, but at least suggests an anomaly of cerebral lateralization among stutterers.

The evidence here is in similar vein to that from the dichotic studies. There is evidence of reversed lateralization and bilateral representation of what are presumably speech-related functions. Again, only right-handed stutterers served as subjects, which may explain why the results are not entirely consistent with those reported by Jones on his series of patients. It seems all the more remarkable, then, that these subjects displayed signs of either reversed dominance or bilaterality.

CONCLUSIONS

Taken overall, there is rather convincing evidence that stutterers often show anomalies of cerebral lateralization. In many cases, however, the anomaly was one of reversal rather than of weak or absent lateralization. Given that nearly all of the subjects who showed reversal were right handed, this might still be taken as evidence of interhemispheric conflict, with one hemisphere specialized for control of the dominant hand and the other for the representation of language. One might even suppose that this inconsistency reflects a switch in handedness—that these subjects were forced to switch to the right hand. In the absence of further evidence that this was so, however, the more cautious interpretation is simply that these stutterers were without any strong predisposition toward consistent lateralization, so that different manifestations of laterality were in conflict.

The evidence also suggested that, in some stutterers at least, there may be bilateral control over speech, leading to interhemispheric conflict. This was especially striking in the case of the four patients described by Jones and was corroborated to some extent by the results of Sussman and MacNeilage for their dichotic tracking task—one of the few tasks designed to measure lateralization for the *production* of speech in normal human subjects. The theory advocated by Orton and Travis is therefore given reasonable support.

We cannot leave our discussion of anomalies of cerebral lateralization without raising an issue that poses a problem for our interpretation of both dyslexia and stuttering. Both afflictions are much more frequent among males than among females, yet the evidence suggests strongly that women are less highly lateralized than men, both with respect to the left-hemispheric representation of language and the right-hemispheric representation of spatial functions. How can we explain this disturbing anomaly? Up to a point, it might be attributed to the higher incidence of cerebral pathology in males; recall, for instance, that a higher proportion of men than women are left handed. Again, the lesser degree of lateralization in women compared with men seems to have been firmly established only among adults, and there is even some evidence that boys lag behind girls in the *development* of lateralization. We suggested earlier that the growth of lateralization may cease earlier in girls than in boys, since girls reach puberty at an earlier age, on average, than boys do. Reading disability and (typically) stuttering develop well before puberty, when lateralization may be if anything more highly developed in girls than in boys.

The more general point to be drawn from the difference between the sexes, perhaps, is that weak lateralization should not be taken as a sufficient cause, either of dyslexia or of stuttering. All we wish to claim is that those who are not strongly lateralized, whether through inheritance or through cerebral pathology, may run the greater risk of falling victim to one or other of these afflictions. It may take some other factor, possibly more closely associated with males than with females, to actually trigger the condition.

PART FOUR

Left, Right, and the Universe

God's in his heaven—
All's right with the world!
[Robert Browning, *Pippa Passes*]

Chapter 13

The Twisted Thread

When a topic is so charged with superstition as is that of left and right, it is hazardous to embark on a thirteenth chapter. The appropriate strategy, perhaps, is to throw caution to the winds and seek at last a cosmic unity in the distinction between left and right. We begin by summarizing the main themes of the book so far. We then suggest that the systematic asymmetries of organisms, including our own handedness and cerebral asymmetry, may depend on the asymmetry of living molecules. Spurred on by demonaic impulses, we then review speculation that biochemical asymmetry may depend in turn on a fundamental asymmetry in the primitive forces of the physical universe.

Throughout this book we have been plagued by an ambivalence. People and animals often have difficulty discriminating left from right, yet they usually can tell them apart. In the appreciation of visual art, a certain degree of left–right symmetry is aesthetically pleasing, but too much symmetry creates an impression of lifelessness and rigidity. Our two hands, like the two sides of our brains, are structurally very much alike, yet they are functionally different in striking ways. Left and right are polar opposites, yet reversing them often has little effect.

We can capture the essence of this ambivalence in terms of whether or not *parity* is conserved. The conservation of parity is a concept much discussed in the realm of physical laws, but we can here give it wider application. If the phenomena of some domain are unaltered by reflection about a plane, as in a mirror, then we may say that parity is conserved within that domain. On the other hand if reflection produces a different set of phenomena, that cannot be mapped onto the original set, then we may say that the conservation of parity does not hold.

Now, parity is in general *not* conserved with respect to *particular* objects or happenings in the everyday physical world. That is, if one could prize the reflections of real-world objects out of the mirror, one could not make them occupy the same space as the original objects, unless those objects happened to be symmetrical about a plane. One is reminded of the predicament posed by the White Knight in Lewis Carroll's *Through the Looking Glass:*

> And now, if e'er by chance I put
> My fingers into glue
> Or madly squeeze a right-hand foot
> Into a left-hand shoe . . .

Similarly, the mirror images of a corkscrew, or a bicycle, or the scene you are looking at now, are not exactly the same as the originals.

With respect to the *generalities* of the everyday, natural, sensible world, parity *is* conserved, at least for the most part. The view of a pastoral scene in a mirror is not the same as the original scene, but it is at least a possible scene. Unless one were familiar with the locale, one could not tell which one was the original and which the mirror image. The laws governing the mirrored scene appear to be exactly the same as those governing the original—laws such as the law of gravity, Newton's laws of motion, the laws governing the reflection of light, and so on. Indeed, until fairly recently, it was thought that all of the laws of physics were invariant with respect to reflection about a plane and thus obeyed the law of conservation of parity. As we shall explain, the exceptions apply principally in the realm of weak nuclear interactions, which are well outside the domain of everyday experience.

The conservation of parity with respect to the generalities of the everyday world underlies the phenomenon of left–right equivalence in the recognition of patterns. Animals tend to treat mirror-image patterns or events as equivalent, and to experience difficulty in telling them apart or in labelling them as distinct. Mirror-image patterns may be readily *perceived* as different, but it is often difficult to tell which is which. We have suggested, for instance, that the natural, innate tendency to mirror-image equivalence partly explains why children often have difficulty learning to read scripts, like English script, that depend on a consistent left–right directionality.

The parity of the everyday laws of nature also explains the high degree of bilateral symmetry exhibited by all freely moving animals. Symmetry is most pronounced with respect to those bodily parts and functions that are most directly involved in interactions with the spatial environment. This symmetry is an adaptation to the equivalence of left and right. The forces, pressures, constraints, and threats of the natural world are indifferent with respect to left and right—they can impinge on either side. We suggested in Chapter 4 that the bilateral symmetry of the brain also underlies the tendency of animals to generalize their experiences to the left–right mirror-images of those experiences and therefore to have difficulty remembering which way round things actually were. Memory is a record of the past, but it is also an adaptation to the future. As such, it is often very largely indifferent with respect to left and right.

Although parity is conserved in the everyday laws of the natural world, it tends not to be in the artificial world of human beings. Many of the objects and institutions of the human habitat bear the asymmetrical imprint of our right handedness. Sometimes the asymmetry is arbitrarily chosen but nevertheless consistent within given cultures. Examples of this include the directionality of script, the construction of automobiles and the side of the road they are driven on, certain rules governing right of way at sea, and so on. These asymmetries do not reflect handedness per se so much as the fact that most humans have a developed sense of which is left and which is right. We have argued that the asymmetries of the human environment reflect the asymmetry of the nervous system, and not vice versa, although there may well have been some reciprocal influence that has tended to preserve the asymmetry of humans within our asymmetrical habitat.

The evolution of cerebral and manual asymmetry can be traced to the evolution of an upright stance, which freed the forelimbs and to a lesser extent the mouth and vocal apparatus for manipulative and communicative skills. Indeed, exceptions to bilateral symmetry can be found thoughout the animal kingdom, and are often associated with manipulation and communication. We discussed these points in Chapters 8 and 9. It is reasonable to suppose, therefore, that symmetry and asymmetry are controlled by evolutionary contingencies. For the most part, bilateral symmetry has proven more adaptive than asymmetry, but in specialized cases symmetry readily yields to asymmetry if that should prove more adaptive.

The same is very largely true even of nonbiological objects. An automobile, for instance, is very largely symmetrical, since it is subject to the same kinds of symmetrical physical constraints as are moving organisms. Yet an automobile is asymmetrical in certain particular ways. Its internal organs—its engine, transmission—are in general asymmetrical, just as the internal organs of animals are asymmetrical, presumably because there is no special reason for symmetry in this respect and because symmetry imposes unnecessary constraints. Even a bicycle is slightly asymmetrical, although the asymmetry is minimized in the interests of efficient linear motion and of accommodation to the symmetry of the human body.

MOLECULAR ASYMMETRY

Parity is not conserved with respect to the molecules of living matter. This remarkable fact was discovered by the French scientist Louis Pasteur (1822–1895). He found that the molecules of tartaric acid could assume either of two mirror-image forms, or *enantiomers,* and that a certain plant mold acted on one but not on the other. This meant in effect that the plant mold could tell left from right! As the reader who followed our reasoning in Chapter 2 will realize, this in turn implies that there is a fundamental asymmetry in the molecular structure of the plant mold. Pasteur saw the asymmetry as the key to life itself: ''This important criterion [of molecular asymmetry],'' he wrote, ''constitutes perhaps the only sharply defined difference which can be drawn at the present time between the chemistry of dead or living matter.'' Prophetically, he went on to seek the origins of asymmetry in the fundamental forces of the universe: ''Life is dominated by asymmetrical actions. I can even imagine that all living species are primordially, in their structure, in their external forms, functions of cosmic asymmetry.''[1]

Subsequent work in molecular biology has amply verified the asymmetrical structure of organic molecules. Most striking of all, perhaps, was the discovery of the helical structure of the deoxyribonucleic (DNA) molecule, documented in lively fashion by James D. Watson in *The Double Helix.*[2] The DNA molecule consists of double strands of nucleotides wound around each other in a clockwise spiral. This molecule cannot be superimposed on its mirror reflection, and thus contravenes the conservation of parity.

We think that molecular asymmetry may well underlie the gross asymmetry of organisms, including the leftward displacement of the heart in vertebrates, or even handedness and cerebral lateralization in humans. The origin of these gross asymmetries must lie in the mechanisms that control the development of spatial structure. Organisms develop from a single fertilized cell that progressively divides to form a complex system consisting of many different cells. In the course of dividing, the genetic information coded in the DNA molecule remains the same in all cells, even though the cells themselves differentiate to form different kinds of tissue, ranging from muscle, bone, and cartilage to nerve cells and blood cells. There are in fact some 200 different kinds of cells in the human body. Each cell therefore carries the genetic information to develop into any one of these different cells, but its actual development depends on its specific location in the growing embryo. That is, the genetic information interacts with some other source of information, which Lewis Wolpert of the Middlesex Hospital Medical School in London has termed "positional information," to determine the actual shape and structure of the organism.[3]

The molecular basis of positional information is unknown, although Wolpert and others have worked out many of its functional properties. In this respect, the science of *morphogenesis,* which is concerned with the growth of structure and form, is in much the same position as genetics was before DNA was identified as the genetic material. The information that identifies whether a cell is on the left or right side of an organism, and that may determine systematic differences in the pattern of growth on the two sides, is but one facet of the positional code. Effectively, however, the mechanism that brings about a systematic difference between the left and right sides must be capable of telling left from right. We can again appeal to our arguments of Chapter 2, and conclude that the mechanism must itself include a structural asymmetry. That is why we think that gross left–right asymmetries must depend on some molecular asymmetry. There seems no other possible source of structural asymmetry that could dictate a systematically asymmetric growth.[4]

Wolpert has concurred with this analysis. "It is hard to see," he writes, "how (left–right asymmetry) could be specified at a cellular or tissue level other than by an underlying molecular or structural asymmetry that could bias the setting up of a gradient across the plane of bilateral symmetry." The details, however, remain, a matter of speculation.[5]

Actual expressions of asymmetry would depend, not simply on this asymmetrical positional information, but on the interaction of positional information with the genetic code. Depending on genetic instructions, the left–right gradient would be expressed in some structures but not in others. The genes themselves do not encode the direction of asymmetry, and are in this sense "left–right agnosic," to borrow M. J. Morgan's phrase. When the gradient is not expressed, we may find random or fluctuating asymmetry. We referred in Chapter 7, for instance, to a strain of mice in which exactly half of the individuals showed reversal of the heart and internal organs, while the remainder exhibited normal situs of these organs. We interpreted this to mean that, due to some genetic anomaly, the left–right gradient is not expressed in these mice. Following Marian Annett, we proposed a similar model for the genetic control of human handedness and cerebral lateralization. In most people, handedness and cerebral lateralization are under the influence of the left–right gradient, resulting in right handedness and the left-cerebral control of speech and other sequential acts. In some minority, however, the gradient is denied expression, and the directions of handedness and cerebral lateralization are assigned randomly and independently—by what R. L. Collins has termed the "asymmetry lottery."

We have suggested that gross biological asymmetries might be traced to the asymmetries of the molecules of living matter. The next question is whether we can trace molecular asymmetry to some even more fundamental asymmetry. Before we tackle this question, we need to consider the remarkable events that led to the nonconservation of parity in the so-called "weak" interactions involved in the spontaneous decay of atomic nuclei.

NONCONSERVATION OF PARITY IN NUCLEAR PHYSICS

There is a strong intuitive belief that the laws of physics should obey the conservation of parity. The world as seen in a mirror seems no different in principle from the real world. If one observes a scene in which mechanical forces are at play, or in which electrical or magnetic interactions occur, there seems no way to determine from these events whether the scene belongs in the real world or whether it is a mirror reflection of a real-world scene.

The intuition that parity is conserved in physical laws is so compelling that any violation may induce shock, or even denial. This is well illustrated by the consternation experienced by Ernst Mach when he discovered that a magnetic needle placed in an electrical field always deflects in the same direction. Characteristically, Mach was aware of the psychological implications.

> Even instinctive knowledge of so great a logical force as the principle of symmetry employed by Archimedes, may lead us astray. Many of my readers will call to mind, perhaps, the intellectual shock they experienced when they heard for the first time that a needle lying in the magnetic meridian is deflected in a definite direction away from the meridian by a wire conducting a current being carried along in a parallel direction above it. The instinctive is just as fallible as the distinctly conscious.[6]

Mach's shock was actually premature, because in terms of what was known at the time, the deflection of the needle did not really violate the conservation of parity. The designations "north" and "south," applied to the poles of the magnetized needle, were essentially arbitrary. If magnetized one way, the needle swings clockwise, but if magnetized the other way, it swings counterclockwise. The reflection in a mirror still represented the action of a possible real-world needle. In other words, there was no way to tell from the behavior of a needle in an electrical field whether it was a real needle or a reflection of a needle, simply because there was no way to tell in any absolute sense which was its north and which its south end. However this problem was resolved in 1957 by the discovery that there *is* an absolute difference between north and south.

Events that occur in the universe are governed by four different kinds of forces—or interactions, to use the term that physicists prefer. The strongest is the nuclear interaction that binds the nucleus of the atom together. Next in order of strength is the electromagnetic interaction that binds electrons to the nucleus, atoms to molecules, and molecules into liquids and solids. The so-called "weak interaction" is a weaker force that has to do with nuclear decay, in which electrons or positrons are emitted from radioactive nuclei. The weakest of all interactions is gravity, the force with which one mass attracts another. This force is so weak as to be negligible at the level of elementary subatomic particles, although we have cause to be grateful to it for keeping our feet on the ground.

In 1956 two physicists of Chinese extraction, T. D. Lee and G. N. Yang, suggested that parity might not be conserved in the weak interactions involved in spontaneous nuclear decay. To many physicists, this notion seemed to challenge our deepest instincts about the nature of the universe. The Nobel Prize-winning physicist Richard Feynman was cautious enough to refuse a bet of a hundred dollars, but he did offer fifty dollars that parity would be conserved. Wolfgang Pauli was more extravagant. In a letter to a friend, he wrote: "I do *not* believe that the Lord is a weak left hander, and I am ready to bet a very high sum that the experiments will give symmetric results."[7] He wrote just two days before the fall of parity.[8]

The critical experiments were conducted by Madame Chien–Shiung Wu early in 1957, and showed in effect that the nucleus of the cobalt-60 atom is more likely to emit electrons from one end than from the other. What this does is to establish an absolute basis for the difference between north and south poles of a magnetic field. If cobalt-60 nuclei are lined up in the magnetic field, then the south pole can be defined as that toward which the greater number of electrons are emitted!

Once we have established which is north and which is south by examining the emission of electrons from a cobalt-60 nucleus, we can use this information to determine whether the deflection of a magnetized needle in an electrical field represents the true state of affairs, or whether it has been mirror-reversed. Picture a wire running north and south beneath a compass, as shown in Figure 13.1. We show the north end of the compass needle as an arrowhead. If a current is sent through the wire from south to north, the needle should swing to the west. If the needle swings to the east, it represents a mirror-reflection.

It is worth noting that a perfectly symmetrical physicist, being unable to tell left from right, would not have been able to make this critical distinction, and thus could not have discovered the nonconservation of parity. We might therefore consider the discovery the pinnacle of the evolution of lateralization, and indeed Lee and Yang justly received the Nobel Prize for their remarkable insight. How appropriate, too, that the discovery that the Lord is a weak left hander should have been made by physicists of Chinese extraction, since the Chinese have traditionally held the left hand in special esteem![9]

Although the discovery of the nonconservation of parity was a triumph of human asymmetry, it remains counterintuitive. Indeed, evidence for nonconservation had been available for some ten years prior to 1957, but had passed unnoticed.[10] The assumption of symmetry had clearly been very strong. One reason for this may have been simply that symmetry is still the dominating principle in the structure of the human

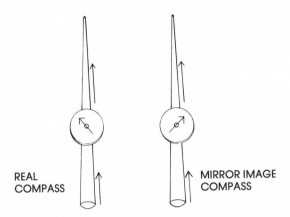

REAL
COMPASS

MIRROR IMAGE
COMPASS

FIGURE 13.1.

If a current is passed through a wire from south to north beneath a compass, the needle swings to the west (**left**). If it swings east (**right**) the compass must be a mirror-image one. This allows an operational distinction to be drawn between left and right, or between the real world and its mirror image. The distinction is only absolute, however, if one can independently establish which is north and which is south, which is positive and which is negative (in electrical charge), and whether time is running forwards or backwards!

brain, and guides our deepest intuitions about the structure of reality. Another reason is that parity does seem to be conserved in other natural laws—although we shall shortly note an exception. Pauli wrote as follows of his own shock at the results reported by Madame Wu:

> I am shocked not so much by the fact that the Lord prefers the left hand but by the fact that he still appears to be left–right symmetric when he expresses himself strongly. In short, the actual problem now seems to be the question why are strong interactions right and left symmetric?[11]

By appealing to still deeper principles, it is possible to argue that even the asymmetry of the decay of the cobalt-60 nucleus need not violate the conservation of parity. In particular, the designations ''positive'' and ''negative,'' applied to electrical charge, might themselves be considered arbitrary. Reversing the charge in Figure 13.1 is equivalent to making the current go the other way, in which event the deflection we have labelled as "mirror-reversed" represents a real-world state of affairs. Again, we might say that the direction of time is essentially arbitrary, and that in witnessing any given interaction we cannot know in any absolute sense whether time is running forward or backward! If time is reversed, then again the situation labeled "mirror-reversed" in Figure 13.1 represents a possible true state of affairs.

These considerations led to the so-called CPT (charge, parity, time) Theorem, formulated by G. Lüders and Pauli. The symmetry of the laws of weak interactions is preserved if any two of these three dimensions are reversed. Thus was Pauli able to preserve his sense of symmetry, and perhaps avoid paying up on his extravagant bet. Only if we know in an absolute sense which is positive and which is negative, and which way time is running, can we use the laws of weak interactions to determine which is left and which is right.

Reversal of charge changes matter to antimatter, in which electrons are replaced by positrons and vice versa. Our own galaxy consists of matter, but there has been speculation that other galaxies might be constructed of antimatter. This must be an issue of concern to intergalactic travellers, since the contact of matter with antimatter would result in a monstrous explosion, and the annihilation of both parties. The physicist Harold P. Furth imagines the scenario:

Well up beyond the tropostrata
There is a region stark and stellar
Where, on a streak of antimatter,
Lived Dr. Edward Anti-Teller.

Remote from Fusion's origin,
He lived unguessed and unawares
With all his anti-kith and kin,
And kept macassars on his chairs.

One morning, idling by the sea,
He spied a tin of monstrous girth
That bore three letters: A.E.C.
Out stepped a visitor from Earth.

Then, shouting gladly o'er the sands,
Met two who in their alien ways
Were like lentils. Their right hands
Clasped, and the rest was gamma rays.[12]

The story of the conservation of parity does not stop there, however.

In 1964 it was discovered that the K-meson, a heavy neutron particle, decays in a way that violates so-called CP invariance.[13] That is, reversal of charge and parity does not leave the interaction invariant, as the CPT Theorem would predict. In his book *The CP Puzzle,* P. B. Kabir is forced to conclude that there is, after all, a fundamental distinction between left and right in the physical laws of the universe.[14] Perhaps, however, someone will point out a deeper level again at which parity can be restored. We shall not attempt to pursue the issue further into the realms of nuclear physics, for it is beyond our competence to do so. Our concerns are primarily psychological, and we may simply observe that the checkered career of the principle of conservation of parity surely reflects in part the conflict between the underlying symmetry and the emerging asymmetry of the human brain. We may remain for ever in two minds about the ultimate distinction between left and right.

We now turn to the final question that completes our mission. If the gross asymmetries of organisms can be traced to the asymmetry of living molecules, can the molecular asymmetry be traced in turn to the asymmetry in the fundamental laws of physics?

THE ULTIMATE ORIGINS

There has long been speculation about the origin of the asymmetry of living molecules. As we have seen, Pasteur wrote of a "cosmic asymmetry," but this was generally considered too ethereal to be taken seriously. Pasteur did have one enthusiastic supporter in Francis Robert Japp, a 19th-century Scottish chemist, who argued that molecular asymmetry must have had an asymmetric cause; "Only asymmetry can beget asymmetry," he declared.[15] Yet it is surely conceivable that the direction of asymmetry might have been a matter of chance, and but for the flip of some metaphorical coin the coiling of living molecules could have gone the other way.

Some theorists have suggested that local asymmetries may have created the particular asymmetry of living molecules. According to this local or "microscopic" view, the asymmetry could just as easily have gone the other way in a different locale or even at a different point in time. Such theories include those based on the influence of elliptically polarized light, which might have combined with the Earth's magnetic field to produce the particular structural twist.[16] Since the magnetic field of the Earth is subject to frequent reversals, the evolution of living molecules at a different period in time could have resulted in the reversed parity. Theories based on polarized light are not generally considered very plausible, however, since any asymmetrical influence would have been extremely small.[17]

The discovery of nonconservation of parity in 1957 opened up the possibility of "macroscopic" theories of the origin of molecular asymmetry—theories that depend on some asymmetry in the universal nature of matter, and that are therefore not constrained by time and place. In other words, here at last was a potential basis for Pasteur's "cosmic asymmetry." At first, the main difficulty seemed to be that asymmetries at the level of weak interactions were outside the domain of the electromagnetic interactions of molecular chemistry. More recently, it has become clear that asymmetries can be detected at the level of electromagnetic interactions, and the nonconservation of parity has been demonstrated experimentally in the electromagnetic transitions of heavy nuclei.[18] According to T.L.V. Ulbricht of the Agricultural Research Council in London, who has offered several speculations as to how parity-violating interactions might play a role in the evolution of asymmetrical molecules, this discovery completely changes the complexion of the problem since the nonconservation of parity has now penetrated "into the heart of chemistry."[19]

Asymmetrical influences manifest at the molecular level are tiny compared with those at the level of weak interactions, and are for most practical purposes negligible. However, the effect may not be negligible over the extremely long periods presumed to be involved in the evolution of life. For instance, V. S. Letokhov of the USSR Academy of Sciences in Moscow has calculated a minuscule difference in energy levels between molecular enantiomers, and writes as follows:

> The difference is quite negligible and can not show itself in chemical reactions of any achievable duration. The chain of biochemical reactions of self-reproducing organisms the duration of which can reach 10^8–10^9 years is an exception to this rule. During such a long period of time even a relative difference in reaction rates of mirror-symmetrical molecules of the order of 10^{-16} is quite sufficient for full selection of either of two stereoisomeric forms of all the amino acids that occur in animate nature.[20]

A very similar argument has been advanced, apparently independently, by Bengt Nordén of the University of Lund in Sweden.[21]

These arguments are speculative, and involve untested assumptions. Nevertheless they do strengthen our conviction that the systematic asymmetries of morphology, molecular biology, and subatomic inter-actions are ultimately linked, and that there is, after all, an absolute, universal distinction between left and right. Pasteur would surely have approved. And yet the paradox remains that it has taken the full force of human ingenuity to discover and articulate the complex and subtle asymmetries of physical laws. In that sense, the distinction between left and right remains uniquely psychological.

Notes

CHAPTER 1
DEFINING LEFT AND RIGHT

1. Schaller and Harris (1975).
2. Cooper and Shepard (1973).
3. Lucretius, "On the Nature of Things" from the translation by Brown (1950, p. 132).
4. *Ibid.*, p. 133.
5. Gardner (1967).
6. This argument is raised by Block (1974).
7. Kant (1783). Kant's dilemma is also lucidly discussed by Gardner (1967) and Bennett (1970).
8. Russell (1897).

CHAPTER 2
TELLING LEFT FROM RIGHT

1. Corballis and Beale (1970).
2. *Ibid.*
3. Benton (1958).
4. Mach (1897), pp. 49–50. Tschirgi (1958) made a similar point.
5. Corballis and Beale (1970).
6. Gardner (1965, p. 10).
7. See, *e.g.*, the correspondence between us and Lila Ghent Braine in *Contemporary Psychology*, 1978, *23*, p. 474 and p. 603.

CHAPTER 3
CAN ANIMALS TELL LEFT FROM RIGHT?

1. Appelle (1972).

2. Lashley (1938).
3. Kinsbourne (1971).
4. Tee and Riesen (1974).
5. Sutherland (1963).
6. *Ibid.*, p. 210.
7. Parriss (1964).
8. Warren (1969).
9. Pavlov (1927).
10. Riopelle, Rahm, Itoigawa, and Draper (1964).
11. Nissen and McCulloch (1973).
12. Sutherland (1957).
13. Sutherland (1960).
14. Mackintosh and Sutherland (1963).
15. Williams (1971).
16. Zeigler and Schmerler (1965).
17. Thomas, Klipec, and Lyons (1966).
18. Beale, Williams, Webster, and Corballis (1972).
19. Clarke and Beale (1972).
20. Elze (1924).
21. Harris and Gitterman (1978); Wolf (1973).
22. Farrell (1979).
23. Maki, Maki, and Marsh (1977).
24. Standing, Conezio, and Haber (1970).
25. Rock (1973).
26. Restle (1957).
27. Douglas (1966).
28. Lawrence (1948).
29. Grindley (1932).
30. Konorski (1934).
31. Bartlett (1932).
32. Hughes (1966).
33. Hughes (1967).
34. Beale and Webster (1971).
35. Hebb (1949).
36. Young (1962).

CHAPTER 4

LEFT–RIGHT EQUIVALENCE AND THE SYMMETRY OF THE BRAIN

1. Weyl (1952).
2. Monod (1969, pp. 16–17).
3. Weyl (1952, p. 27).
4. Gardner (1967, p. 70).
5. Galaburda, LeMay, Kemper, and Geschwind (1978); see also Chapter 8 of this book.
6. See Corballis and Beale (1976), and also Chapter 6 of this book.
7. Bornstein, Gross, and Wolf (1978). Similar results have been reported by Fagan and Shepherd (1979).
8. Herrnstein, Loveland, and Cable (1976).
9. See *e.g.*, Deutsch (1973) or Mark (1974) for reviews.
10. Cumming (1970); Sperry (1962).
11. Corballis and Beale (1970).
12. Morrell (1963).
13. Marinoni (1974, p. 60).
14. These cases are cited by Critchley (1928).
15. Hécaen and Ajuriaguerra (1964).

16. Clark (1957).
17. Hewes (1949).
18. Ireland (1881, p. 367).
19. Critchley (1928).
20. Cardinal Luis' observation is cited by Ireland (1881, p. 365). Burt (1937, p. 343) notes that Leonardo's mirror writing dates from the age of 20 years and cites Fra Sabba de Castiglione as stating that Leonardo had always been left-handed.
21. Lennon (1945), cited by Gardner (1965).
22. Gardner (1965, p. 183).
23. Critchley (1928).
24. Milisen and Van Riper (1939).
25. Ray and Emley (1964, 1965).
26. Luria (1966).
27. Mello (1965).
28. Mello (1966).
29. Noble (1966, 1968).
30. Berlucchi and Marzi (1970).
31. Hamilton and Tieman (1973).
32. Beale and Corballis (1968).
33. Corballis and Beale (1976).
34. Pavlov (1927).
35. Beale, Williams, Webster and Corballis (1972).
36. Achim and Corballis (1977).
37. Gross (1973).
38. Gross, Lewis and Plaisier (1975).

CHAPTER 5

THE PERCEPTION OF SYMMETRY

1. Weyl (1952).
2. Ruskin (1907, p. 391).
3. Quoted from *Quarterly Review,* March, 1855, pp. 423–28.
4. Day (1968).
5. Barron (1958).
6. This quote and the previous one are from Weyl (1952, pp. 13, 16).
7. Clark (1969, p. 202).
8. Gardner (1967).
9. "Envoi," from *Selected Poems* by Anna Wickham. Reprinted by permission of the author's literary estate and Chas. L. Windus, Ltd.
10. Feynman, Leighton, and Sands (1963, pp. 52–12 [*sic*]).
11. From the translation by Stewart (1950, p. 491).
12. Julesz (1969).
13. Mach (1898, p. 94).
14. Goldmeier (1935).
15. Chipman and Mendelson (1979).
16. Corballis and Roldan (1974).
17. Locher and Nodine (1973).
18. Delius and Habers (1978).
19. Clark (1969, p. 202).
20. From the translation by Stewart (1950, p. 491).
21. Mach (1898, p. 96).
22. Mach (1897, p. 53).
23. Mach (1898, p. 99). Notice that Mach begins by discussing the problem of people missing an eye *from birth*, but then, presumably to ease the burden of explanation, he discusses the consequences of *losing* an eye.

24. Julesz (1971).
25. See Corballis and Beale (1976, pp. 67–70), and Sperry (1962).
26. Brindley and Lewin (1968).
27. Trevarthen (1970).
28. Levy, Trevarthen, and Sperry (1972).
29. Julesz (1971).
30. Mach (1897, p. 46).
31. Shepard (1978).
32. Corballis and Roldan (1975).
33. Rock and Leaman (1963).

CHAPTER 6
THE ORIGINS OF RIGHT HANDEDNESS

1. Hertz (1909; translated 1960).
2. Wieschhoff (1938); this is reprinted in Needham (1973), which provides extensive documentation of left–right symbolism throughout the world, ancient and modern. The next three articles are also reprinted there.
3. Hertz (1909; translated 1960).
4. Lloyd (1962).
5. Needham (1967).
6. Rigby (1966).
7. Hertz (1909; translated 1960).
8. Fritsch (1968).
9. Cited by Russell (1946, p. 72), who wisely preserves the anonymity of the poet.
10. Mittwoch (1977).
11. Levy and Levy (1978); we have ourselves failed to replicate these bizarre results.
12. Fliess (1923).
13. Freud (1948).
14. Freud (1954).
15. Adolf Erlenmayer, according to a letter in the *British Medical Journal* (Anon. 1883).
16. Hewes (1949).
17. Blau (1946).
18. Wile (1934) and Wilson (1872) provide extensive discussion on this.
19. Wilson (1872).
20. Erman (1894).
21. Cited in Wilson (1872, p. 225).
22. Cited in Wile (1934, p. 20).
23. Coren and Porac (1977).
24. Wilson (1872, p. 208).
25. Blau (1946); Wile (1934).
26. De Mortillet (1890).
27. De Mortillet (1882).
28. Sarasin (1918).
29. Wile (1934).
30. Blau (1946).
31. Harris (1980a).
32. Dart (1949).
33. LeGros Clark (1965).
34. Schaller (1963).
35. Cited by Lancaster (1973).
36. Finch (1941).
37. Cole (1957); Lehman (1978).
38. Peterson (1934).
39. Collins (1969, 1970).
40. Cole (1955).

41. Friedman & Davis (1938).
42. *The Sinistral Mind,* a conference held on March 3–4 1977, in San Francisco, California, and organized by J. Herron of the Langley Porter Institute, San Francisco.
43. Collins (1975).
44. Plato, *de Legibus* (cited by Wile, 1934).
45. Aristotle, *De Partibus Animalium* (cited by Wile, 1934).
46. Jowett translation (1953).
47. Rousseau (1780).
48. Reade (1878); cited by Harris (1980a) whose valuable review provided us with much of the information on early theories of handedness.
49. Hertz (1909); cited in translation by Needham (1973, p. 3).
50. Jackson (1905).
51. Annett (1973).
52. Teng, Lee, Yang and Chang (1976).
53. Hertz (1909); cited in translation by Needham (1973, p. 5).
54. Browne (1646).
55. Bacon (1852).
56. Torgerson (1950).
57. Baillie (1809). This is a reprint of the original paper of 1788.
58. Fitch (1852), cited by Wile (1934).
59. Buchanan (1862).
60. Wilson (1872).
61. Comte (1828).
62. Overstreet (1938).
63. Browne (1646).
64. Darwin (1877).
65. Hall and Hartwell (1884).
66. Woolley (1910).
67. Gesell and Ames (1947).
68. Seth (1973).
69. Chorazyna (1976).
70. Finch (1941).
71. Gesell and Ames (1947).
72. A contingency table with the three categories of tonic neck reflex set against left and right handedness yields a chi-squared value of 5.63, $.05 < p < .10$ (see e.g., Ferguson, 1977).
73. Turkewitz (1977).
74. Milner (1975).
75. Witelson (1977b).

CHAPTER 7
VARIATIONS IN HANDEDNESS

1. Oldfield (1971).
2. *Ibid.*
3. Bryden (1977).
4. Woo and Pearson (1927).
5. Annett (1970).
6. Bruner (1968).
7. Oldfield (1969).
8. Barnsley and Rabinovitch (1970).
9. Rigal (1974a,b) gives a description of six tests which he chose to represent the factors identified by Barnsley and Rabinovitch, and suggests a way to incorporate the six measures into a single index of handedness.
10. Kimura and Vanderwolf (1970).
11. Coren and Porac (1978).
12. Chaurasia and Goswami (1975).

13. Blau (1946).
14. Bakan (1971, 1975, 1978); Bakan, Dibb and Reed (1973).
15. Hicks, Evans and Pellegrini (1975) review five studies and conclude that, taken together, they fail to support the relation. Bakan (1977) provides some counter-evidence.
16. Barnes (1975).
17. McManus (1980).
18. Ramaley (1913).
19. Trankell (1955). Other theories based on partial penetrance or limited expressivity have been proposed by Rife (1940) and Annett (1964). See Corballis and Beale (1976) for more extensive review.
20. We have tried to explain genetic concepts as we go along.
21. Collins (1970).
22. Peterson (1934).
23. Collins (1975).
24. The trend is evident in surveys by Chamberlain (1928), Ramaley (1913) and Rife (1940) but not in a more recent survey by Hicks and Kinsbourne (1976).
25. Collins (1970).
26. The actual distribution does not quite match that generated by throwing dice, because the probability of a twin being right handed is slightly more than $5/6$. In the tabulation by Collins (1970), shown in Table 7.2., the probability was .864, and the distribution of right-handed, mixed, and left-handed pairs is well matched by the binomial probabilities $.864^2$, $2 \times .864 \times .136$, and $.136^2$. In a later tabulation by Zazzo (1960), the probability of a twin being right handed was .838, which is quite close to $5/6$ (.833).
27. Collins (1970).
28. Nagylaki and Levy (1973).
29. Newman (1928). The notion of mirror imaging remains controversial, however—see Springer and Searleman (1980) for more up-to-date discussion.
30. Torgerson (1950).
31. Springer and Searleman (1980).
32. Morgan (1977); Morgan and Corballis (1978).
33. Nagylaki and Levy (1973).
34. Diver and Andersson-Kottö (1938).
35. Morgan (1978).
36. See, *e.g.*, Levy and Nagylaki (1972).
37. Annett (1972, 1978).
38. Annett argues that lack of right shift is due to lack of a gene. We are suggesting instead that presence or absence of the right shift is due to different alleles of the same gene locus. The issue as to which version is correct does not seem to be a substantive one, at least at our present state of knowledge.
39. Annett (1974).
40. Peters and Durding (1979).
41. Friedlander (1971).
42. Olson and Laxar (1974).
43. Rife (1955).
44. Levy (1976).
45. Morgan (1976).
46. Layton (1976).
47. Zazzo (1960).
48. See Annett (1978) and Corballis (1980) for somewhat conflicting attempts to fit Annett's theory mathematically to the data. The issue is further discussed by Corballis (1978).

CHAPTER 8
LANGUAGE AND THE LEFT CEREBRAL HEMISPHERE

1. Dax (1865).
2. Broca (1861).

3. Wernicke (1874).
4. Chomsky (1957).
5. Buckingham and Kertesz (1974).
6. Strub and Gardner (1974).
7. Whitaker (1976).
8. Bogen and Vogel (1963).
9. Sperry (1969).
10. Gazzaniga and Sperry (1967).
11. Nebes and Sperry (1971).
12. Zaidel (1975).
13. Orbach (1953); McKeever and Huling (1971).
14. Cohen (1972); Geffen, Bradshaw and Wallace (1971).
15. Milner, Taylor, and Sperry (1968).
16. Kimura (1961, 1967).
17. See White (1969) for a review.
18. Kimura (1961, 1967).
19. Curry and Rutherford (1967).
20. Treisman and Geffen (1968).
21. Studdert-Kennedy and Shankweiler (1970).
22. Weiss and House (1973).
23. Kimura and Folb (1968).
24. Zurif (1974).
25. Sussman (1971); Sussman and MacNeilage (1975).
26. Geschwind (1975).
27. Kimura and Archibald (1974).
28. Jackson (1864).
29. Broca (1865).
30. Jackson (1868).
31. Penfield and Roberts (1959).
32. Milner (1975).
33. Wada and Rasmussen (1960).
34. Milner (1975).
35. Rossi and Rosadini (1967).
36. Warrington and Pratt (1973).
37. Goodglass and Quadfasel (1954).
38. Blumstein, Goodglass, and Tartter (1975).
39. Geffen, Traub, and Stierman (1978).
40. We have no reason to suggest that Australians are not normal.
41. Curry and Rutherford (1967); Hines and Satz (1974).
42. Levy and Reid (1976, 1978).
43. Annett (1972, 1978).
44. Hécaen and Sauguet (1971); Hines and Satz (1974); Zurif and Bryden (1969). Bryden (1975) did not observe this relation, however, and Warrington and Pratt (1973) found that the *familial* group showed the stronger left-cerebral dominance.
45. LeMay (1977).
46. Hines and Satz (1974).
47. We have no evidence for this assertion whatsoever.
48. Geschwind and Levitsky (1968).
49. Wada, Clarke and Hamm (1975).
50. *Ibid.*
51. Chi, Dooling, and Gilles (1977).
52. *Ibid.*
53. Molfese, Freeman, and Palermo (1975).
54. Entus (1977).
55. Vargha–Khadem and Corballis (1979) failed to replicate the right-ear advantage for speech sounds.

56. Ingram (1975).
57. Basser (1962).
58. Lenneberg (1967).
59. Dennis and Whitaker (1976).
60. Dennis and Kohn (1975).
61. For a review, see Searleman (1977).
62. Romer (1962).
63. Wilson (1903).
64. Nottebohm (1971, 1972).
65. Nottebohm (1976).
66. See Morgan (1977) and Morgan and Corballis (1978) for a review and further discussion.
67. Fromkin, Krashen, Curtiss, Rigler and Rigler (1974).
68. Hrdlicka (1907); Hadziselimovic and Cuś (1966).
69. Hoadley and Pearson (1929) describe the measurements of the Egyptian skulls; they do not subscribe to the theory that the ancient Egyptians were left handed, but they cite others who do.
70. Gundara and Zivanovic (1968).
71. LeMay (1976).
72. LeMay (1975).
73. Yeni–Komshian and Benson (1976).
74. Gardner and Gardner (1969).
75. Premack (1970).
76. Patterson (1978).
77. Petersen, Beecher, Zoloth, Moody, and Stebbins (1978).
78. Dart (1959, p. 219).
79. Hewes (1973).
80. Kimura (1973a, b).
81. Brain (1945).
82. Roberts (1949, p. 567).
83. Neville (1976).
84. Trevarthen (1978).
85. Fincher (1977).
86. Burt (1937, p. 287).
87. Hardyck, Petrinovich, and Goldman (1976).
88. Dimond and Beaumont (1974).
89. Peterson and Lansky (1974).
90. Deutsch (1978).
91. Young (1962).

Chapter 9

Complementary Specialization in the Two Cerebral Hemispheres

1. Hone Tuwhare, "The River is an Island," *NZ Listener,* Feb. 24, 1979, p. 12. Reprinted with permission of the author.
2. Jackson (1864).
3. Rudyard Kipling, "The Two-Sided Man," from *Kim.* Reprinted with the permission of the National Trust (London) and Macmillan London Limited.
4. Bogen and Gazzaniga (1965); Le Doux, Wilson and Gazzaniga (1977).
5. See Weinstein (1978) for a recent review.
6. Geffen, Bradshaw, and Wallace (1971).
7. *E.g.,* Hellige (1978).
8. Kimura (1966).
9. Atkinson and Egeth (1973).
10. Durnford and Kimura (1971).

11. Davidoff (1976).
12. Davidoff (1975).
13. Gilbert and Bakan (1973).
14. Kimura (1964).
15. Blumstein and Cooper (1974).
16. Kallman and Corballis (1975).
17. Gordon (1970).
18. Chaney and Webster (1966).
19. Curry (1967).
20. Witelson (1974).
21. Harris (1980b).
22. Brooks (1973).
23. Bryden and Allard (1976).
24. Hatta (1978).
25. Papcun, Krashen, Terbeek, Remington and Harshman (1974).
26. Gordon (1978b).
27. Gordon (1978a).
28. Alajouanine (1948).
29. Luria, Tsvetkova, and Futer (1965).
30. Cohen (1972); Geffen, Bradshaw, and Nettleton (1972).
31. Levy and Trevarthen (1976). "Metacontrol of Hemispheric Function in Human Split-Brain Patients," *Journal of Experimental Psychology: Human Perception and Performance,* 1976, 2, 299–312. Reprinted with the permission of the American Psychological Association and J. Levy.
32. Kinsbourne (1975).
33. Goodglass, Shai, Rosen, and Berman (1971); but see also Gardner and Branski (1976), who failed to replicate either this result or that of Kinsbourne.
34. Kinsbourne (1975).
35. We include this last example for the benefit of our Australian friends.
36. For a review and critique of this research, see Ehrlichman and Weinberger (1978).
37. Battersby, Bender, Pollack, and Kahn (1965); Critchley (1953); De Renzi (1978).
38. Bisiach and Luzzatti (1978).
39. Janet (1907).
40. Gainotti (1972).
41. Terzian (1964).
42. Carmon and Nachshon (1973).
43. Haggard and Parkinson (1971).
44. Ley and Bryden (1979).
45. *Ibid.*
46. *E.g.,* Milner (1958).
47. Humphrey and Zangwill (1951).
48. *E.g.,* Zangwill (1960).
49. Bogen (1969a, b); Bogen and Bogen (1969).
50. Ornstein (1972).
51. Quoted by Massis (1926, p. 487).
52. Snow (1959).
53. *Los Angeles Times,* November 6, 1977.
54. Garrett (1976).
55. Bogen and Bogen (1969).
56. Zangwill (1976, p. 309).
57. Erlichman and Weinberger (1978).
58. Ornstein and Galin (1976).
59. Arndt and Berger (1978).
60. McGlone (1977, 1978).
61. The volume edited by White (1974) contains several uncritical references to Geller's exploits.
62. Targ and Puthoff (1974). This work is critically examined by Marks and Kammann (1978).

63. *E.g.*, Roll (1974, p. 420).
64. Zangwill (1960).
65. Eccles (1965, pp. 30–31). The same view is reiterated in Popper and Eccles (1977).
66. Rossi and Rosadini (1967).
67. Jaynes (1976).
68. Zangwill (1976, p. 304).
69. Griffin (1976).
70. Patterson (1978).
71. Milner (1971).
72. Neville (1976).
73. Guthrie–Smith (1936).
74. Hay (1979).
75. Examples from Neville (1976).
76. Wolff, Hurwitz, and Moss (1977).
77. Bosshardt and Hörmann (1975); Efron (1963a, b, c); Gordon (1967).
78. We have pursued this theme elsewhere; see Corballis (1980), Corballis and Beale (1976) and Corballis and Morgan (1978).
79. Webster (1977).
80. Harris (1978).
81. McGlone (1977, 1978).
82. Harris (1978).
83. Newman (1977); see also Corballis and Beale (1978).
84. DeSante (1973).
85. Critchley (1953); Piercy and Smyth (1962).
86. Mountcastle, Lynch, Georgopoulos, Sakata, and Acuna (1975).
87. Le Doux, Wilson and Gazzaniga (1977, p 746).
88. Eimas, Siqueland, Jusczyk, and Vigorito (1971).
89. Kohn and Dennis (1974, p 45).
90. Cited by Sutherland (1976).

CHAPTER 10

DEVELOPMENT OF THE LEFT–RIGHT SENSE

1. Belmont and Birch (1963); Piaget (1928); Swanson and Benton (1955).
2. Davidson (1935).
3. French (1976).
4. Vogel (1979).
5. Cäron (1967).
6. Siqueland (1964).
7. Rudel and Teuber (1963).
8. Serpell (1971).
9. Bryant (1969, 1973); Corballis and Zalik (1977); Fellows and Brooks (1973); Over and Over (1967a, b).
10. Olson (1970).
11. Bryant (1969, 1973, 1976).
12. Fellows and Brooks (1973).
13. Corballis and Zalik (1977).
14. Jeffrey (1958).
15. Jeffrey (1966). Notice that this experiment adds further support to the view that the primary difficulty in discriminating mirror-image obliques has to do with telling left from right, rather than with the fact that the lines are oblique.
16. Clarke and Whitehurst (1974).
17. Fernald (1943).
18. Hill, McCullum, and Sceau (1967).
19. *E.g.*, by Kephart (1960), Tansley (1967).

20. Bijou (1968).
21. Described by Ray and Sidman (1969).
22. Harper (1978).
23. Benton (1959).
24. *Ibid.*
25. Geffner and Hochberg (1971); Kimura (1967); Knox and Kimura (1970).
26. Miller and Turner (1973).
27. Ingram (1975).
28. Entus (1977); but recall that Entus' results were not replicated by Vargha-Khadem and Corballis (1979).
29. Geffen (1976, 1978).
30. Bryden and Allard (1978).
31. Tomlinson-Keasey, Kelly, and Burton (1978).
32. Waber (1977).

CHAPTER 11
DYSLEXIA

1. Orton (1937) gives a review of his theories and clinical observations.
2. Bannatyne (1971, p. 6).
3. Mattis, French and Rapin (1975).
4. MacMeeken (1939).
5. Rutter, Graham, Yule, and Birch (1970).
6. Clark (1970).
7. Eisenberg (1966).
8. Miles (1971); Naidoo (1971).
9. Critchley (1964, p. 111).
10. Thompson (1971).
11. Critchley (1970).
12. Naidoo (1972). The first two clusters are based on the similarities of subgroups identified by Kinsbourne and Warrington (1963), Ingram (1964), and Johnson and Myklebust (1967).
13. Makita (1960).
14. Rozin, Poritsky, and Sotsky (1971).
15. Reported in the *APA Monitor,* December, 1976, p. 10.
16. Orton (1925, p. 607).
17. Zangwill (1960, p. 14).
18. Orton (1931, p. 166).
19. Orton (1937, p. 151).
20. Bennett (1942); Hermann (1959); Monroe (1928); Schonell (1942).
21. Ginsberg and Hartwick (1971).
22. Liberman, Shankweiler, Orlando, Harris, and Berti (1971); Lovell, Shapton and Warren (1964); Croxen and Lytton (1971); Lovell and Gorton (1968).
23. Sidman and Kirk (1974); Irwin and Newland (1977).
24. Monroe (1928).
25. Galifret-Granjon (1951).
26. Wolfe (1939).
27. Orton (1937, p. 151).
28. Lesevre (1966); Rubino and Minden (1973); Taylor (1966).
29. Zangwill (1960).
30. Zangwill and Blakemore (1972, p. 371).
31. Blau (1946).
32. Critchley (1970, p. 31).
33. Orton (1937).
34. Zangwill (1960).
35. Eames (1934); Ettlinger and Jackson (1955); Ingram and Reid (1956); Monroe (1932); Schonell (1940, 1941); Shearer (1968).

36. Dearborn (1933); Wall (1945, 1946); Zlab (1970).
37. Gates and Bond (1936); Jackson (1944); Smith (1950); Wolfe (1941).
38. Belmont and Birch (1965); Corballis and Beale (1976, p 166, 169); Naidoo (1972).
39. Zangwill (1978).
40. Naidoo (1972).
41. Denckla (1979).
42. Dunlop, Dunlop and Fenelon (1973).
43. The right-field advantage was reduced or absent among poor readers in studies by Kershner (1977), Marcel, Katz, and Smith (1974), and Marcel and Rajan (1975). McKeever and Huling (1970) failed to observe this effect, and according to a review by Satz (1976, p. 287) studies by Yeni–Komshian, Isenberg, and Goldberg (1975) and Witelson (1976) are ambiguous.
44. Satz (1976).
45. Satz and Sparrow (1970).
46. Shankweiler, Liberman, Mark, Fowler, and Fischer (1979).
47. Marcel and Rajan (1975).
48. Witelson (1977a).
49. *E.g.*, Kershner (1977), Masland (see Footnote 15).
50. Hines and Satz (1974).
51. Gordon (1980).
52. Cited by Geschwind (1979).
53. A useful review of evidence on the nature of eye movements in reading is provided by Rayner (1978).
54. Sklar and Hanley (1972).
55. Delacato (1966).
56. Balow (1971).
57. Witelson (1976).
58. Critchley (1970).
59. In the preface to *The Diaries of Evelyn Waugh*, Davie (1976) notes that "Waugh's spelling was invariably poor."
60. These facts emerged from an interview with Smothers in *The Gazette* of Montreal on July 31, 1979.

CHAPTER 12

STUTTERING

1. "Stuttering" may be defined as an impediment of speech in which the rhythm is disrupted by repetitions, blocks, or spasms, or by the prolongation of syllables. It is usually preferred in technical usage to the more general term "stammering," which need not imply pathology; thus one may stammer (but not stutter) with embarrassment.
2. Wood (1966).
3. Pudney (1952). The photograph is on p. 94.
4. Travis (1931).
5. Johnson (1955).
6. *Ibid.*, p. 9.
7. Johnson (1959).
8. Lee (1950); Cherry and Sayers (1956).
9. Neelley (1961).
10. Van Riper (1971).
11. *Ibid.*
12. Jones (1966).
13. Andrews, Quinn, and Sorby (1972); Lussenhop, Boggs, LaBorwit, and Walle (1973).
14. Guillaume, Mazars, and Mazars (1957); Mazars, Hécaen, Tzavaras, and Merreune (1970).
15. Brady and Berson (1975); Curry and Gregory (1969); Quinn (1972); Perrin (1969); Sommers, Brady and Moore (1975); Tsunoda and Moriyama (1972).
16. Slorach and Noehr (1973); Sussman and MacNeilage (1975).

17. Sussman and MacNeilage (1975).
18. Moore (1976).
19. Zimmermann and Knott (1974).
20. Moore and Lang (1977).

CHAPTER 13
THE TWISTED THREAD

1. These quotations are taken from the book on Pasteur by Dubos (1960, p. 36).
2. Watson (1968).
3. For a lucid popular account of these matters see Wolpert (1978a).
4. See Morgan (1977, 1978) and Morgan and Corballis (1978) for more extensive discussion.
5. The quotation is from Wolpert (1978b, p. 325), who goes on to speculate as follows: "There are several macromolecules and organelles associated with cell structure and motility that have both a left–right asymmetry—they are helical of fixed handedness—and a polarity. Examples of these include the protein actin, microtubules that are built out of protein subunits, and cilia, which contain microtubules. It is attractive to think that the handedness of these structures underlies left–right asymmetry. The problem is to translate this structural asymmetry at the molecular or organelle level to the cellular and tissue level. Our colleague, Dr. J. Lewis, has suggested that under certain conditions, the unwinding of a helix could exert an asymmetric force that might provide a directed bias to a structure like the heart or gut, which develops asymmetrically. Another possibility, suggested by Dr. L. Honig, is that the molecular asymmetry could cause asymmetric transport."
6. Mach (1893, p. 27).
7. Quoted by Salam (1958, p. 103). We have also drawn heavily on Gardner's (1967) entertaining account of these momentous events.
8. According to Gardner (1967), Feynman paid up on his bet. We do not know whether Pauli was ever held accountable for his rash prophecy.
9. Granet (1973).
10. Salam (1958).
11. *Ibid.* (p. 103).
12. "Perils of Modern Living," by Harold P. Furth. From *The New Yorker* (Nov. 10, 1956). Reprinted by permission.
    We do not have to travel so far to find evidence for the reversal of time, for was it not of *Time* that Wolcott Gibbs wrote his famous description: "Backward ran the sentences until reeled the mind"?
13. Christenson, Cronin, Fitch, and Turlay (1964).
14. Kabir (1968).
15. Japp (1898, p. 458).
16. The idea that polarized daylight might be responsible for molecular asymmetry was first suggested by Byk (1904), and is more recently championed by Mörtberg (1971).
17. Ulbricht (1975).
18. Henley (1969).
19. Ulbricht (1975, p. 313).
20. Letokhov (1975, p. 275). We have taken slight liberties with Letokhov's English.
21. Nordèn (1978).

Bibliography

Achim, A., and Corballis, M. C. Mirror-image equivalence and the anterior commissure. *Neuropsychologia* 15 (1977):475-78.

Alajouanine, J. Aphasia and artistic realization. *Brain* 71 (1948):229-41.

Andrews, G., Quinn, P. T., and Sorby, W. A. Stuttering: An investigation into cerebral dominance for speech. *Journal of Neurology, Neurosurgery, and Psychiatry,* 35 (1972):414-18.

Annett, M. The growth of manual preference and speed. *British Journal of Psychology 61,* (1970):545-58.

Annett, M. The distribution of manual asymmetry. *British Journal of Psychology* 63 (1972):343-58.

Annett, M. Handedness in families. *Annals of Human Genetics* 37 (1973):93-105.

Annett, M. Handedness in the children of two left-handed parents. *British Journal of Psychology* 65 (1974):129-31.

Annett, M. Throwing loaded and unloaded dice. *Behavioral and Brain Sciences* 2 (1978):278-79.

Appelle, S. Perception and discrimination as a function of stimulus orientation: The "oblique effect" in man and animals. *Psychological Bulletin* 78 (1972):226-78.

Arndt, S. T., and Berger, D. E. Cognitive mode and asymmetry in cerebral functioning. *Cortex* 14 (1978):78-86.

Atkinson, J., and Egeth, H. Right hemisphere superiority in visual orientation matching. *Canadian Journal of Psychology* 27 (1973):152-58.

Bacon, F. *The Works of Francis Bacon, Vol. II.* Philadelphia: A. Hart, 1852.

Baillie, M. A remarkable transposition of the viscera. *The Philosophical Transactions of the Royal Society* 16 (1809):483–89 (reprint of original 1788 paper).

Bakan, P. Birth order and handedness. *Nature* 229 (1971): 195.

Bakan, P. Are left handers brain damaged? *New Scientist* 67 (1975):200–02.

Bakan, P. Left handedness and birth order revisited. *Neuropsychologia* 15 (1977):837–39.

Bakan, P. Why left handedness? *The Behavioral and Brain Sciences* 2 (1978):279–80.

Bakan, P., Dibb, G., and Reed, P. Handedness and birth stress. *Neuropsychologia* 11 (1973):363–66.

Bannatyne, A. *Language, Reading and Learning Disabilities.* Springfield, Ill: Charles C. Thomas, 1971.

Balow, B. Perceptual motor activities in the treatment of severe reading disability. *The Reading Teacher* 24 (1971):513–42.

Barnes, F. Temperament, adaptability, and left handedness. *New Scientist* 62 (1975):202–3.

Barnsley, R. H., and Rabinovitch, M. S. Handedness: Proficiency versus stated preference. *Perceptual and Motor Skills* 30 (1970):343–62.

Barron, F. The psychology of imagination. *Scientific American* 199 (1958):151–66.

Bartlett, F. C. *Remembering: A Study in Experimental and Social Psychology.* Cambridge, England: Cambridge University Press, 1932.

Basser, L. S. Hemiplegia of early onset and the faculty of speech with special reference to the effects of hemispherectomy. *Brain* 85 (1962):427–60.

Battersby, W. S., Bender, M. B., Pollack, M., and Kahn, R. L. Unilateral "spatial agnosia" ("inattention") in patients with cerebral lesions. *Brain* 88 (1965):675–86.

Beale, I. L., and Corballis, M. C. Beak shift: An explanation for interocular mirror-image reversal in pigeons. *Nature* 220 (1968):82–83.

Beale, I. L., and Webster, D. M. The relevance of leg-movement cues, to turn alternation in woodlice (*Porcellio scabor*). *Animal Behaviour* 19 (1971):353–56.

Beale, I. L., Williams, R. J., Webster, D. M., and Corballis, M. C.

Confusion of mirror-images by pigeons and interhemispheric commissures. *Nature* 238 (1972):348–49.

Belmont, L., and Birch, H. G. Lateral dominance and right-left awareness in normal children. *Child Development* 34 (1963): 257–70.

Bennett, A. An analysis of errors in word recognition made by retarded readers. *Journal of Educational Psychology* 33 (1942):25–38.

Bennett, J. The difference between right and left. *American Philosophical Quarterly* 7 (1970):175–91.

Benton, A. L. Significance of systematic reversal in right–left discrimination. *Acta Psychiatrica et Neurologica (Kopenhagen)* 33 (1958):129–37.

Benton, A. L. *Right–Left Discrimination and Finger Localization: Development and Pathology*. New York: Hoeber–Harper, 1959.

Berlucchi, G., and Marzi, C. A. Veritical interocular transfer of lateral mirror-image discriminations in split-chasm cats. *Journal of Comparative and Physiological Psychology* 72(1970): 1–7.

Bijou, S. W. Studies in the experimental development of left–right concepts in retarded children using fading techniques. In N. R. Ellis (ed.), *International Review of Research in Mental Retardation*. Vol. 3. New York: Academic Press, 1968.

Bisiach, E., and Luzzatti, C. Unilateral neglect of representational space. *Cortex* 14 (1978):129–33.

Blau, A. *The Master Hand*. Research Monograph No. 5. New York: American Orthopsychiatric Association, Inc., 1946.

Block, N. J. Why do mirrors reverse right/left but not up/down? *Journal of Philosophy* 71 (1974):259–77.

Blumstein, S., and Cooper, W. E. Hemispheric processing of intonation contours. *Cortex* 10 (1974):146–58.

Blumstein, S., Goodglass, H., and Tartter, V. The reliability of ear advantage in dichotic listening. *Brain and Language* 2 (1975):226–36.

Bogen, J. E. The other side of the brain, I: Dysgraphia and dyscopia following cerebral commissurotomy. *Bulletin of the Los Angeles Neurological Society* 34 (1969):73–105. (a).

Bogen, J. E. The other side of the brain, II: An appositional mind. *Bulletin of the Los Angeles Neurological Society* 34 (1969):135–62. (b).

Bogen, J. E., and Bogen, G. M. The other side of the brain, III: The corpus callosum and creativity. *Bulletin of the Los Angeles Neurological Society* 34 (1969):191–220.

Bogen, J. E., and Gazzaniga, M. S. Cerebral commissurotomy in man:

Minor hemisphere dominance for certain visuo–spatial functions. *Journal of Neurosurgery* 23 (1965):394–99.

Bogen, J. E., and Vogel, P. J. Treatment of generalized seizures by cerebral commissurotomy. *Surgical Forum* 14 (1963):431.

Bornstein, M. H., Gross, C. G., and Wolf, J. Z. Perceptual similarity of mirror images in infancy. *Cognition* 6 (1978):89–116.

Bosshardt, H. G., and Hörmann, H. Temporal precision of coding as a basic factor of laterality effects in the retention of verbal auditory stimuli. *Acta Psychologica* 39 (1975):1–12.

Brady, J. P., and Berson, J. Stuttering, dichotic listening, and cerebral dominance. *Archives of General Psychiatry* 32 (1975):1449–52.

Brain, R. Speech and handedness. *Lancet* 249 (1945):837–41.

Brindley, G. S., and Lewin, W. S. The sensations produced by electrical stimulation of the visual cortex. *Journal of Physiology (London)* 196 (1968):479–93.

Broca, P. Remarques sur le siége de la faculté du language articulé, suivies d'une observation d'aphémie (perte de la parole). *Bulletins de la Société Anatomique* 6 (1861):330–57.

Broca, P. Sur le siẏe de la faculté du langage articulé. *Bulletins de la Société d'Anthropologie de Paris* 6 (1865):377–93.

Brooks, L. R. Treating verbal stimuli in a novel manner. Unpublished paper presented at Eastern Psychological Association Meeting in Washington, 1973.

Brown, W. H. (translator) *Lucretius' On the Nature of Things.* New Brunswick, N.J.: Rutgers University Press, 1950.

Browne, T. *Pseudodoxia Epidemica, or Enquiries into Very Many Received Tenets, and Commonly Presumed Truths.* London, printed by T. H. for Edward Dod, 1646.

Bruner, J. S. *Processes of Cognitive Growth: Infancy.* Vol. III. Heinz Werner Memorial Lecture Series. Worcester, Massachusetts: Clark University Press, 1968.

Bryant, P. E. Perception and memory of the orientation of visually presented lines by children. *Nature* 224 (1969):1331–32.

Bryant, P. E. Discrimination of mirror images by young children. *Journal of Comparative and Physiological Psychology* 82 (1973):415–25.

Bryant, P. E. *Perception and Understanding in Young Children: An Experimental Approach.* London: Methuen, 1974.

Bryden, M. P. Speech lateralization in families: A preliminary study using dichotic listening. *Brain and Language* 2 (1975):201–11.

Bryden, M. P. Measuring handedness with questionnaires. *Neuropsychologia* 15 (1977):617–24.

Bryden, M. P., and Allard, F. Visual hemifield differences depend on typeface. *Brain and Language* 3 (1976):191–200.

Bryden, M. P., and Allard, F. Dichotic listening and the development of linguistic processes. In M. Kinsbourne (ed.), *Asymmetrical Function of the Brain*. New York: Cambridge University Press, 1978.

Buchanan, A. Mechanical theory of the predominance of the right hand over the left; or, more generally, of the limbs of the right side over the left side of the body. *Proceedings of the Philosophical Society of Glasgow* 5 (1862):142–67.

Buckingham, H. W., Jr., and Kertesz, A. A linguistic analysis of fluent aphasia. *Brain and Language* 1 (1974):29–42.

Burt, C. *The Backward Child*. New York: Appleton–Century, 1937.

Byk, A. The question of the resolution of racemic compounds by circularly polarized light, a contribution to the primary origin of optically active substances. *Zeitschrift für Physikalische Chemie* 49 (1904):641.

Cäron, R. F. Visual reinforcement in young infants. *Journal of Experimental Child Psychology* 5 (1967):489–511.

Carmon, A., and Nachshon, I. Ear asymmetry in perception of emotional non-verbal stimuli. *Acta Psychologica* 37 (1973):351–57.

Chamberlain, A. F. Right-handedness. *Science* 18 (1903):788–89.

Chaney, R. B., and Webster, J. C. Information in certain multidimensional sounds. *Journal of the Acoustical Society of America* 40 (1966):449–55.

Chaurasia, B. D., and Goswami, H. K. Functional asymmetry in the face. *Acta Anatomica* 91 (1975):154–60.

Cherry, C., and Sayers, B. McA. Experiments on the total inhibition of stammering by external control, and some clinical results. *Journal of Psychosomatic Research* 1 (1956):233–46.

Chi, J. G., Dooling, E. C., and Gilles, F. H. Left-right asymmetries of the temporal speech areas of the human fetus. *Archives of Neurology* 34 (1977): 346–48.

Chipman, S. F., and Mendelson, M. J. Influence of six types of visual structure on complexity judgments in children and adults. *Journal of Experimental Psychology: Human Perception and Performance* 5 (1979):365–78.

Chomsky, N. *Syntactic structures*. The Hague: Mouton, 1957.

Chorazyna, H. Shifts in laterality in a baby chimpanzee. *Neuropsychologia* 14 (1976):381–84.

Christenson, J. H., Cronin, J. W., Fitch, V. L., and Turlay, R. Evidence for the 2π decay of the K_2° meson. *Physical Review Letters* 13 (1964):138–40.

Clark, K. *Civilisation: A Personal View.* London: British Broadcasting Corporation and John Murray, 1969.

Clark, M. M. *Left-handedness.* London: University of London Press, 1957.

Clark, M. M. *Reading Difficulties in Schools.* London: Penguin Papers in Education, 1970.

Clarke, J. C., and Beale, I. L. Selective stimulus control in discrimination of lateral mirror images by pigeons. *Animal Behaviour* 20 (1972):656–61.

Clarke, J. C., and Whitehurst, G. J. Asymmetrical stimulus control and the mirror-image problem. *Journal of Experimental Child Psychology* 17 (1974):147–66.

Cohen, G. Hemispheric differences in a letter classification task. *Perception and Psychophysics* 11 (1972):139–42.

Cole, J. Paw preference in cats related to hand preference in animals and man. *Journal of Comparative and Physiological Psychology* 48 (1955):137–40.

Cole, J. Laterality in the use of the hand, foot, and eye in monkeys. *Journal of Comparative and Physiological Psychology* 50 (1957):296–99.

Collins, R. L. On the inheritance of handedness: II. Selection for sinistrality in mice. *Journal of Heredity* 60 (1969):117–19.

Collins, R. L. The sound of one paw clapping: An inquiry into the origins of left handedness. In G. Lindzey and D. D. Thiessen (eds.), *Contributions to Behavior-Genetic Analysis—the Mouse as a Prototype.* New York: Meredith Corporation, 1970.

Collins, R. L. When left-handed mice live in right-handed worlds. *Science* 187 (1975):181–84.

Comte, A. J. Recherches anatomico—physiologiques, relative á la prédominance du bras droite sur le bras gauche. Paris, chez l'auteur, 1828. (No. 7 in a volume of pamphlets with binder's title: *Mémoires Physiologie Système Nerveux.* ''Mémoire lue á l'Academie des Sciences le 25 février 1828'').

Cooper, L. A., and Shepard, R. N. Chronometric studies of the rotation of mental images. In W. G. Chase (ed.), *Visual Information Processing.* New York: Academic Press, 1973.

Corballis, M. C. Brain twisters and hand wringers. *The Behavioral and Brain Sciences* 1 (1978):331–36.

Corballis, M. C. Is left-handedness genetically determined? In J. Herron (ed.), *Neuropsychology of Left-handedness*. New York: Academic Press, 1980.

Corballis, M. C., and Beale, I. L. Bilateral symmetry and behavior. *Psychological Review* 77 (1970):451–64.

Corballis, M. C., and Beale, I. L. *The Psychology of Left and Right.* Hillsdale, N.J.; Lawrence Erlbaum Associates, 1976.

Corballis, M. C. and Beale, I. L. Left and right in navigation. Letters to the Editor, *Bulletin of the British Psychological Society* 31 (1978):136.

Corballis, M. C., and Morgan, M. J. On the biological basis of human laterality: I. Evidence for maturational left–right gradient. *The Behavioral and Brain Sciences* 1 (1978):261–69.

Corballis, M. C., and Roldan, C. E. On the perception of symmetrical and repeated forms. *Perception and Psychophysics* 16 (1974):136–42.

Corballis, M. C., and Roldan, C. E. Detection of symmetry as a function of angular orientation. *Journal of Experimental Psychology: Human Perception and Performance* 1 (1975):221–30.

Corballis, M. C., and Zalik, M. Why do children confuse mirror-image obliques? *Journal of Experimental Child Psychology* 24 (1977):516–23.

Coren, S., and Porac, C. Fifty centuries of right-handedness: The historical record. *Science* 198 (1977):631–32.

Coren, S., and Porac, C. The validity and reliability of self-report items for the measurement of lateral preference. *British Journal of Psychology* 69 (1978):207–12.

Critchley, M. *Mirror-writing.* Psyche Miniature Medical Series. London: Kegan, Paul, Trench, Trubner & Co. Ltd., 1928.

Critchley, M. *The Parietal Lobes.* London: Arnold, 1953.

Critchley, M. *Developmental Dyslexia.* London: Heinemann, 1964.

Critchley, M. *The Dyslexic Child.* London: Heinemann, 1970.

Croxen, M. E., and Lytton, H. Reading disability and difficulties in finger localization and right–left discrimination. *Developmental Psychology* 5 (1971):256–62.

Cumming, W. J. K. An anatomical review of the corpus callosum. *Cortex* 6 (1970):1–18.

Curry, F. K. W. A comparison of left-handed and right-handed subjects on verbal and nonverbal dichotic listening tasks. *Cortex* 3 (1967):343–52.

Curry, F. K. W., and Gregory, H. H. The performance of stutterers on dichotic listening tasks thought to reflect cerebral dominance. *Journal of Speech and Hearing Research* 12 (1969):73–82.

Curry, F. K. W., and Rutherford, D. R. Recognition and recall of dichotically presented verbal stimuli by right- and left-handed persons. *Neuropsychologia* 5 (1967):119–26.

Dart, R. A. The predatory implemental technique of *Australopithecus*. *American Journal of Physical Anthropology* 7 (1949):1–38.

Dart, R. A. (with Dennis Craig). *Adventures with the Missing Link*. London: H. Hamilton, 1959.

Darwin, C. A biological sketch of an infant. *Mind* 2 (1877):285–94.

Davidoff, J. B. Hemispheric differences in the perception of lightness. *Neuropsychologia* 13 (1975):121–24.

Davidoff, J. B. Hemispheric sensitivity differences in the perception of colour. *Quarterly Journal of Experimental Psychology* 28 (1976):387–94.

Davidoff, J. B. Hemispheric differences in dot detection. *Cortex* 13 (1977):434–44.

Davidson, H. P. A study of the confusing letters *b, d, p, q*. *Journal of Genetic Psychology* 47 (1935):458–68.

Davie, M. (ed.), *The Diaries of Evelyn Waugh*. London: Weidenfeld and Nicolson, 1976.

Day, H. I. The importance of symmetry and complexity in the evaluation of complexity, interest, and pleasingness. *Psychonomic Science* 10 (1968):339–40.

Dax, M. Lésions de la moitié gauche de l'encéphale coincident avec l'oubli des signes de la pensée. (Read at Montpelier, 1836). *Gazette Hebdomadaire* 11 (1865):259–60.

Dearborn, W. F. Structural factors which condition special disability in reading. *Proceedings of the 57th Annual Session of the American Association for Mental Deficiency* 38 (1933):266–83.

Delacato, C. H. *The Treatment and Prevention of Reading Problems*. Springfield, Illinois: Charles, C. Thomas, 1966.

Delius, J. D., and Habers, G. Symmetry: Can pigeons conceptualize it? *Behavioral Biology* 22 (1978):336–42.

De Mortillet, G. *Le préhistorique antiquité de l'homme*. Paris: Reinwald, 1882.

De Mortillet, G. Formations des variétés, albinisme et gauchissement. *Bulletin de la Société d'Anthropologie de Paris,* Séeance de 3 Juillet, 1890.

Denckla, M. B. Childhood learning disabilities. In K. M. Heilman and E. Valenstein (eds.). *Clinical Neuropsychology.* New York: Oxford, 1979.

Dennis, M., and Kohn, B. Comprehension of syntax in infantile hemiplegics after cerebral hemidecortication: Left hemiplegics superiority. *Brain and Language* 2 (1975):472–82.

Dennis, M., and Whitaker, H. A. Language acquisition following hemidecortication: Linguistic superiority of the left over the right hemisphere. *Brain and Language* 3 (1976):404–33.

De Renzi, E. Hemispheric asymmetry as evidenced by spatial disorders. In M. Kinsbourne (ed.), *Asymmetrical Function of the Human Brain.* New York: Academic Press, 1978.

De Sante, D. F. *An Analysis of the Fall Occurrences and Nocturnal Orientations of Vagrant Wood Warblers (Parulidae) in California.* Unpublished doctoral dissertation, Stanford University, 1973.

Deutsch, D. Pitch memory: An advantage for the left-handed. *Science* 199 (1978):559–60.

Deutsch, J. A. *Physiological Basis of Memory.* New York: Academic Press, 1973.

Dimond, S., and Beaumont, G. Hemispheric function and paired associate learning. *British Journal of Psychology* 65 (1974):275–78.

Diver, C. D., and Andersson–Kottö, I. Sinistrality in Limnaea peragra (Mollusca, Pulmonata): The problems of mixed broods. *Journal of Genetics* 35 (1938):447–525.

Douglas, R. J. Cues for spontaneous alternation. *Journal of Comparative and Physiological Psychology* 62 (1966):171–83.

Dubos, R. *Pasteur and Modern Science.* London: Heinemann, 1960.

Dunlop, B., Dunlop, P., and Fenelon, B. Vision-laterality analysis in children with reading disability: The result of new techniques of examination. *Cortex* 9 (1973):227–36.

Durnford, M., and Kimura, D. Right hemisphere specialization for depth perception reflected in visual field differences. *Nature* 231 (1971):394–95.

Eames, T. H. The anatomical basis of lateral dominance anomalies. *American Journal of Orthopsychiatry* 4(1934):524–28.

Eccles, J. C. *The Brain and the Unity of Conscious Experience.* Cambridge: Cambridge University Press, 1965.

Efron, R. The effect of handedness on the perception of simultaneity and temporal order. *Brain* 86 (1963):261–84. (a).

Efron, R. The effect of stimulus intensity on the perception of simultaneity in right- and left-handed subjects. *Brain* 86 (1963):285–94. (b).

Efron, R. Temporal perception, aphasia, and déjà vu. *Brain* 86 (1963):403–24. (c).

Ehrlichman, H., and Weinberger, A. Lateral eye movements and hemispheric asymmetry: A critical review. *Psychological Bulletin* 85 (1978):1080–1101.

Eimas, P. D., Siqueland, E., Jusczyk, P., and Vigorito, J. Speech perception in infants. *Science* 171 (1971):303–306.

Eisenberg, L. The epidemiology of reading retardation and a programme of preventive intervention. In J. Money (ed.). *The Disabled Reader*. Baltimore: Johns Hopkins Press, 1966.

Elze, K. Rechtslinksempfinden und Rechtslinksblindheit. *Zeitschrift für angewandte Psychologie* 24 (1924):129–35.

Entus, A. K. Hemispheric asymmetry in processing of dichotically presented speech and nonspeech by infants. In S. J. Segalowitz and F. Gruber (eds.), *Language Development and Neurological Theory*. New York: Academic Press, 1977.

Erlenmeyer, D. Quoted by *British Medical Journal* 1 (1883):1161.

Erman, A. *Life in ancient Egypt* (trans. by H. M. Tirard). London: Macmillan, 1894.

Ettlinger, G., and Jackson C. V. Organic factors in developmental dyslexia. *Proceedings of the Royal Society of Medicine* 48 (1955):998–1000.

Fagan, J. F., and Shepherd, P. A. Infants' perception of face orientation. *Infant Behavior and Development* 2 (1979):227–34.

Farrell, W. S. Coding left and right. *Journal of Experimental Psychology: Human Perception and Performance* 5 (1979):42–51.

Fellows, B. J., and Brooks, B. An investigation of the role of matching and mismatching frameworks upon the discrimination of differently oriented line stimuli in young children. *Journal of Child Psychology and Psychiatry* 14 (1973):292–99.

Ferguson, G. A. *Statistical Analysis in Psychology and Education*. 4th ed. New York: McGraw-Hill, 1977.

Fernald, G. M. *Remedial Techniques in Basic School Subjects*. New York: McGraw–Hill, 1943.

Feynman, R. P., Leighton, R. B., and Sands, M. *The Feynman Lectures on Physics, Vol. 1.* New York: Addison–Wesley, 1963.

Finch, G. Chimpanzee's handedness. *Science* 94 (1941):117–18.

Fincher, J. *Sinister People: The Looking-Glass World of the Lefthander.* New York: G. P. Putman's Sons, 1977.

Fitch, S. S. *Six Discourses on the Function of the Lungs,* 1852, quoted by G. R. Penn, London, *Daily Mail,* March 16, 1933, p. 10.

Fliess, W. *Der Ablauft des Lebens.* Vienna: Deuticke, 1923.

French, M. J. *Discrimination of Mirror Images and Up–Down Inversions by Young Children at Three Age Levels: Effects of Varying Instructions and Stimuli.* Unpublished Master's thesis: University of Auckland, 1976.

Freud, S. *Leonardo da Vinci: A Psychological Study of an Infantile Reminiscence.* London: Routledge, 1948.

Freud, S. *The Origins of Psychoanalysis. Letters to Wilhelm Fliess, Drafts and Notes: 1887–1902.* London: Imago Publishing Co. Ltd., 1954.

Friedlander, W. J. Some aspects of eyedness. *Cortex* 7 (1971):357–71.

Friedman, H., and Davis, M. Left handedness in parrots. *Auk* 55 (1938):478–80.

Fritsch, V. *Left and Right in Science and Life.* London: Barrie & Rockliff, 1968.

Fromkin, V. A., Krashen, S., Curtiss, S., Rigler, D., and Rigler, M. The development of language in Genie: A case of language acquisition beyond the ''critical period.'' *Brain and Language* 1 (1974):81–107.

Gainotti, G. Emotional behavior and the hemispheric side of the lesion. *Cortex* 8 (1972):41–54.

Galaburda, A. M., LeMay, M., Kemper, T. L., and Geschwind, N. Right–left asymmetries in the brain. *Science* 199 (1978):852–56.

Galifret–Granjon, N. Le probleme de l'organisation spatiale dans les dyslexics d'évolution. *Enfance* 5 (1951):445.

Gardner, E. B., and Branski, D. M. Unilateral cerebral activation and perception of gaps: a signal detection analysis. *Neuropsychologia* 14 (1976):43–53.

Gardner, M. *The Annotated Alice.* Harmondsworth, England: Penguin Books, 1965.

Gardner, M. *The Ambidextrous Universe.* London: Allen Lane, The Penguin Press, 1967.

Gardner, R. A., and Gardner, B. Teaching sign language to a chimpanzee. *Science* 165 (1969):664–72.

Garrett, S. V. Putting our whole brain to use: A fresh look at the creative process. *Journal of Creative Behavior* 10 (1976):239–49.

Gates, A. I., and Bond, G. L. Reading readiness. A study of factors determining success and failure in beginning reading. *Teacher's College Record* 37 (1936):679–85.

Gazzaniga, M. S., and Sperry, R. W. Language after section of the cerebral commissures. *Brain* 90 (1967):131–48.

Geffen, G. The development of hemispheric specialization for speech perception. *Cortex* 12 (1976):337–46.

Geffen, G. The development of the right ear advantage in dichotic listening with focused attention. *Cortex* 14 (1978):169–77.

Geffen, G., Bradshaw, J. L., and Nettleton, N. C. Hemispheric asymmetry: verbal and spatial coding of visual stimuli. *Journal of Experimental Psychology* 95 (1972):25–31.

Geffen, G., Bradshaw, J. L., and Wallace, G. Interhemispheric effects on reaction times to verbal and nonverbal stimuli. *Journal of Experimental Psychology* 87 (1971):415–22.

Geffen, G., Traub, E., and Stierman, I. Language laterality assessed by unilateral ECT and dichotic monitoring. *Journal of Neurology, Neurosurgery, and Psychiatry* 41 (1978):354–60.

Geffner, D. S., and Hochberg, I. Ear laterality performance of children from low and middle socioeconomic levels on a verbal dichotic listening task. *Cortex* 7 (1971): 193–203.

Geschwind, N. The apraxias: Neural mechanisms of disorders of learned movement. *American Scientist* 63 (1975):188–95.

Geschwind, N. Specializations of the human brain. *Scientific American* 241 (1979):158–71.

Geschwind, N., and Levitsky, W. Human brain: Left–right asymmetries in temporal speech region. *Science* 161 (1968):186–87.

Gesell, A., and Ames, L. B. The development of handedness. *Journal of Genetic Psychology* 70 (1947):155–75.

Gilbert, C., and Bakan, P. Visual asymmetry in the perception of faces. *Neuropsychologia* 11 (1973):355–62.

Ginsberg, Y. P., and Hartwick, A. Directional confusion as a sign of dyslexia. *Perceptual and Motor Skills* 32 (1971):535–43.

Goldmeier, E. Über Ähnlichkeit bei gesehenen Figuren. *Psychologische Forschung* 21 (1935):146–208.

Goodglass, H., and Quadfasel, F. A. Language laterality in left handed aphasics. *Brain* 77 (1954):521–48.

Goodglass, H., Shai, A., Rosen, W., and Berman, M. New observations on right-left differences in tachistoscopic recognition of verbal and nonverbal stimuli. Paper presented at the International Neuropsychological Society Meeting, Washington, D.C., 1971.

Gordon, H. W. Hemispheric asymmetries in the perception of musical chords. *Cortex* 6 (1970):387–98.

Gordon, H. W. Hemispheric asymmetry for dichotically presented chords in musicians and non-musicians, males and females. *Acta Psychologica* 42 (1978):383–95. (a).

Gordon, H. W. Left hemisphere dominance for rhythmic elements in dichotically-presented melodies. *Cortex* 14 (1978):58–70. (b).

Gordon, H. W. Cognitive asymmetry in dyslexic families. *Neuropsychologia* 18 (1980):645–56.

Gordon, M. C. Reception and retention factors in tone duration discriminations by brain-damaged and control patients. *Cortex* 3 (1967):233–49.

Granet, M. Right and left in China. In R. Needham (ed.), *Right and Left: Essays on Dual Symbolic Classification*. Chicago: University of Chicago Press, 1973.

Griffin, D. R. *The Question of Animal Awareness*. New York: Rockefeller University Press, 1976.

Grindley, G. C. The formation of a simple habit in guinea pigs. *British Journal of Psychology* 23 (1932):127–47.

Gross, C. G. Inferotemporal cortex and vision. In E. Stellar and J. M. Sprague (eds.), *Progress in Physiological Psychology, Vol. 5*. New York: Academic Press, 1973.

Gross, C. G., Lewis, M., and Plaisier, D. Inferior temporal cortex lesions do not impair discrimination of lateral mirror images. *Neurosciences Abstracts* 1 (1975):73.

Guillaume, J., Mazars, G., and Mazars, Y. Intermédiare epileptique dans certains types de bégaiement. *Revue Neurologique* 96 (1957):59–61.

Gundara, N., and Zivanovic, B. Asymmetry in East African skulls. *American Journal of Physical Anthropology* 28 (1968):331–38.

Guthrie–Smith, H. *Sorrows and Joys of a New Zealand Naturalist*. Dunedin, New Zealand: Reed, 1936.

Hadziselimovic, H., and Cuś, M. The appearance of the internal structures of the brain in relation to the configuration of the human skull. *Acta Anatomica* 63 (1966):289–99.

Haggard, M. P., and Parkinson, A. M. Stimulus task factors as determinants of ear advantages. *Quarterly Journal of Experimental Psychology* 23 (1971):168–77.

Hall, G. S., and Hartwell, E. M. Research and discussion, bilateral asymmetry of function. *Mind* 9 (1884):93–109.

Hamilton, C. R., and Tieman, S. B. Interocular transfer of mirror-image discriminations by chiasm-sectioned monkeys. *Brain Research* 64 (1973):241–55.

Hardyck, C., and Petrinovich, L. F. Left-handedness. *Psychological Bulletin* 84 (1977):385–404.

Hardyck, C., Petrinovich, L., and Goldman, R. Left handedness and cognitive dificit. *Cortex* 12 (1976):266–78.

Harper, C. M. Training mirror-image discrimination in retardates. Unpublished Master's thesis: University of Waikato, 1978.

Harris, L. J. Sex differences in spatial ability: Possible environmental, genetic, and neurological factors. In M. Kinsbourne (ed.), *Asymmetrical Function of the Human Brain.* Cambridge: Cambridge University Press, 1978.

Harris, L. J. Left-handedness: Early theories, facts and fancies. In J. Herron (ed.), *Neuropsychology of Left-handedness.* New York: Academic Press, 1980. (a).

Harris, L. J. Which hand is the "eye" of the blind?—A new look at an old question. In J. Herron (ed.), *Neuropsychology of Left-handedness.* New York: Academic Press, 1980. (b).

Harris, L. J., and Gitterman, S. R. Sex and handedness differences in well-educated adults' self-descriptions of left–right confusability. *Archives of Neurology* 35 (1978):773.

Hatta, T. Recognition of Japanese *Kanji* and *Hirakana* in the left and right visual fields. *Japanese Psychological Research* 20 (1978):51–59.

Hay, R. The wrybill—one of the world's ornithological oddities. *Forest and Bird* 13 (1979):13–17.

Hebb, D. O. *Organization of Behavior.* New York: John Wiley & Sons Inc., 1949.

Hécaen, H., and Ajuriaguerra, J. de. *Left Handedness.* New York: Grune & Stratton, 1964.

Hécaen, H., and Sauguet, J. Cerebral dominance in left-handed subjects. *Cortex* 7 (1971):1940.

Hellige, J. B. Visual laterality patterns for pure- versus mixed-list presentations. *Journal of Experimental Psychology: Human Perception and Performance* 4 (1978):121–31.

Henley, E. M. Parity and time-reversal invariance in nuclear physics. *Annual Review of Nuclear Science* 19 (1969):367–427.

Hermann, K. *Reading Disability*. Copenhagen: Munksgaard, 1959.

Herrnstein, R. J., Loveland, D. H., and Cable, C. Natural concepts in pigeons. *Journal of Experimental Psychology: Animal Behavior Processes* 2 (1976):285–302.

Hertz, R. La prééminence de la main droite: étude sur la polarité religieuse. *Revue Philosophique* 68 (1909):553–80. (Trans. in Hertz, 1960.)

Hertz, R. *Death and the Right Hand* (trans. by R. Needham). Aberdeen: Cohen & West, 1960.

Hewes, G. W. Lateral dominance, culture, and writing systems. *Human Biology* 21 (1949):233–45.

Hewes, G. W. Primate communication and the gestural origin of language. *Current Anthropology* 14 (1973):5–24.

Hicks, R. E., Evans, E. A., and Pellegrini, R. J. Correlation between handedness and birth order: Compilation of five studies. *Perceptual and Motor Skills* 46 (1975):53–54.

Hicks, R. E., and Kinsbourne, M. Human handedness: A partial cross-fostering study. *Science* 192 (1976):908–10.

Hill, S. D., McCullum, A. H., and Sceau, A. G. Relation of training in motor activity to development of right–left directionality in mentally retarded children: Exploratory study. *Perceptual and Motor Skills* 24 (1963):363–66.

Hines, D., & Satz, P. Cross-modal asymmetries in perception related to asymmetry in cerebral function. *Neuropsychologia* 12 (1974):239–47.

Hoadley, N. F., and Pearson, K. On measurement of the internal diameters of the skull in relation: (I) To the prediction of its capacity, (II) To the "pre-eminence" of the left hemisphere. *Biometrika* 21 (1929):85–123.

Hrdlicka, A. Measurement of the cranial fossa. *Proceedings of the U.S. National Museum* 32 (1907):117–232.

Hughes, R. N. Some observations of correcting behaviour in woodlice. *Animal Behaviour* 14 (1966): 319.

Hughes, R. N. Turn alternation in woodlice *(Porcellio scaber). Animal Behaviour* 15 (1967):282–86.

Humphrey, M. E., and Zangwill, O. L. Cessation of dreaming after brain injury. *Journal of Neurology, Neurosurgery, and Psychiatry* 14 (1951):322–25.

Ingram, D. Cerebral speech lateralization in young children. *Neuropsychologia* 13 (1975):103–6.

Ingram, T. T. S. The dyslexic child. *World Blind Bulletin* 1 (1964):1.

Ingram, T. T. S., and Reid, J. F. Developmental aphasia observed in a department of child psychiatry. *Archives of Diseases of Childhood* 31 (1956):161.

Ireland, W. W. On mirror-writing and its relation to left-handedness and cerebral disease. *Brain* 4 (1881):361–67.

Irwin, R. J., and Newland, J. K. Children's knowledge of left and right. *Journal of Child Psychology and Psychiatry* 18 (1977):271–77.

Jackson, J. *Ambidexterity or Two-handedness and Two-brainedness.* London: Kegan Paul, Trench, Trubner & Co. Ltd., 1905.

Jackson, J. A. A survey of psychological, social and environmental differences between advanced and retarded readers. *Journal of Genetic Psychology* 65 (1944):113–31.

Jackson, J. H. Clinical remarks on cases of defects of expression (by words, writing, signs, etc.) in diseases of the nervous system. *Lancet* 2 (1864):604.

Jackson, J. H. Defect of intellectual expression (aphasia) with left hemiplegia. *Lancet* 1 (1868):457.

Janet, P. *The Major Symptoms of Hysteria.* New York: Macmillan, 1907.

Japp, F. R. Stereochemistry and vitalism. *Nature* 58 (1898):452–60.

Jaynes, J. *The Origin of Consciousness in the Breakdown of the Bicameral Mind.* Boston: Houghton Mifflin, 1976.

Jeffrey, W. E. Variables in early discrimination training: I. Motor responses in the training of left–right discrimination. *Child Development* 29 (1958):269–75.

Jeffrey, W. E. Discrimination of oblique lines by children. *Journal of Comparative and Physiological Psychology* 62 (1966):154–56.

Johnson, D. J., and Myklebust, H. R. *Learning Disabilities: Educational Principles and Practice.* New York: Grune & Stratton, 1967.

Johnson, W. (Ed.) *Stuttering in Children and Adults.* Minneapolis: University of Minnesota Press, 1955.

Johnson, W. *The Onset of Stuttering.* Minneapolis: University of Minnesota Press, 1959.

Jones, R. K. Observations on stammering after localized cerebral injury. *Journal of Neurology, Neurosurgery, and Psychiatry* 29 (1966):192–95.

Jowett, B. (trans.). *The Dialogues of Plato, Vol. IV.* Oxford, England: Oxford University Press, 1953.

Julesz, B. Binocular depth perception. In W. Reichardt (ed.), *Processing of Optical Data by Organisms and by Machines.* New York: Academic Press, 1969.

Julesz, B. *Foundations of Cyclopean Perception.* Chicago, Illinois: University of Chicago Press, 1971.

Kabir, P. K. *The CP Puzzle.* New York: Academic Press, 1968.

Kallman, H. J., and Corballis, M. C. Ear asymmetry in reaction time to musical sounds. *Perception and Psychophysics* 17 (1975):368–70.

Kant, I. *Prolegomena to Any Future Metaphysics. c.* 1783. Trans. by P. G. Lucas. Manchester, England: Manchester University Press, 1953.

Kephart, N. C. *The Slow Learner in the Classroom.* Columbus, Ohio: Charles E. Merrill, 1960.

Kershner, J. R. Lateralization in normal six-year-olds as related to later reading disability. *Developmental Psychobiology* 11 (1977):309–19.

Kimura, D. Some effects of temporal-lobe damage on auditory perception. *Canadian Journal of Psychology* 15 (1961):156–65. (a).

Kimura, D. Cerebral dominance and the perception of verbal stimuli. *Canadian Journal of Psychology* 15 (1961):166–71. (b).

Kimura, D. Left-right differences in the perception of melodies. *Quarterly Journal of Experimental Psychology* 16 (1964):355–58.

Kimura, D. Dual functional asymmetry of the brain in visual perception. *Neuropsychologia* 4 (1966):275–85.

Kimura, D. Functional asymmetry of the brain in dichotic listening. *Cortex* 3 (1967):163–78.

Kimura, D. Manual activity during speaking. I. Right-handers. *Neuropsychologia* 11 (1973):45–50. (a).

Kimura, D. Manual activity during speaking. II. Left-handers. *Neuropsychologia* 11 (1973):51–55. (b).

Kimura, D., and Archibald, Y. Motor functions of the left hemisphere. *Brain* 97 (1974):337–50.

Kimura, D., and Folb, S. Neural processing of backwards-speech sounds. *Science* 161 (1968):395–96.

Kimura, D., and Vanderwolf, C. H. The relation between hand preference and the performance of individual finger movements by the left and right hands. *Brain* 93 (1970):769–74.

Kinsbourne, M. Discrimination of orientation by rats. *Psychonomic Science* 22 (1971):50.

Kinsbourne, M. The mechanism of hemispheric control of the lateral gradient of attention. In P.M.A. Rabbitt and S. Dornic (eds.), *Attention and Performance V*. New York: Academic Press, 1975.

Kinsbourne, M., and Warrington, E. K. Developmental factors in reading and writing backwardness. *British Journal of Psychology* 54 (1963):145–56.

Knox, C., and Kimura, D. Cerebral processing of nonverbal sounds in boys and girls. *Neuropsychologia* 8 (1970):227–37.

Kohn, B., and Dennis, M. Patterns of hemispheric specialization after hemidecortication for infantile hemiplegia. In M. Kinsbourne & W. L. Smith (eds.), *Hemispheric Disconnection and Cerebral Function*. Springfield, Illinois: Charles C. Thomas, 1974.

Konorski, J. On the mechanism of instrumental conditioning. In *Proceedings of the 17th International Congress of Psychology*. Amsterdam: North Holland Publishing Co., 1964.

Lancaster, J. B. On the evolution of tool-using behavior. In C. L. Brace and J. Metress (eds.), *Man in Evolutionary Perspective*. New York: Wiley, 1973.

Lashley, K. S. The mechanism of vision, XV. Preliminary studies of the rats' capacity for detailed vision. *Journal of General Psychology* 18 (1938):123–93.

Lawrence, D. H. Acquired distinctiveness of cues: I. Transfer between discriminations on the basis of familiarity with the stimulus. *Journal of Experimental Psychology* 39 (1948):770–84.

Layton, W. M. Random determination of a developmental process: Reversal of normal visceral asymmetry in the mouse. *Journal of Heredity* 67 (1976):336–38.

LeDoux, J. E., Wilson, D. H., and Gazzaniga, M. S. Manipulo-spatial aspects of cerebral lateralization: Clues to the origin of lateralization. *Neuropsychologia* 15 (1977):743–50.

Lee, B. S. Effects of delayed speech feedback. *Journal of the Acoustical Society of America* 22 (1950):824–26.

LeGros Clark, W. E. *History of the Primates: An Introduction to the Study of Fossil Man*. 9th Edition. London: Trustees of the British Museum (Natural History), 1965.

Lehman, R. A. W. Lateralized preferences and right–left discrimination in the monkey: Choice of mirror-image shape, position of recovered food and hand usage. *Cortex* 14 (1978):530–39.

LeMay, M. The language capacity of Neanderthal man. *American Journal of Physical Anthropology* 42 (1975):19–24.

LeMay, M. Morphological cerebral asymmetries of modern man, fossil man, and nonhuman primate. *Annals of the New York Academy of Sciences* 280 (1976):349–66.

LeMay, M. Asymmetries of the skull and handedness. *Journal of the Neurological Sciences* 32 (1977):243–53.

Lenneberg, E. H. *Biological Foundations of Language.* New York: Wiley, 1967.

Lennon, F. B. *Victoria Through the Looking-glass: The Life of Lewis Carroll.* New York: Simon & Schuster, 1945.

Lesevre, N. Les mouvements oculaires d'exploration. *Word Blind Bulletin* 1 (1966):(cited by Bannatyne, 1971).

Letokhov, V. S. On differences of energy levels of left and right molecules due to weak interactions. *Physics Letters* 53A (1975):275–76.

Levy, J. A review of evidence for a genetic component in the determination of handedness. *Behavior Genetics* 6 (1976):429–53.

Levy, J., and Levy, J. M. Human lateralization from head to foot: Sex-related factors. *Science* 200 (1978):1291–92.

Levy, J., and Nagylaki, T. A model for the genetics of handedness. *Genetics* 72 (1972):117–28.

Levy, J., and Reid, M. Variations in writing posture and cerebral organization. *Science* 194 (1976):337–39

Levy, J., and Trevarthen, C. Metacontrol of hemispheric function in human split-brain patients. *Journal of Experimental Psychology: Human Perception and Performance* 2 (1976):299–312.

Levy, J., Trevarthen, C. B., and Sperry, R. W. Perception of bilateral chimeric figures following hemispheric deconnection. *Brain* 95 (1972):61–78.

Ley, R. G., and Bryden, M. P. Hemispheric differences in processing emotions and faces. *Brain and Language* 7 (1979):127–38.

Liberman, I. Y., Shankweiler, D., Orlando, C., Harris, K. S., and Berti, F. B. Letter confusions and reversals of sequence in the beginning reader: Implications for Orton's theory of developmental dyslexia. *Cortex* 7 (1971):127–42.

Lloyd, G. Right and left in Greek philosophy. *Journal of Hellenic Studies* 82 (1962):56–66.

Locher, P. J., and Nodine, C. F. Influence of stimulus symmetry on visual scanning patterns. *Perception and Psychophysics* 13 (1973):408–12.

Lovell, K., and Gorton, A. A study of some differences between backward and normal readers of average intelligence. *British Journal of Educational Psychology* 38 (1968):240–48.

Lovell, K., Shapton, O., and Warren, N. S. A study of some cognitive and other disabilities in backward readers of average intelligence as assessed by a non-verbal test. *British Journal of Educational Psychology* 34 (1964):58–64.

Luria, A. R. *Human brain and psychological processes.* New York: Harper & Row, 1966.

Luria, A. R. The functional organization of the brain. *Scientific American* 222 (1970):66–79.

Luria, A. R.; Tsvetkova, L. S.; and Futer, D. S. Aphasia in a composer. *Journal of Neurological Science* 2 (1965):288–92.

Lussenhop, A. J., Boggs, J. S., LaBorwit, L. J., and Walle, E. L. Cerebral dominance in stutterers determined by Wada Testing. *Neurology* 23 (1973):1190–92.

McGlone, J. Sex differences in the cerebral organization of verbal functions in patients with unilateral brain lesions. *Brain* 100 (1977):755–93.

McGlone, J. Sex differences in functional brain asymmetry. *Cortex* 14 (1978):122–28.

Mach, E. *The Science of Mechanics.* Chicago, Illinois: Open Court Publishing House, 1893.

Mach, E. *The Analysis of Sensations.* Chicago, Illinois: Open Court Publishing House, 1897.

Mach, E. *Popular Scientific Lectures.* Chicago, Illinois: Open Court Publishing House, 1898.

McKeever, W. F., and Huling, M. D. Lateral dominance in tachistoscopic word recognitions of children at two levels of ability. *Quarterly Journal of Experimental Psychology* 22 (1970):600–04.

McKeever, W. F., and Huling, M. D. Lateral dominance in tachistoscopic word recognition performance obtained with simultaneous visual input. *Neuropsychologia* 9 (1971):15–20.

Mackintosh, J., and Sutherland, N. S. Visual discrimination by the goldfish: The orientation of rectangles. *Animal Behaviour* 11 (1963):135–41.

McManus, I. C. *Handedness and Birth Stress.* Unpublished manuscript, University of Cambridge, 1980.

MacMeekan, M. *Ocular Dominance in Relation to Developmental Aphasia.* London: University of London Press, 1939.

Maki, R. H., Maki, W. S., and Marsh, L. G. Processing locational and orientational information. *Memory and Cognition* 5 (1977):602–12.

Makita, K. The rarity of reading disability in Japanese children. *American Journal of Orthopsychiatry* 38 (1968):599–614.

Marcel, T., Katz, L., and Smith, M. Laterality and reading proficiency. *Neuropsychologia* 12 (1974):131–39.

Marcel, T., and Rajan, P. Lateral specialization for recognition of words and faces in good and poor readers. *Neuropsychologia* 13 (1975):489–98.

Marinoni, A. Leonardo's literary legacy. In L. Reti (ed.), *The Unknown Leonardo.* New York: McGraw–Hill, 1974.

Mark, R. F. *Memory and Nerve Cell Connections.* London: Oxford University Press, 1974.

Marks, D., and Kammann, R. Information transmission in remote viewing experiments. *Nature* 274 (1978):680.

Massis, H. Defense of the West, II. *The Criterion* 4 (1926):476–93.

Mattis, S., French, J. H., and Rapin, I. Dyslexia in children and young adults: Three independent neurological syndromes. *Developmental Medicine and Child Neurology* 17 (1975):150–63.

Mazars, G., Hécaen, H., Tzavaras, A., and Merreune, L. Contribution à la chirurgie de certains bégaiements et à la compréhension de leur physiopathologie. *Revue Neurologique* 122 (1970):213–20.

Mello, N. K. Interhemispheric reversal of mirror-image oblique lines after monocular training in pigeons. *Science* 148 (1965):252–54.

Mello, N. K. Concerning the interhemispheric transfer of mirror-image oblique lines after monocular training in pigeons. *Physiology and Behavior* 1 (1966):293–300.

Miles, T. R. Symposium on reading disability: I. More on dyslexia. *British Journal of Educational Psychology* 41 (1971):1–5.

Milisen, R., and Van Riper, C. Differential transfer of training in a rotary activity. *Journal of Experimental Psychology* 24 (1939):640–46.

Miller, L. K., and Turner, S. Development of hemifield differences in word recognition. *Journal of Educational Psychology* 65 (1973):172–76.

Milner, B. Psychological defects produced by temporal lobe excision. *Research Publications of the Association for Nervous and Mental Diseases* 36 (1958):244–57.

Milner, B. Interhemispheric differences in the localization of psychological processes in man. *British Medical Bulletin* 27 (1971):272–77.

Milner, B. Psychological aspects of focal epilepsy and its neurosurgical management. In D. P. Purpura, J. K. Penry, and R. D. Walters (eds.), *Advances in Neurology,* Vol. 8. New York: Raven Press, 1975.

Milner, B., Taylor, L., and Sperry, R. W. Lateralized suppression of dichotically presented digits after commissural section in man. *Science* 161 (1968):184–86.

Mittwoch, U. To be right is to be born male. *New Scientist* 73 (1977):74–76.

Molfese, D. L., Freeman, R. B. Jr., and Palermo, D. S. The ontogeny of brain lateralization for speech and nonspeech sounds. *Brain and Language* 2 (1975):356–68.

Monod, J. On symmetry and function in biological systems. In A. Engstom, and B. Strandberg (eds.), *Symmetry and Function of Biological Systems at the Macromolecular Level.* New York: John Wiley & Sons, Inc., 1969.

Monroe, M. Methods for diagnosis and treatment of cases of reading disability. *Genetic Psychology Monographs* 4 (1928), Nos. 4 and 5.

Monroe, M. *Children Who Cannot Read.* Chicago: University of Chicago Press, 1932.

Moore, W. H. Bilateral tachistoscopic word perception of stutterers and normal subjects. *Brain and Language* 3 (1976):434–42.

Moore, W. H., and Lang, M. K. Alpha asymmetry over the right and left hemispheres of stutterers and control subjects preceding massed oral readings: A preliminary investigation. *Perceptual and Motor Skills* 44 (1977):223–30.

Morgan, M. J. Embryology and inheritance of asymmetry. In S. R. Harnad; R. W. Doty; L. Goldstein; J. Jaynes; and G. Krauthamer (eds.), *Lateralization in the Nervous System.* New York: Academic Press, 1977.

Morgan, M. J. Genetic models of asymmetry should be asymmetrical. *The Behavioral and Brain Sciences* 1 (1978):325–31.

Morgan, M. J., and Corballis, M. C. On the biological basis of human laterality: II The mechanisms of inheritance. *The Behavioral and Brain Sciences* 1 (1978):270–77.

Morrell, P. Information storage in nerve cells. In W. S. Fields and W. Abbott (eds.), *Information Storage and Neural Control.* Springfield, Illinois: Charles C. Thomas, 1963.

Mörtberg, L. Nonbiotic origin of optical activity. *Nature* 232 (1971):105–7.

Mountcastle, V. B., Lynch, J. C., Georgopoulos, A., Sakata, H., and Acuna, C. Posterior parietal association areas of the monkey: Command functions for operations in extrapersonal space. *Journal of Neurophysiology* 38 (1975):871.

Nagylaki, T., and Levy, J. "The sound of one paw clapping" isn't sound. *Behavior Genetics* 3 (1973):279–92.

Naidoo, S. Symposium on reading disability: IV. Specific developmental dyslexia. *British Journal of Educational Psychology* 41 (1971):19–22.

Naidoo, S. *Specific Dyslexia.* London: Pitman, 1972.

Nebes, R. D., and Sperry, R. W. Hemispheric deconnection syndrome with cerebral birth injury in the dominant arm area. *Neuropsychologia* 9 (1971):247–59.

Needham, R. (ed.). *Right and Left: Essays on Dual Symbolic Classification.* Chicago, Illinois: University of Chicago Press, 1974.

Needham, R. Right and left in Nyoro symbolic classification. *Africa* 37 (1967):425–51.

Neelley, J. N. A study of the speech behavior of stutterers and non-stutterers under normal and delayed auditory feedback. *Journal of Speech and Hearing Disorders, Monograph Supplement No. 7,* 1961.

Neville, A. C. *Animal Asymmetry.* London: Edward Arnold, 1976.

Newman, H. H. Asymmetry reversal or mirror imaging in identical twins. *Biological Bulletin* 55 (1928):298–315.

Newman, S. Review of *The Psychology of Left and Right. Bulletin of the British Psychological Society* 30 (1977):387.

Nissen, H. W., and McCulloch, T. L. Equated and non-equated stimulus conditions in discrimination learning by chimpanzees: I. Comparison with unlimited response. *Journal of Comparative Psychology* 23 (1937):165–89.

Noble, J. Mirror-images and the forebrain commissures of the monkey. *Nature* 211 (1966):1263–65.

Noble, J. Paradoxical interocular transfer of mirror-image discrimination in the optic chiasm sectioned monkey. *Brain Research* 10 (1968):127–51.

Norden, B. The asymmetry of life. *Journal of Molecular Evolution* 11 (1978):313–32.

Nottebohm, F. Neural lateralization of vocal control in a passerine bird. I. Song. *Journal of Experimental Zoology* 177 (1971):229–62.

Nottebohm, F. Neural lateralization of vocal control in a passerine bird. II. Subsong, calls, and a theory of vocal learning. *Journal of Experimental Zoology* 179 (1972):25–50.

Nottebohm, F. Phonation in the orange-winged Amazon parrot, *Amazona amazonica*. *Journal of Comparative Psysiology, Series A* 108 (1976):157–70.

Oldfield, R. C. Handedness in musicians. *British Journal of Psychology* 60 (1969):91–99.

Oldfield, R. C. The assessment and analysis of handedness: The Edinburgh inventory. *Neuropsychologia* 9 (1971):97–114.

Olson, D. R. *Cognitive Development: The Child's Acquisition of Diagonality.* New York: Academic Press, 1970.

Olson, G. M., and Laxar, K. Processing the terms *right* and *left*: A note on left handers. *Journal of Experimental Psychology* 102 (1974):1135–37.

Orbach, J. Retinal locus as a factor in the recognition of visually perceived words. *American Journal of Psychology* 65 (1953):555–62.

Ornstein, R. E. *The Psychology of Consciousness.* San Francisco: Freeman, 1972.

Ornstein, R. E., and Galin, D. Physiological studies of consciousness. In P. Lee, R. E. Orenstein, D. Galin, A. Deikman, and C. Tart (eds.), *Symposium on Consciousness.* New York: Viking Press, 1976.

Orton, S. T. "Word-blindness" in school children. *Archives of Neurology and Psychiatry* 14 (1925):581–615.

Orton, S. T. Special disability in reading. *Bulletin of the Neurological Institute of New York* 1 (1931):159–92.

Orton, S. T. *Reading, Writing and Speech Problems in Children.* New York: W. W. Norton & Co. Ltd., 1937.

Over, R., and Over, J. Detection and recognition of mirror-image obliques by young children. *Journal of Comparative and Physiological Psychology* 64 (1967):467–70. (a).

Over, R., and Over, J. Kinesthetic judgements of the direction of line by young children. *Quarterly Journal of Experimental Psychology* 19 (1967):337–40. (b).

Overstreet, R. An investigation of prenatal position and handedness. *Psychological Bulletin* 35 (1938):520–21.

Papcun, G., Krashen, S., Terbeek, D., Remington, R., and Harshman, R. Is the right hemisphere specialized for speech, language, and/or something else? *Journal of the Acoustical Society of America* 55 (1974):319–27.

Parriss, J. R. A technique for testing cats' discrimination of differently oriented rectangles. *Nature* 202 (1964):771–73.

Patterson, F. Conversations with a gorilla. *National Geographic* 154 (1978):438–66.

Pavlov, I. P. *Conditioned Reflexes.* London: Oxford University Press, 1927.

Penfield, W., and Roberts, L. *Speech and Brain Mechanisms.* Princeton: Princeton University Press, 1959.

Perrin, K. L. An examination of ear preference for speech and non-speech stimuli in a stuttering population. Unpublished PhD dissertation, Stanford University, 1969.

Peters, M., and Durding, B. M. Footedness of left- and right-handers. *American Journal of Psychology* 92 (1979):133–42.

Petersen, M. R., Beecher, M. D., Zoloth, S. R., Moody, D. B., and Stebbins, W. C. Neural lateralization of species specific vocalizations by Japanese macaques *(Macaca fuscata). Science* 202 (1978):324–27.

Peterson, G. M. Mechanics of handedness in the rat. *Comparative Psychology Monographs* 9 (1934), No. 46.

Peterson, J. M., and Lansky, L. M. Left-handedness among architects: Some facts and speculation. *Perceptual and Motor Skills* 38 (1974):547–50.

Piaget, J. *Judgement and Reasoning in the Child.* London: Routledge and Kegan Paul, 1928.

Piercy, M., and Smyth, V. O. G. Right hemisphere dominance for certain nonverbal intellectual skills. *Brain* 85 (1962):775–90.

Popper, K., and Eccles, J. C. *The Self and Its Brain.* Berlin: Springer, 1977.

Premack, D. A functional analysis of language. *Journal of the Experimental Analysis of Behavior* 14 (1970):107–25.

Pudney, J. *His Majesty King George VI: A Study.* London: Hutchinson, 1952.

Quinn, P. Stuttering, cerebral dominance and the dichotic word test. *Medical Journal of Australia* 2 (1972):639–43.

Ramaley, F. Inheritance of left handedness. *American Naturalist* 47 (1913):730–38.

Ray, B. A., and Sidman, M. Reinforcement schedules and stimulus control. In W. N. Schoenfeld (ed.), *The Theory of Reinforcement Schedules*. New York: Appleton–Century–Crofts, 1969. Pp. 187–215.

Ray, O. S., and Emley, G. Time factors in interhemispheric transfer of learning. *Science* 144 (1964):76–78.

Ray, O. S., and Emley, G. Interhemispheric transfer of learning. *Life Sciences* 4 (1965):823–26.

Rayner, K. Eye movements in reading and information processing. *Psychological Bulletin* 85 (1978):618–60.

Restle, F. Discrimination of cues in mazes: A resolution of the "place-vs-response" question. *Psychological Review* 64 (1957):217–28.

Rife, D. C. Handedness with special reference to twins. *Genetics* 25 (1940):178–86.

Rife, D. C. Hand prints and handedness. *American Journal of Human Genetics* 7 (1955):170–79.

Rigal, R. A. Hand efficiency and right–left discrimination. *Perceptual and Motor Skills* 38 (1974):219–24. (a).

Rigal, R. A. Determination of handedness using hand-efficiency tests. *Perceptual and Motor Skills* 39 (1974):253–54. (b).

Rigby, P. Dual symbolic classification among the Gogo of Central Tanzania. *Africa* 36 (1966):1–16.

Riopelle, A. J., Rahm, U., Itoigawa, N., and Draper, W. A. Discrimination of mirror-image patterns by rhesus monkeys. *Perceptual and Motor Skills* 19 (1964):383–89.

Roberts. W. W. The interpretation of some disorders of speech. *Journal of Mental Science* 95 (1949):567–88.

Rock, I. *Orientation and Form*. New York: Academic Press, 1973.

Rock, I., and Leaman, R. An experimental analysis of visual symmetry. *Acta Psychologica* 21 (1963):171–83.

Roll, W. G. Survival research: Problems and possibilities. In J. White (ed.), *Psychic Exploration: A Challenge for Science*. New York: Putman, 1974.

Romer, A. S. *The Vertebrate Body*. London: W. B. Saunders, 1962.

Rossi, G. F., and Rosadini, G. Experimental analysis of cerebral dominance in man. In C. H. Millikan and F. L. Darley (eds.), *Brain Mechanisms Underlying Speech and Language*. New York: Grune & Stratton, 1967.

Rousseau, J. J. *Émile* (trans. B. Foxley). London: J. M. Dent & Sons Ltd, 1911. (First published 1780).

Rozin, P., Poritsky, S., and Sotsky, R. American children with reading problems can easily learn to read English represented by Chinese characters. *Science* 171 (1971):1264–67.

Rubino, C. A., and Minden, H. A. An analysis of eye-movements in children with a reading disability. *Cortex* 9 (1973):217–20.

Rudel, R. G., and Teuber, H–L. Discrimination of direction of line in children. *Journal of Comparative and Physiological Psychology* 56 (1963):892–98.

Ruskin, J. *The Seven Lamps of Architectures*. London: George Allen & Sons, 1907.

Russell, B. R. *An Essay on the Foundations of Geometry*. London: Cambridge University Press, 1897.

Russell, B. R. *A History of Western Philosophy*. London: George Allen & Unwin Ltd, 1946.

Rutter, M., Graham, P., Yule, W., and Birch, H. *A Neuropsychiatric Study in Childhood Clinics in Developmental and Medical Child Neurology*. London: Spastics International Medical Publications and Heinemann, 1970.

Salam, A. Elementary particles and space–time symmetries. *Endeavour* 17 (1958):97–105.

Sarasin, P. Über rechts–und links–Händigheit in der Praehistorie und die rechts-Händigheit in der historischen Zeit. *Naturforschende Gesellschaft in Basel, Verhandlingen* 29 (1918):122–96.

Satz, P. Cerebral dominance and reading disability: An old problem revisited. In R. M. Knights & D. J. Bakker (eds.), *The Neuropsychology of Learning Disorders*. Baltimore: University Park Press, 1976.

Satz, P., and Sparrow, S. Specific developmental dyslexia: A theoretical formulation. In D. J. Bakker and P. Satz (eds.), *Specific Reading Disability: Advances in Theory and Method*. Rotterdam: Rotterdam University Press, 1970.

Schaller, G. B. *The Mountain Gorilla: Ecology and Behavior*. Chicago, Illinois: University of Chicago Press, 1963.

Schaller, M., and Harris, L. J. "Upright" orientations of forms change with subject age and with features of form. *Perception and Psychophysics* 17 (1975):179–88.

Schonell, F. J. The relation of reading disability to handedness and certain ocular factors: Part 1. *British Journal of Educational Psychology* 10 (1940):227–37.

Schonell, F. J. The relation of reading disability to handedness and certain ocular factors: Part 2. *British Journal of Educational Psychology* 11 (1941):20–27.

Schonell, F. J. *Backwardness in the Basic Subjects.* London: Oliver & Boyd, 1942.

Searleman, A. A review of right hemisphere linguistic capabilities. *Psychological Bulletin* 84 (1977):503–28.

Serpell, R. Discrimination of orientation by Zambian children. *Journal of Comparative and Physiological Psychology* 75 (1971):312–16.

Seth, G. Eye-hand co-ordination and 'handedness': a developmental study of visuo-motor behavior in infancy. *British Journal of Educational Psychology* 43 (1973):35–49.

Shankweiler, D., Liberman, I. Y., Mark, L. S., Fowler, C. A., and Fischer, F. W. The speech code and learning to read. *Journal of Experimental Psychology: Human Learning and Memory* 5 (1979):531–45.

Shearer, E. Physical skills and reading backwardness. *Educational Research* 10 (1968):197–206.

Shepard, R. N. The mental image. *American Psychologist* 33 (1978):125–37.

Sidman, M., and Kirk, B. Letter reversals in naming, writing, and matching to sample. *Child Development* 45 (1974):616–25.

Siqueland, E. R. Operant conditioning of headturning in four month infants. *Psychomonic Science* 1 (1964):223–24.

Sklar, B., and Hanley, J. A multifontal alphabet for dyslexic children. *Journal of Learning Disabilities* 5 (1972):46–50.

Slorach, N., and Noehr, B. Dichotic listening in stuttering and dyslexic children. *Cortex* 9 (1973):295–300.

Smith, L. C. A Study of laterality characteristics of retarded readers and reading achievers. *Journal of Experimental Education* 18 (1950):321–29.

Snow, C. P. *The Two Cultures and the Scientific Revolution.* Cambridge: Cambridge University Press, 1959.

Sommers, R. K.; Brady, W.; and Moore, W. H. Jr. Dichotic ear preferences of stuttering children and adults. *Perceptual and Motor Skills* 41 (1975):931–38.

Sperry, R. W. Some general aspects of interhemispheric integration. In V. B. Mountcastle (ed.), *Interhemispheric Relations and Cerebral Dominance.* Baltimore: Johns Hopkins Press, 1962.

Sperry, R. W. A modified concept of consciousness. *Psychological Review* 76 (1969):532–36.

Springer, S. P., and Searleman, A. Left-handedness in twins: Implications for the mechanisms underlying cerebral asymmetry of function. In J. Herron (ed.), *Neuropsychology of Left-handedness.* New York: Academic Press, 1980.

Standing, L., Conezio, J., and Haber, R. N. Perception and memory for pictures: Single-trial learning of 2,500 visual stimuli. *Psychonomic Science* 19 (1970);73–74.

Stewart, H. F. *Pascal's Pensées.* London: Routledge and Kegan Paul, Ltd, 1950.

Studdert–Kennedy, M., and Shankweiler, D. Hemispheric specialization for speech perception. *Journal of the Acoustical Society of America* 48 (1970):579–94.

Strub, R. L, and Gardner, H. The repetition deficit in conduction aphasia. *Brain and Language* 1 (1974):241–56.

Sussman, H. M. The laterality effect in lingual-auditory tracking. *The Journal of the Acoustical Society of America* 49 (1971):1874–80.

Sussman, H. M., and MacNeilage, P. F. Hemispheric specialization for speech production and perception in stutterers. *Neuropsychologia* 13 (1975):19–26. (a).

Sussman, H. M., and MacNeilage, P. F. Studies of hemispheric specialization for speech production. *Brain and Language* 2 (1975):131–51. (b).

Sutherland, N. S. Visual discrimination of orientation and shape by *Octopus. Nature* 179 (1957):11–13.

Sutherland, N. S. Theories of shape discrimination in *Octopus. Nature* 186 (1960):840–44.

Sutherland, N. S. Cats' ability to discriminate oblique rectangles. *Science* 139 (1963):209–10.

Sutherland, N. S. *Breakdown.* London: Weidenfeld and Nicolson Ltd, 1976.

Swanson, R., and Benton, A. L. Some aspects of the genetic development of right–left discrimination. *Child Development* 26 (1955):123–33.

Tansley, A. E. *Reading and Remedial Reading.* London: Routledge & Kegan Paul, 1967.

Targ, R., and Puthoff, H. Information transmission under conditions of sensory shielding. *Nature* 251 (1974):602–7.

Taylor, S. E. *The Fundamental Reading Skill as Related to Eye Movement Photography and Visual Anomalies.* Springfield, Ill.: Charles C. Thomas, 1966.

Tee, K. S., and Riesen, A. H. Visual left–right confusions in animal and man. In G. Newton & A. H. Riesen (eds.), *Advances in Psychobiology.* Vol. 2. New York: John Wiley & Sons, Inc., 1974.

Teng, E. L., Lee, P–H., Yang, K–S., and Chang, P. C. Handedness in a Chinese population: Biological, social, and pathological factors. *Science* 193 (1976):1148–50.

Terzian, H. Behavioral and EEG effects of intracarotid sodium amytal injection. *Acta Neurochirurgia* (Wien.) 12 (1964):230–39.

Thomas, D. R., Klipec, W., and Lyons, T. Investigations of a mirror-image transfer effect in pigeons. *Journal of the Experimental Analysis of Behavior* 9 (1966):567–71.

Tomlinson–Keasey, C., Kelly, R. R., and Burton, J. K. Hemispheric changes in information processing during development. *Developmental Psychology* 14 (1978):214–23.

Torgerson, J. Situs inversus, asymmetry, and twinning. *American Journal of Human Genetics* 2 (1950):361–70.

Trankell, A. Aspects of genetics in psychology. *American Journal of Human Genetics* 7 (1955):264–76.

Travis, L. E. *Speech Pathology.* New York: Appleton–Century–Crofts, 1931.

Treisman, A., and Geffen, G. Selective attention and cerebral dominance in perceiving and responding to speech messages. *Quarterly Journal of Experimental Psychology* 20 (1968):139–50.

Trevarthen, C. B. Experimental evidence for a brain-stem contribution to visual perception in man. *Brain, Behavior, and Evolution* 3 (1970):338–52.

Trevarthen, C. B. Manipulative strategies of baboons and origins of cerebral asymmetry. In M. Kinsbourne (ed.), *Asymmetrical Function of the Brain.* London: Cambridge University Press, 1978.

Tschirgi, R. D. Spatial perception and central nervous system asymmetry. *Arquivos de Neuropsiquiatria* 16 (1958):364–66.

Tsunoda, T., and Moriyama, H. Specific patterns of cerebral dominance for various sounds in adult stutterers. *Journal of Auditory Research* 12 (1972):216–27.

Turkewitz, G. The development of lateral preferences in the human infant. In S. Harand, R. W. Doty, L. Goldstein, J. Jaynes, and G. Krauthamer (eds.), *Lateralization in the Nervous System.* New York: Academic Press, 1977.

Ulbricht, T.L.V. The origin of optical asymmetry on earth. *Origins of Life* 6 (1975):303–15.

Van Riper, C. *Nature of Stuttering.* Ref. ed. New York: Prentice-Hall, 1971.

Vargha–Khadem, F., and Corballis, M. C. Cerebral asymmetry in infants. *Brain and Language* 8 (1979):1–9.

Vogel, J. M. The influence of verbal descriptions versus orientation codes on kindergartners' memory for the orientation of pictures. *Child Development* 50 (1979): 239–42.

Waber, D. P. Six differences in mental abilities, hemispheric lateralization and the rate of physical growth in adolescence. *Developmental Psychology* 13 (1977):29–38.

Wada, J. A., and Rasmussen, T. Intracarotid injection of sodium amytal for the lateralization of cerebral speech dominance: Experimental and clinical observations. *Journal of Neurosurgery* 17 (1960):266–82.

Wada, J. A., Clarke, R., and Hamm, A. Cerebral hemispheric asymmetry in humans. *Archives of Neurology* 32 (1975):239–46.

Wall, W. D. Reading backwardness among men in the army. I. *British Journal of Educational Psychology* 15 (1945):28–40.

Wall, W. D. Reading backwardness among men in the army. II. *British Journal of Educational Psychology* 16 (1946):133–48.

Warren, J. M. Discrimination of mirror images by cats. *Journal of Comparative and Physiological Psychology* 69 (1969):9–11.

Warrington, E. K., and Pratt, R. T. C. Language laterality in left handers assessed by unilateral E.C.T. *Neuropsychologia* 11 (1973): 423–28.

Watson, J. D. *The Double Helix.* London: Weidenfeld & Nicholson, 1968.

Webster, W. G. Territoriality and the evolution of brain asymmetry. In S. J. Dimond, and D. A. Blizard, (eds.), *Evolution and Lateralization of the Brain.* New York: New York Academy of Sciences, 1977.

Weinstein, S. Functional cerebral hemisphere asymmetry. In M. Kinsbourne (ed.), *Asymmetrical Function of the Brain.* London: Cambridge University Press, 1978.

Weiss, M. S., and House, A. S. Perception of dichotically presented vowels. *Journal of the Acoustical Society of America* 53 (1973):51–58.

Wernicke, C. Der aphasiche symptomencomplex. *Eine psychologische studie auf anatomischer basis.* Breslau: Cohen & Weigert, 1874.

Weyl, H. *Symmetry.* Princeton, N.J.: Princeton University Press, 1952.

Whitaker, H. A. A case of the isolation of the language function. In H. Whitaker and H. A. Whitaker (eds.), *Studies in Neurolinguistics, Vol. 1.* New York: Academic Press, 1976.

White, J. *Psychic Exploration: A Challenge for Science.* New York: Putnam, 1974.

White, M. J. Laterality differences in perception: A review. *Psychological Bulletin* 72 (1969):387–405.

Wickham, A. *Selected Poems.* London: Chatto & Windus, 1971.

Wieschhoff, H. A. Concepts of right and left in African cultures. *Journal of the American Oriental Society* 58 (1938):202–17.

Wile, I. S. *Handedness: Right and Left.* Boston: Lothrop, Lee, & Shepard, 1934.

Williams, R. J. Discrimination of Mirror Images by the Pigeon. Unpublished Master's thesis, University of Auckland, 1971.

Wilson, D. Right handedness. *The Canadian Journal* No. 75 (1872):193–230.

Wilson, E. B. Notes on the reversal of asymmetry in the regeneration of chelae in *Alpheus heterochelis. Biological Bulletin* (of the Marine Biological Laboratory, Woods Hole, Mass.) 4 (1903):197–210.

Witelson, S. F. Hemispheric specialization for linguistic and nonlinguistic tactual perception using a dichotomous stimulation technique. *Cortex* 10 (1974):3–17.

Witelson, S. F. Abnormal right hemisphere specialization in developmental dyslexia. In R. M. Knights and D. J. Bakker (eds.), *The Neuropsychology of Learning Disorders.* Baltimore, Md: University Park Press, 1976.

Witelson, S. F. Developmental dyslexia: Two right hemispheres and none left. *Science* 195 (1977):309–11. (a).

Witelson, S. F. Early hemispheric specialization and interhemispheric plasticity: An empirical and theoretical review. In S. J. Segalowitz and F. A. Gruber (eds.), *Language Development and Neurological Theory.* New York: Academic Press, 1977. (b).

Wolf, S. M. Difficulties in right–left discrimination in a normal population. *Archives of Neurology* 29 (1973):128–29.

Wolfe, L. S. An experimental study of reversals in reading. *American Journal of Psychology* 52 (1939):533–61.

Wolfe, L. S. Differential factors in specific reading disability. *Journal of Genetic Psychology* 58 (1941):45–70.

Wolff, P. H., Hurwitz, I., and Moss, H. Serial organization of motor skills in left- and right-handed adults. *Neuropsychologia* 15 (1977):539–46.

Wolpert, L. Pattern formation in biological development. *Scientific American* 239 (1978):124–37. (a).

Wolpert, L. The problem of directed left–right asymmetry in development. *The Behavioral and Brain Sciences* 2 (1978):324–25. (b).

Woo, T. L., and Pearson, K. Dextrality and sinistrality of hand and eye. *Biometrika* 19 (1927):165–99.

Wood, J. P. *The Snark was a Boojum: A Life of Lewis Carroll.* New York: Pantheon Books, 1966.

Woolley, H. T. The development of right handedness in a normal infant. *Psychological Review* 17 (1910):37–41.

Yeni–Komshian, G. H., and Benson, D. A. Anatomical study of cerebral asymmetry in the temporal lobes of humans, chimpanzees, and rhesus monkeys. *Science* 192 (1976):387–89.

Yeni–Komshian, G. H., Isenberg, D., and Goldberg, H. Cerebral dominance and reading disability: left visual field deficit in poor readers. *Neuropsychologia* 13 (1975):83–94.

Young, J. Z. Why do we have two brains? In V. B. Mountcastle (ed.), *Interhemispheric Relations and Cerebral Dominance.* Baltimore: Johns Hopkins Press, 1962.

Zaidel, E. A technique for presenting lateralized visual input with prolonged exposure. *Vision Research* 15 (1975):283–89.

Zangwill, O. L. *Cerebral Dominance and Its Relation to Psychological Function.* Edinburgh: Oliver & Boyd, 1960.

Zangwill, O. L. Thought and the brain. *British Journal of Psychology* 67 (1976):301–14.

Zangwill, O. L. Dyslexia and cerebral dominance: A reassessment. In L. Oettinger, Jr., and E. V. Majovski (eds.), *The Psychologist, the School, and the Child with MBD/LD.* New York: Grune & Stratton, 1978.

Zangwill, O. L. and Blakemore, C. Dyslexia: Reversal of eye-movements during reading. *Neuropsychologia* 10 (1972):371–73.

Zazzo, R. *Les jumeaux: Le couple et la personne.* Paris: Presses Universitaires de France, 1960.

Zeigler, H. P., and Schmerler, S. Visual discrimination of orientation by pigeons. *Animal Behaviour* 13 (1965): 475–77.

Zimmermann, G. W., and Knott, J. R. Slow potentials of the brain related to speech processing in normal speakers and stutterers. *Electroencephalography and Clinical Neurophysiology* 37 (1974):599–607.

Zlab, Z. Laterality and left–right orientation in developmental disorders of reading and writing. *Psychológia a Patopsychologia Dieťaťa* 5 (1970):303–17.

Zurif, E. B. Auditory lateralization: Prosodic and syntactic factors. *Brain and Language* 1 (1974):391–404.

Zurif, E. B., and Bryden, M. P. Familial handedness and left–right differences in auditory and visual perception. *Neuropsychologia* 7 (1969):179–87.

Name Index

301

Subject Index

Ambidexterity, 7, 99, 107–8, 113–14, 120, 122, 125, 134, 137, 151; and dyslexia, 215–17; and stuttering, 230

Anterior commissure, and left-right equivalence, 71, 73. *See also* Interhemispheric reversal; Split-brain preparation

Aphasia. *See* Language: disorders of

Apraxia, 133

Asymmetry: advantages of, 150, 172–81, 198; in animals, 7, 121, 143–44, 147–48, 170–73, 241–43; and conservation of parity, 241; emergence of, 89–102; of internal organs, 56, 100–101, 243; of living moelcules, 6, 56, 171, 242, 249–51; of man-made world, 241–42; of physical laws, 6, 244–51; of tonic neck reflex, 103–4, 124, 187. *See also* Cerebral asymmetry; Handedness; Hemispheric specialization

Bilateral symmetry. *See* Symmetry

Birdsongs, 143, 170–71

Braille, 156

Broca's area, 127–29

Cerebral asymmetry: anatomical, 138, 140–41, 145–47; and apraxia, 133; biological perspective on, 171–81; in birds, 143–44, 170–71; and consciousness, 168–71; development of, 141–45, 178–80, 200–201; and dyslexia, 205–8, 211–13, 218–25; and equipotentiality, 142–44, 179–80; and hallucinations, 169; and handedness, 104, 124, 133–40, 148–49; and language, 127–52; in nonhuman

primates, 147–48, 170; origins of, 145–49; in prehistoric humans, 145–46, 241; in split-brain patients, 129–31; in stutterers, 231–34; tests for, 129–36. *See also* Dichotic listening; Hemispheric specialization

Cerebral lateralization. *See* Cerebral asymmetry; Dichotic listening; Hemispheric specialization

Conservation of parity, 25–26, 239; and bilateral symmetry, 241; and CP invariance, 249; and CPT theorem, 248; in electromagnetic interactions, 250; and left-right equivalence, 240; and living molecules, 242, 249–51; in nuclear physics, 244–49; in weak interactions, 245–49. *See also* Left-right equivalence

Corpus callosum. *See* Interhemispheric reversal; Split-brain preparation

Denial, role of, in hemispheric bias, 161–62

Development of left-right sense, 183–202; and cerebral lateralization, 200–201; effective teaching in, 191–98; and eye dominance, 199; and growth of structural asymmetries, 198–201; and handedness, 198–99; role of response asymmetries in, 191–94; use of fading techniques in, 195–98

Dexterity, defined, 7

Dichotic listening, 132, 136, 141–42, 156, 158–59, 163, 200–201; and dyslexia, 218–20; and stuttering, 232–33. *See also* Cerebral asymmetry; Hemispheric specialization

309